POLITICAL EMPOWERMENT OF WOMEN
THE NETHERLANDS AND OTHER COUNTRIES

NIJHOFF LAW SPECIALS

VOLUME 59

The titles published in this series are listed at the end of this volume

POLITICAL EMPOWERMENT OF WOMEN
THE NETHERLANDS AND OTHER COUNTRIES

by

Monique Leyenaar

MARTINUS NIJHOFF PUBLISHERS
LEIDEN / BOSTON

A C.I.P. Catalogue record for this book is available from the Library of Congress

Cover illustration: "Danseuse", Sonia Delaunay (1916).
© L & M Services B.V. Amsterdam 20040603

Printed on acid-free paper

ISBN 90 04 14099 9

©2004 Koninklijke Brill NV

Brill Academic Publishers incorporates the imprint of Martinus Nijhoff Publishers.
http://www.brill.nl

This publication is protected by international copyright law.
All rights reserved. No part of this publication may be reproduced, stored in a retrieval system, or transmitted in any form or by any means, electronic, mechanical, photocopying, recording or otherwise, without the prior permission of the publisher.

CONTENTS

ACKNOWLEDGEMENTS xi

CHAPTER 1
INTRODUCTION 1
THE POLITICS OF GENDER REPRESENTATION 2
THE POLICY OF GENDER REPRESENTATION 6
POSITIVE CONTRIBUTION 7
THE CASE OF THE NETHERLANDS 8
PLAN OF THE BOOK 10

PART I:
DEMOCRATIC DEFICIT: A COMPARATIVE PERSPECTIVE

CHAPTER 2
POLITICAL REPRESENTATION OF WOMEN IN FIFTEEN EUROPEAN
COUNTRIES 17
WOMEN IN POLITICS IN THE 15 EUROPEAN COUNTRIES 18
    Scandinavian Countries 21
    Greece, Italy, Portugal and Spain 25
    France, Belgium and Luxembourg 30
    Britain and Ireland 36
    Germany and Austria 43
EUROPEAN UNION 48
EVALUATING EUROPE 53

Contents

CHAPTER 3
AN EXPLANATORY FRAMEWORK FOR WOMEN'S POLITICAL
REPRESENTATION 56
VOTING 58
RECRUITMENT 62
    Social and Cultural Climate 62
    Gender Division of Labour and Gender Equality 63
    Civil Society and Corporatism 64
    Structural Factors 64
    Situational Factors 65
    Psychological Factors 66
SELECTION 67
    Electoral System 68
    Selection Process 71
    Selection Criteria 73
    Affirmative Action 75
    Women's Factions 75
    Party System/Party Competition 77
    Political and Civic Expertise 78
    Quality of Life 78
ELECTION 79
    Preferential Voting and Electoral Attractiveness 80
REPRESENTATION 81
    Culture of Politics 82
CONCLUSION 82

**PART II:
THE CASE OF THE NETHERLANDS**

CHAPTER 4
THE NETHERLANDS: POLITICAL RIGHTS FOR WOMEN 87
'NO GENDER BARRIER AT THE POLLING BOOTH' 88
POLITICAL SYSTEM 89
ELECTORAL SYSTEM 90

PARTY SYSTEM 92
    Pillarisation 96
PARTIES' ATTITUDE TOWARDS THE INTEGRATION OF WOMEN IN
    POLITICS 98
    Women's Suffrage 99
    After 1919: the Confessional Parties 102
    After 1919: the Liberal and Socialist Parties 104
    After 1945 107
WOMEN'S PARTIES 112
CONCLUSION 117

CHAPTER 5
FROM TOKEN TO PLAYER 119

1917-1946: PIONEERS 120
1946-1975: TOKENS OR GROUP REPRESENTATIVES 123
1975-1989: DEFENDERS OF WOMEN'S INTERESTS 128
1990S: PLAYERS 133
LOCAL AND REGIONAL LEVEL 138
EUROPEAN LEVEL 145
CONCLUSION 146

CHAPTER 6
EXPLAINING THE CHANGE IN ATTITUDE 148

SOCIAL AND ECONOMIC POSITION OF WOMEN 149
    Employment and Education 149
    Equality Policies 153
WOMEN'S ORGANISATIONS 157
POLITICAL PARTIES 164
    Party Membership 165
    Women's Factions 167
    Selection Criteria 171
    Affirmative Action Plans by Parties 173
GOVERNMENT 175
CONCLUSION 184

Contents

CHAPTER 7
EMPOWERMENT OF WOMEN IN THE 21ST CENTURY: LONG-LASTING DEVELOPMENT OR SHORT-TERM UPHEAVAL? ... 186

THE 2002 AND 2003 ELECTIONS ... 187
    Parliamentary Elections ... 187
    Local and Provincial Elections ... 193
THE PRIME MOVERS IN THE 21ST CENTURY ... 195
    Women's Movement ... 195
    Political Parties ... 198
    Government ... 201
        Combining Work and Care ... 202
        Empowerment ... 206
        Gender Mainstreaming and Empowerment ... 208
CONCLUSION ... 211

PART III:
DEBATES AND DEVELOPMENTS IN EUROPE

CHAPTER 8
PARTY QUOTAS, PARITY AND 'PANDA' LAWS ... 217

VOLUNTARY QUOTAS INTRODUCED BY PARTIES ... 218
QUOTA LEGISLATION ... 226
FRANCE ... 228
    Arguments in Favour of Legally Imposed Quotas ... 228
    Arguments against Legally Imposed Quotas ... 231
        From Theoretical Concept into Law of the Land ... 232
BELGIUM ... 236
GREECE ... 241
ITALY ... 242
PORTUGAL ... 245
DISCUSSION ... 247

CHAPTER 9
WINDOW OF OPPORTUNITY: THE CRISIS OF POLITICS 252

THE CRISIS OF PARTY POLITICS 254
A REACTION: POLITICAL REFORM 257
GENDER AND POLITICAL REFORM 261
A NEW INSTITUTIONAL REGIME FOR SELECTING MEPS 267
CONCLUSION 277

CHAPTER 10
THE FUTURE OF EUROPEAN GENDER DEMOCRACY 279

RESULTS OF 30 YEARS' STRUGGLE FOR REPRESENTATION 280
    The 15 European Countries 280
    The Dutch Case 283
    An Enlarged Europe 284
EXPLAINING THE SUCCESS 285
    Voting 285
    Recruitment 285
    Selection 286
    Election 287
    Representation 287
DANGERS THAT LIE IN WAIT 289
TIME FOR NEW POLITICS 293
    New Politics and Gender 295
GENDER DEMOCRACY AS A CONDITION OF GOOD EUROPEAN
    GOVERNANCE 296

APPENDIX
ABBREVIATIONS OF POLITICAL PARTIES 299

BIBLIOGRAPHY 301

INDEX 315

ACKNOWLEDGEMENTS

Despite the 20 years I have spent studying the under-representation of women in politics, I still become enraged at seeing all-male political panels on television, at the appointment of just one woman in a cabinet of 14 and at the fact that there are only 12 per cent women MPs in the French National Assembly. The fact that there were only 16 per cent female participants in the European Convention, charged with drafting European Constitution, made me want to organise a Europe-wide protest movement of women demanding full participation and representation in these matters, under the threat of not acknowledging the legality of this Constitution.

Why are women in the 21st century not participating in political decision-making on equal terms with men, keeping politics as one of the most traditional, archaic, elitist and alienated sectors of society at a time that wide inclusion and support is so necessary? Finding an answer to this question has been a guiding principle in my work. This book is the reflection of 20 years of research resulting in papers for conferences, chapters in edited books, lectures, and many consultancies for government ministries on the participation of women in politics. Some parts of the text have therefore been published before. Sometimes these publications were co-authored and I would like to thank the co-authors of these papers for letting me use this work here.

Participating in many conferences on the issue of Women and Politics has been very stimulating and has made it possible to share results and new insights. The five-year existence of the European Network 'Women in Decision-Making' has been another inspiring experience. The twice-yearly meetings with women experts from other EU countries has resulted in many concrete ideas on policies directed towards achieving a more balanced participation of women and men in political bodies. I am grateful to all 14 other experts in the Network, and especially to the chair, Sabine de Bethune, for the many stimulating discussions we have had on the empowerment of women in Europe. I have often relied on the work of the Network when writing about developments in different European countries. I thank

Acknowledgements

Marila Guadagnini, Petra Meier, Anna van der Vleuten, Lenita Freidenvall, Yvonne Galligan, Maria Tsolaki, Maddy Mulheims and Jaana Kuusipalo for commenting on the descriptions of their respective countries and on the paragraph on the European Union in chapter two.

A special word of thanks to four colleagues and friends, Kees Niemöller, Michael Laver, Lies Janssen and Hella van de Velde, who commented on (parts of) the text and whose critical remarks I took gratefully into account.

Finally I want to dedicate this book to my parents who have supported me unstintingly throughout my professional life.

Alphen a/d Maas,
May 2004

CHAPTER 1

INTRODUCTION

The problem of ensuring that women are at the heart of political decision-making is now very topical in Europe. This is because, despite all of the international agreements, the research, the recommendations and the untold other efforts, the participation of women in political bodies remains low in all European countries. European governance, in short, still fails to include 50 per cent of women in its political decision-making.

It is a familiar sight, on television and in newspapers, to see at the start of a summit or other high-level political meeting, a group of men in dark suits discussing the strength of the euro, the restoration of peace in Northern Ireland, Israel and Palestine, or the quality of the health service or education. Often women participants at these meetings are very few or non-existent. The same is true for the pictures of newly installed parliaments: only a few brightly coloured dresses among the dark grey or dark blue suits.

The core of the problem of the under-representation of women in politics is that it is such a persistent phenomenon as well as a global one. According to the Inter-Parliamentary Union, we find, in the 183 existing parliaments in the world as of 31 May 2004, that only 15 per cent of legislators are women. Looking at both Upper and Lower Houses combined, there are 18 per cent women parliamentarians in Europe, 18 per cent in the Americas, 12 per cent in the Pacific countries, 14 per cent in the sub-Saharan countries, 15 per cent in Asia and 6 per cent women legislators in the Arab States. The participation of women in national cabinets is often lower. In many countries, the enfranchisement of women became a reality in the beginning of the 20th century. At the beginning of a new century, one would expect to find women taking part on an equal footing with men in political decision-making. Nevertheless, the contrary is true. It seems that while women have in most countries the right to be elected as well as to vote, *de facto*, they continue to be under-represented at all levels of political decision-making.

The empowerment of women is not, however, a neglected issue. Already in 1960, the International Covenant on Civil and Political Rights stated: 'The States party to the present covenant undertake to ensure the equal right of men and women to the enjoyment of all civil and political rights set forth in the present covenant'. In addition, in 1995 the European Council of Ministers adopted the following resolution: 'The Council affirms that balanced participation in decision-making in every sphere of life constitutes an important condition for equality between men and women'.

Why do political leaders attach importance to this issue? The under-representation of women in national parliaments poses a problem in terms of both the practice and the theory of politics. In practical terms, the under-representation of women in political leadership is even more remarkable when one realises that women have succeeded in gaining access to other sectors of society in many European countries. Moreover, equality between men and women is now a leading political principle all over Europe. Taking part in decision-making however, in politics as well as in the private sector, typically remains a male privilege. Let us first discuss the under-representation of women from a political point of view.

THE POLITICS OF GENDER REPRESENTATION

The persistent under-representation of women in politics poses a problem for the functioning of representative democracy. Europe is a continent of long-established democracies. Since the modern political systems are responsible for large numbers of citizens and complex interactions are involved in most of the decision-making, the only effective way to do this is to delegate many decisions to elected representatives. All European democracies, therefore, are representative democracies or, to be more accurate, representative party democracies. In a modern state with millions of voters and thousands of aspiring candidates for political office, there is an obvious need to bring some structure to the decisions made by voters. In most contemporary systems, political parties provide this structured choice. Political parties provide the candidates and the reasons, other than personal acquaintance for people to choose one candidate rather than another. Since different parties must compete for the support of voters at election time, the key assumption underlying representative party democracy is that political parties and party candidates respond to and articulate the views of voters. The problem now is that the public representatives are almost never a microcosm or cross-section of the public they represent. Every study of political recruitment shows that legislatures almost always include more men than women, more well than badly educated, more affluent than poor, more middle-aged than young, more people working in the public sector than in the private sector and more urban than rural representatives.

The one-sided composition of the legislature in terms of gender poses a problem to the legitimacy of the outcome of political decision-making, if women, as a group in society, have interests that differ from those of men and if women politicians articulate and defend their interests better than their male colleagues. Women as a group have the following in common:

- a historical deprivation of (political) rights;
- a lower participation rate in the labour force, and one which exhibits both horizontal and vertical segregation;
- a capability to bear children, which has resulted, among others, in a gendered division of domestic labour – women are the 'carers' in society.

The interests arising from this collective situation of women can be defined as objective women's interests, in the sense that they are an empirical description of the group situation in which women have found themselves, and are therefore independent of any subjective evaluation. Based on this definition, concrete women's interests can be presented. The first category concerns matters of political equality: women's rights, equal decision-making, equal pay, equal education, individualisation of taxes and social security. The second category concerns matters such as the re-distribution of paid and unpaid labour, work-life balance and childcare facilities. A third group of women's interests follows from the biological difference between men and women. Examples are matters such as health care, the banning of sexual violence against women, and the traffic of women and children (prostitution). The idea is further that women will be more aware, for example, of the need to have control over their own bodies, and therefore of the need for access to family planning, of the need for proper provision in the care of children and others who are physically dependent, and of the need for more protection against sexual violence and harassment.

Early empirical studies of gender differences in parliamentary behaviour and in role and issue orientation confirm the existence of women's and men's specific interests, which is reflected in parliamentary behaviour. In general, given their experiences and interests, women politicians have expanded the scope of politics. Issues such as child care, sexuality and family planning, which were once confined to the private sphere, have only been seen as political since a fair number of women have entered the political bodies. For example Skeije (1990) reported that two-thirds of Norwegian MPs confirmed the existence of gender-structured interests, with no consistent variations between men and women or between the members of

Chapter 1

different parties.[1] Other Scandinavian researchers concluded that women MPs in the 1970s concerned themselves with bills related to social legislation, and to cultural and educational policies, while men concerned themselves with transport, public utilities and economic policy.[2] In a study of British MPs the following reference is made to the representation of women's issues:

> The twenty-five Private Members' Bills which have been successfully introduced by women do seem to show a preference for women's concerns. No less than three relate to alcohol or drunkenness, three to protection of animals, nine to women and children directly and four to consumer interests.[3]

In the Netherlands too, women MPs have tended to occupy themselves more with social functions customarily attributed to women: welfare, health, education, emancipation and the like.[4] Later studies show that these clear gender differences, especially in the division of parliamentary committee work, gradually disappear. Women MPs are being represented in all parliamentary committees, including the 'harder' ones. Studies carried out in the 1990s and 2000s still report, however, on the impact women MPs make to the policy agenda and on the fact that women politicians are more likely than men to act pro-women, for example by prioritising gender equality. Political and party constraints, such as voting discipline enforced by party leadership, cause women MPs to surrender their more feminist point of view at least in their voting behaviour.[5] A study of parliamentary records of 2000 and 2001 of the Scottish Parliament together with interviews showed, for example,

---

[1] H. Skeije, 'Norway: a Case History of Political Integration', paper presented at the UNESCO meeting of experts, February 1990, pp. 18, 19.

[2] S. Sinkkonen and E. Haavio-Mannila, 'The Impact of the Women's Movement and Legislative Activity of Women MPs on Social Development', in M. Rendel (ed.) *Women, Power and Political Systems*, London, Croom Helm, 1981, p. 21. See also C. Bergqvist *et al.* (eds.), *Equal Democracies? Gender and Politics in the Nordic Countries*, Oslo, Scandinavian University Press, 1999.

[3] E. Vallance, *Women in the House. A Study of Women Members of Parliament*, London, Athlone Press, 1979, p. 107.

[4] M. Leyenaar, *De Geschade Heerlijkheid. Politiek Gedrag van Vrouwen en Mannen in Nederland, 1918-1988*. Den Haag, Staatsuitgeverij, 1989, p. 269.

[5] J. Lovenduski and P. Norris, 'Westminster Women: The Politics of Presence', in *Political Studies*, vol. 51, 2003, p. 91.

Introduction

only a few differences in political conduct and styles. However the women MPs themselves perceived different behaviour. According to them they worked 'in a low-profile solution-oriented way', they were 'more outward facing and collectively oriented', and 'they placed less emphasis on oratory and a capacity for thinking on one's feet, and more on establishing a dialogue based on evidence and prior preparation'.[6] And Childs's (2001, 2002) study of British women MPs in 1997 reports further on the strong perception of female representatives that they made a difference for women.[7] Lovenduski and Norris (2003) find, using survey results of 999 interviewed parliamentary candidates and MPs in Britain, no evidence for the claim that women politicians have different values and attitudes than men do. Women showed almost similar scores on the pro-European scale, on the pro-moral traditionalism scale and on the pro-free market economy scale. Significant gender differences only occurred on issues dealing with women's interests, gender equality or the use of affirmative action. Male respondents, regardless of the party, were significantly less in favour.[8]

The functioning of a representative democratic system and the image it projects to the public at large have a fundamental impact on the whole of society. The ideal of democracy rests on the ideals of progress and social justice. Reflection on how to realise these ideals implies a permanent examination of the characteristics of those who can legitimately claim to represent the people and partake in decision-making in the name of them all. Who talks and who decides? Who, by his or her presence, personifies public power? In terms of the gender of public representatives, the current answer is that, for the most part, it is men who do this. Men, especially at the highest levels of decision-making, have held a quasi-monopoly of political power. Consequently, holders of public office and democratically elected

---

[6] F. Mackay, F. Meyers and A. Brown, 'Towards a New Politics? Women and the Constitutional Change in Scotland', in A. Dobrowolsky and V. Hart (eds.) *Women Making Constitutions: New Politics and Comparative Perspectives*, Basingstoke and New York, Palgrave, 2003, p. 92.

[7] S. Childs, 'In Their Own Words: New Labour Women and the Substantive Representation of Women', in *British Journal of Politics and International Relations*, vol. 3:2, 2001, pp. 173-190; S. Childs, ' Hitting the Target: Are Labour Women MPs "Acting for" Women?', in K. Ross (ed.) *Women, Politics and Change,* Hansard Society Series in Politics and Government, Oxford University Press, 2002, p. 152. In the same volume see also J. Freedman, 'Women in the European Parliament', pp. 184, 185.

[8] J. Lovenduski and P. Norris, 2003, pp. 94, 95.

representatives have given a masculine image to the role of 'representative of the people'.

Democracy is based upon the participation of *all* citizens in political decision-making. A clearly one-sided composition of representative bodies poses the problem of the legitimacy of existing political structures. The current public mistrust towards the representative system may be a result of the exclusiveness of politics.

THE POLICY OF GENDER REPRESENTATION

The under-representation of women in politics poses also a problem to decision-makers, because in a way it is a failure of policy-making. Equality legislation that can be found in most Western European countries and specific policies to increase the participation of women have so far failed. Equality of the sexes is considered a basic human right in western democracies. Today, equality of rights for all, including the right to full participation in all areas of life, is widely recognised in both national (constitutions) and international legal instruments. One can say that a culture of equality is increasingly detectable in Europe, identifiable on the agendas of national governments as well as of inter- and transnational organisations. In most of the 15 countries under investigation[9] there is a certain willingness in both state and society to promote and implement policy initiatives aimed at achieving an equal distribution of economic, social and political resources between men and women. A product of this culture of equality has been the establishment of various governmental institutions that are responsible for dealing with different aspects of the advancement of women. What we also see is that in most of the 15 countries the overall position of women has improved. Compared to the 1950s, when in many countries women were legally not persons, the economic and social position of women has clearly improved. In most countries, the majority of adult women are gainfully employed and women have caught up with men in education. Tax systems and pension-schemes have been individualised and made independent of marital status. Moreover, especially in those countries where a critical mass of women MPs have been participating in decision-making, like the Scandinavian countries, we find a wide range of child-care policies and parental benefit and parental leave policies.

---

[9] When we refer in this book to the '15 countries' we talk about the 15 Member States of the European Union before 1 May 2004.

However, so far equality policies have not yet resulted in changing those structures in society that contribute to and sustain the under-representation of women in politics. A good example is the organisation of the labour market. In the majority of the 15 countries, the organisation of labour is still not geared to combine work with parental responsibilities. Structural changes in this regard would involve in all countries the introduction of extensive public child care, parental benefits and parental leave for both women and men and the right for both parents to shorten their working hours when their children are small. Time constraints still form an important reason for women *not* to pursue a political career. Other examples are the gender biases in procedures for selecting candidates for representative offices. We come across to a Catch 22 situation: still too many obstacles keep women away from leadership positions in politics, while at the same time women are needed in these high-level powerful positions, because then they can take decisions in order to change the underlying structural mechanisms that favour men.

POSITIVE CONTRIBUTION

There are other, more pragmatic reasons to consider the one-sided composition of representative bodies a problem. Given the demographic changes and specifically the low birth rate that we find in many EU Member States, an efficient use of human resources is vital in order to face the challenges of tomorrow's Europe. In the Netherlands, the expected future shortage of labour in most economic sectors make women employees an important target, since only 53 per cent of women are employed for more than 12 hours a week, with a majority of them working part-time. Private companies and governmental organisations are setting up campaigns to attract women potential employees, also for the highest levels.

Another change from 20 years ago is that women are no longer viewed as victims in need of special treatment. Policy-makers and high-level decision-makers are more aware of the fact that substantively important input is lacking when there is a one-sided composition of the management team. We see that, in the realm of politics, parties have become more and more aware that a greater representativeness of their parliamentary party leads to a greater legitimacy (more people are inclined to accept the decisions that were taken), to a higher responsiveness (women politicians are in general more receptive to the problems of their own group) and to higher levels of support (women operate in other networks so they will involve other people in their political work). In the economic sector women's contribution to leadership and management is much more valued these days. A tough, hierarchical organisational structure causes too much dependence on the part of employees. More commitment and responsibility from the staff is necessary, however, when companies need to be flexible in order to compete. Company leaders are looking for high-level management in which masculine and feminine leadership qualities can be combined. Leaders of the future have to be able to build relations with others, to communicate and to share information and power. The new trend in corporate governance is that companies operate more like a family and less like an army. And women are traditionally seen by most people as better equipped to lead a family.[10]

These days there are no longer many people who hold the opinion that a woman should not become a politician. To the contrary, there are many reasons why a gender-balanced representation in cabinet and parliament is preferable over a male-dominated legislation or government. It strengthens the equality principle and the democratic character of the political bodies and it means an efficient use of potential talent and ability. And as long as women and men perform different tasks and therefore have separate political interests, a balance of women and men MPs articulating and defending interests will increase the legitimate power and responsiveness of political decision-making. Recruitment officers have become more and more aware of the fact that without the full participation of women in political decision-making, the political process will be less effective than it should be.

THE CASE OF THE NETHERLANDS

The practical situation is that we find a great variety in levels of representation of women in the legislatures of the different countries under investigation. In Sweden, Finland, Denmark, the Netherlands, Belgium, Austria and Germany, women take more than 30 per cent of the seats in parliament. In Greece, France, Italy and Ireland women's representation is less than 15 per cent, while in Luxembourg, Portugal, Spain and the UK the percentage of women MPs is between 15 and 30. The explanatory framework presented in the next chapters will show that women face many barriers and opportunities along the path to a seat in the legislature. All these factors help us to explain the variety in women's representation among the 15 states. For example the progress in the Scandinavian countries can be traced to

---

[10] A. van Vianen and A. Fischer, 'Sexeverschillen in voorkeuren voor een 'mannelijke' organisatiecultuur', in *Gedrag en Organisatie,* vol. 11:5, 1998, pp. 249-264.

Introduction

the setting of quotas in the largest parties in the 1970s, but also to the party system and the fact that one party, the Social Democratic Party, has been the dominant party for years. The low figures for representation in the Southern European countries can be explained by the electoral system (France, Italy), but also by the influence of the church and its stance on the role of women in society and, often related to this, the culture of gender equality.

The Netherlands can be placed between these two extremes. Here, we find a relatively high proportion (36 per cent) of women in parliament, despite the traditional division of gender roles that lasted until the 1960s, the dominance of the Christian Democratic Party and the fact that quotas were never really applied. Other factors explain the positive attitude towards the political integration of women, especially the role of government policy. A case study of the Netherlands is used to explore a range of issues surrounding the empowerment of women in Europe. The reason this case study is important is that it shows ways in which the active pursuit of public policies promoting the integration of women into politics may have a substantial and lasting impact.

In the context of this book, the Dutch case is interesting for other reasons as well. First, there is its historical heritage of strong social and political segregation along the lines of religion and class combined with a stable political system.[11] This 'consociational democracy' and pillarisation (*verzuiling*) are relevant in understanding the political role of women. For example, the strong religious overtones in society diminished the possibilities for women to participate in the political arena. In general, the practice of religion encouraged and strengthened the *de facto* inequality of women in the family and in society by perpetuating the idea that a woman's place is in the home. A second interesting characteristic is the contradiction in norms and values related to gender roles. We find at the one hand the long-term structure of breadwinners and conservative family policies. On the other hand, there is a considerable freedom of thought on sexual matters, for instance the legislation on abortion. Bussemaker and Voet (1998) refer to the images of the preacher and the merchant which can be both found in the Dutch national character. The Netherlands is liberal and feminist as far as attitudes and ideas are concerned, but more conservative in behaviour and in organisational structures. They give two examples such as the fact that full participation of women in the labour market is viewed as desirable, but in practice many women are working part-time because

---

[11] A. Lijphart, *Verzuiling, Pacificatie en Kentering in de Nederlandse Politiek*, Amsterdam, De Bussy, 1968.

of the structural difficulties in combining work and care. Another example is the broad public support for an equal division of the caring tasks between men and women, but again surveys show that in practice women perform most of the caring tasks.[12]

PLAN OF THE BOOK

This book thus sets out to explain the high level of current concern for the under-representation of women in politics. It explores the reasons behind recent favourable attitudes towards sharing political power with women in the Netherlands and in other European countries. The book consists of three parts. Generally, the first part of the book sets up the problems for women's representation in Europe while the case study of the Netherlands in the second part of the book permits us to make concrete many of the obstacles and strategies we identify. It also points to future expectations about the representation of women in Europe that are explored in the third part of the book. Is the setting of quotas the solution for tackling the under-representation of women? Alternatively, should governments themselves introduce legislation that forces parties to nominate women? More generally, the third part concerns the circumstances under which political players can be influenced to change institutions and procedures in favour of newcomers to politics. In this regard, the current 'crisis of politics' opens a window of opportunity for changing the underlying male-biased structures.

We thus begin in the next chapter with a sketch of the political representation of women in the 15 countries that are the object of this study. In most European countries, the political empowerment of women happened slowly, but at the turn of the century, we find that women representatives became more visible. Of special interest is the difference between the countries in the increase rate. For several groups of countries we will briefly describe the development in political involvement of women focussing on the electoral system of the countries analysed, the party system, the impact of the integrated and autonomous women's movement and the role the government has played over the years in stimulating or blocking the participation of women in parliament. We also look at the European level and the representation figures of women in the ten countries that joined the EU on 1 May 2004. The chapter concludes with an evaluation of the progress that has

---

[12] J. Bussemaker and R. Voet, *Gender, Participation and Citizenship in the Netherlands*, Aldershot Ashgate, 1998, p. 8.

Introduction

been made in the 15 countries. The objective of this chapter is to give the readers a feel for the persistent character of the under-representation of women in politics and the (lack of) progress after 80 years of gaining the right to vote and the right to be elected.

In chapter 3, a theoretical framework is presented of possible barriers for women to enter politics. Based on a large body of academic research it is now possible to develop a framework to characterise the obstacles that women find on their path towards a political position.

The second part of this book homes in on the Netherlands. Chapter 4 starts with a description of the political system and its consequences for the participation of women. Then we focus on the development of the Dutch party system and the political parties' attitude towards the integration of women in their midst. The narrative on women's political empowerment starts at the end of the 19th century when women demanded the right to vote and be elected. We follow the steps of Aletta Jacobs, the first woman ever to challenge the electoral laws by registering as a voter. The struggle for women's suffrage has taken about 25 years, in the face of opposition based mainly on the conception that a woman's proper role was raising a family.

Chapter 5 describes the process of political empowerment of women in the Netherlands. Four periods are distinguished: the period of the *pioneers*, the women who entered parliament between 1917-1946; the period of the *tokens* or *group representatives*, the women MPs from 1946 until the mid-1970s; the period of the *defenders of women's interests* from 1975-1990 and the 1990s that can be characterised by the *players*. We will see that in the first period there was no conscious activity to select women as MPs. Only unmarried, upper class and highly educated women were acceptable to the party leadership. In the second period parties accepted that they should select at least one woman in the parliamentary party or cabinet. Those women were selected because they were women and they were expected only to deal with the interests of women as mothers and home-makers. From the mid-1970s on, the under-representation of women in political decision-making became an issue on the agenda of parties, women's organisations and the government. The mid-1970s mark a turning-point in the political representation of women. From that time on many more women MPs defended and articulated women's issues, now much more broadly defined, and a parliamentary committee on gender equality was established. In the final period, the 1990s and 2000s the number of women MPs has reached the critical mass of 35 per cent. Parties and policy-makers recognise the fact that having more women in their midst is an asset for the organisation. Interestingly enough we will see that, with many more women

Chapter 1

MPs present, special attention for women's issues and gender equality is less than in the previous periods.

At the end of this chapter we discuss the participation at the local level, since, in contrast with other representative bodies, here there is hardly any progress in the numerical participation of women in the councils.

Chapter 6 attempts to explain the willingness of most parties to share power with women by describing the activities of three relevant players in this process: women's organisations, political parties and the Netherlands government. The chapter deals with the current strategies and policies of each of these sets of players as well as the philosophy behind them. The chapter concludes by pointing to the government as an important player in getting more women into the representative bodies. We describe the concrete policies the government set out to increase the number of women in high-level political decision-making, like providing grants to political parties and influencing the nomination processes of the appointment of mayors.

Based on the previous chapters conclusions on the empowerment of women in the Netherlands are drawn in chapter 7. It focuses on the question of whether the increase in representation is a long lasting development or a short upheaval in Dutch politics by analysing the results of the parliamentary elections in 2002 and 2003. In this chapter we will look again into the activities of women's organisations, of the political parties and of the government in order to judge their performance with regard to the political empowerment of women.

The third and last part of the book explores recent debates and developments in Europe on this issue of gender representation. Chapter 8 reviews the debate on 'parity democracy', a concept that is embraced by women in the southern countries, where it is seen as a leading principle to get more women in leadership positions. In the northern countries however, the concept is rejected since it takes sexual differences as fundamental. Here we find quotas set by the parties, and, especially in the Scandinavian countries, these quotas certainly had their uses. The chapter also discusses the most recent developments in this context, the parity law that was accepted by the French parliament in 1999. This regulation put the principle into practice and adopted a law ruling that 50 per cent of the representative bodies should consist of women. The chapter discusses the implication of this law and other concrete examples of quota legislation in Europe.

Chapter 9 deals with another European debate, the so-called crisis of politics. The fact that a large proportion of citizens now turn their back on (party) politics is crucial in this context, since this increases the pressure on the political system both to change and to find ways of involving more people, including women. What this chapter does is to analyse the crisis of politics using a gender perspective and

Introduction

present possible ways to change these institutions in such a way that women can begin to take part in equal numbers in the decision-making process. A concrete example of how to use an institutional change for the benefit of women (and other newcomers to the political system) is the plan to have elections to the European Parliament conducted according to a common electoral system. In this chapter, we present a woman-friendly electoral system, based on best practices of gender and representation.

Will politics in Europe be dealt with by women and men on an equal basis, once the Belgium and French example of quota-legislation are followed by the other Member States? On the basis of the historical and cultural analysis of the political empowerment of women in Europe an attempt is made in the last chapter to answer questions about the future role of women in politics. Is it possible to predict future trends and outcomes with regard to political leadership of women, while taking into account developments such as globalisation, the dislocation of political decision-making, the technological developments concerning communication and the changing role of both women and men in society as well as the demands for political representation of other newcomers, for example the increasing group of ethnic minorities?

PART I:
DEMOCRATIC DEFICIT: A COMPARATIVE PERSPECTIVE

CHAPTER 2

POLITICAL REPRESENTATION OF WOMEN IN FIFTEEN EUROPEAN COUNTRIES

This second chapter takes a comparative perspective by analysing the relative increase in the representation of women in different European national legislatures. In most European countries, the political empowerment of women happened at a slow pace but, at the turn of the century, we find that women representatives became more visible. Of special interest is the difference between countries in the rate of increase of women's representation. For several groups of countries, we will briefly describe the development in political involvement of women, focusing on the electoral system of the countries analysed, the party system, the impact of the integrated and autonomous women's movement, and the role government has played over the years in stimulating or blocking the participation of women in parliament. The following groups of countries will be analysed: the Scandinavian countries Finland, Denmark and Sweden; the southern countries, Greece, Spain, Portugal and Italy; France, Belgium and Luxembourg; the two Anglo-Saxon countries Britain and Ireland; and Germany and Austria. The Netherlands is missing from this detailed overview since part two of this book is devoted to an analysis of the empowerment of Dutch women.

The European Union as an intergovernmental institution has also been instrumental in convincing Member States to applying gender equality in political decision-making. The chapter concludes with an overview of these EU activities and with an evaluation of the progress that has been made in the separate states.

The overview presented in this chapter is based on the description of developments in separate countries. In the next chapter, however, a more structured analysis will be presented by putting the separate findings into an analytical framework.

Chapter 2

WOMEN IN POLITICS IN THE 15 EUROPEAN COUNTRIES

Studying the political systems of the 15 countries under investigation, one is inclined to conclude that the only thing these countries have in common is their location on the same continent. There is a great variety in political and party systems as there is in the representation of women in legislatures. In all 15 states, members of representative bodies such as national legislatures, regional and local councils, are chosen using popular elections, but the methods used to elect representatives differ widely from country to country. While elections in every state involve citizens in casting votes for candidates and political parties, it is a remarkable fact that no two Member States use precisely the same electoral system. There is considerable variation even in the general types of electoral laws that determine how votes cast by the public are transformed into representatives holding seats in the legislature. As well as differing in their electoral systems, the 15 countries also vary widely in the way in which parties select their candidates. Even within a single country, different parties typically use different candidate selection procedures. Table 2.1 shows some key features of electoral systems in the 15 countries.

Previous research has shown all of these different aspects of the electoral and party system to have an impact on the political representation of women.[1] But Table 2.1 also makes it clear that these institutional factors do not fully explain why in some countries more women rule in politics. In October 2003 we find more than one-third women MPs in the Scandinavian countries, the Netherlands, Belgium and Austria, while in Greece, France, Ireland and Italy less than 15 per cent of seats in parliament are held by women. We need to take other factors into account, including the level of participation of women in the labour market, the level of education, the equality index of a country and the predominant religion. In table 2.2 we find information on the percentages of employed women together with the percentages of women MPs and the date women got the vote.

In all countries female employment has expanded considerably over the postwar period, resulting in the percentages in Table 2.2. The highest percentages of employed women are found in Denmark and Sweden, closely followed by Finland, the Netherlands, the United Kingdom, Austria and Portugal. Another related development (not reported in the table), is the narrowing of the gender gap in employment. Spain, Greece, Italy and Luxembourg show the largest gaps, while

---

[1] See M. Leyenaar, *How to Create a Gender Balance in Political Decision-Making*, Brussels, European Commission, 1996.

Table 2.1: Key features of European electoral systems

Country	Electoral system	No. MPs	No. constituencies	Electoral threshold	Pref'l voting	Party system[1]	% Women MPs[2]
Austria	List-PR	183	43	1 seat/4%	Yes	4.5	34
Belgium	List-PR	150	20	No	Yes	11.7	35
Denmark	List-PR	175	17	2%	Yes	9.0	38
Finland	List-PR	200	15	No	Yes	9.7	37
France	2-ballot SMP	577	577	No	No	7.0	12
Germany	AMS	± 603	299	3 seats/5%	No	5.0	32
Greece	List-PR	300	56	3%	Yes	5.0	9
Ireland	STV	166	41	No	Yes	7.0	13
Italy	AMS	630	475	4%	No	19.3	11
Luxembourg	List-PR	60	4	No	Yes	5.5	17
Netherlands	List-PR	150	1	0.67%	Yes	10.5	37
Portugal	List-PR	230	20	No	No	4.7	19
Spain	List-PR	350	52	No	No	11.5	28
Sweden	List-PR	349	29	4%/12% in 1 const.	Yes	7.0	45
UK	SMP	659	659	No	No	9.0	18

Source: adapted from M. Gallagher *et al.*, 2001, pp. 304, 322.
[1] Actual number of different parties in parliament in the 1990s (average).
[2] Source: Website IPU, data are from 30 October 2003.

at the opposite end of the ranking are again Sweden and the other Scandinavian countries.

Despite the fact that in nine of the 15 countries women were legally allowed to enter parliament around 1920-1925, by 1980, some 60 years later, not many had managed to do so. In more than half of the 15 countries there were fewer than

Chapter 2

Table 2.2: Percentage of employed women, the date of women's suffrage and the percentage of women MPs.

Country	% Women labour market 2002*	Date women's vote	% Women MPs, October 2003
Austria	63	1919	34
Belgium	51	1948	35
Denmark	72	1915	38
Finland	66	1906	37
France	57	1944	12
Germany	59	1919	32
Greece	43	1952	9
Ireland	55	1922	13
Italy	42	1945	11
Luxembourg	52	1918	17
Netherlands	66	1919	37
Portugal	61	1974	19
Spain	44	1931	28
Sweden	72	1919	45
UK	65	1928	18
Average EU	56		26

* Source: Eurostat 2002. Percentages of women who are employed for more than *one* hour a week in the age range of 15-64.

10 per cent women MPs. By the beginning of the 1990s representation of women had improved in most countries, but the percentages in Belgium, France, Greece and Britain were still very low. In 2003, parliament comprised more than 25 per cent female MPs in eight countries. In countries such as Greece, Ireland and Italy, however, there had been hardly any progress at all.

Scandinavian Countries[2]

What do the three Scandinavian countries have in common to explain the large number of women in politics, something that stands out in contrast to women's electoral fortunes in the other countries? First, in all three countries, the electoral system is seen as encouraging women's representation through proportional representation in large multi-member constituencies, with preferential voting and electoral thresholds (in Denmark and Sweden) that keep small parties at bay. For example, in Finland where open lists are used, parties have from the beginning nominated women on their lists, who then got a substantial part of the vote.[3] Secondly, citizens in all three countries are either secular or Protestant and, contrary to the ethos of the Catholic Church, there never has been a strong tradition that women should not become involved in politics. Thirdly, especially in Sweden and Denmark, electoral support for Social Democratic Parties has been high. In general, leftist parties are more inclined to integrate women in the party than are right-wing parties. In the period 1950-2000, between 40 and 45 per cent of all voters in Sweden, and in Denmark between 32 and 40 per cent, voted for a Social Democratic Party.[4] In Finland the SDP share of the vote averaged around 25 per cent. Another consequence of social democratic rule is a social and political climate that values equality, including gender equality. The acceptance of gender equality as an important organising principle in politics and society and the long tradition of working towards this goal has made it easier to institutionalise equal representation of women and men in decision-making.

What also helped was the passing of equality legislation in all three countries, guaranteeing a balanced composition of public committees and boards.[5] For example, the Finnish Act on Equality between Women and Men that was passed in

---

[2] Parts of the texts on Sweden has been published before in: M. Leyenaar, B. Niemoller, M. Laver and Y. Galligan: *Electoral Systems in Europe: a Gender Impact Assessment*, European Commission, 1999. I thank my colleagues for letting me use these parts for this book.

[3] S. Bergman, 'Frauen in die Finnischen Politik: Auf dem weg zur Halfte der Macht?', in B. Hoecker (ed.), *Handbuch Politische Partizipation von Frauen in Europa*, Leske & Budrich, 1998, p. 102.

[4] M. Gallagher, M. Laver and P. Mair, *Representative Government in Modern Europe*, McGraw and Hill, 2001, p. 204.

[5] A. Borchorst, 'What is Institutionalised Gender Equality?', in C. Berqvist *et al.* (eds.), 1999, pp. 161-164.

1987 states that promotion of the equality of the sexes is an official duty of public authorities. It also prescribes a minimum percentage of both women and men in government committees, advisory boards and other corresponding bodies; in municipal bodies, exclusive of municipal councils, this is 40 per cent, unless there are special reasons to the contrary.[6] The existence of this kind of legislation made it more acceptable for political parties to introduce methods to increase the number of women in their midst.

Fifthly, women involved in the new women's movement of the 1960s and 1970s did not turn their back to party politics. Unlike in other Western European countries, where a considerable part of women's new-found political focus was channelled into feminist and protest politics, in Sweden and Denmark one of the important effects of the new women's movement was to revitalise existing women's organisations such as the women's groups of political parties. This also led to an intensification of women's activity in the party organisations as a whole. Thus, instead of working for change from outside the party system, newly mobilised women in the Scandinavian countries sought to work within the parties.

The women's factions have always offered a power base for politically ambitious women. Between 1920 and 1935 women formed their own organisations inside the parties and, although the overall attitude towards women's groups was negative, their existence was tolerated because of their role in attracting female electoral support.[7] Women's party organisations continually sought increased female political representation. They provided parties with a ready supply of politically skilled women for recruitment to high-level party positions and cabinet posts. In doing so, women's factions provided a means for women to enhance their political qualifications. Thus a major route to parliament for Scandinavian women has been through achieving prominence in the women's organisations of the political parties.[8]

A sixth explanation is the participation of women at the *local* political level. From the 1970s on, women party members became very active in their local party branches and, over time, came to equal men in holding party office at this level. This too became an important route to parliament. A final explanation is the

---

[6] See www.db-decision.de.

[7] E. Haavio-Manilla *et al.* (eds.), *Unfinished Democracy. Women in Nordic Politics*, Oxford, Pergamon Press, 1985, p. 17.

[8] *Ibid.*, p. 22.

extensive use of quotas, in Finland with regard to governmental bodies and in Denmark and Sweden in electoral bodies. When in the 1970s the participation of women in the party ranks and in the representative bodies stayed far behind that of men, the women's factions in Denmark and Sweden started to increase pressure on party leadership, arguing that women's under-representation was a contradiction of democratic principles and equal rights. In order to gain support for the introduction of quotas, women first demanded quotas for internal bodies and committees. Here it was easy to enlarge the size of the committee to allow seats for women without having to get rid of men.[9] The second step was then to establish quotas for the parliamentary party. By 1972 the Swedish Liberal Party had already adopted a recommendation that a gender quota of 40 per cent was to be used for seats on district or constituency boards. In 1974 the recommendation was extended to include the nomination to party lists in elections. The Green Party in Sweden introduced the first internal party quotas in 1981 and expanded this to the electoral bodies in 1987. The Left Party introduced quotas in 1987 as well. The largest Swedish party, the Social Democratic Party waited until 1993 to adopt a zipper system: men and women were to be alternated on the electoral lists.[10] 'Each sex has the right to a representation of at least 40 per cent of the Social Democratic candidates for local and regional elections'.

The Danish Social Democratic Party adopted internal party quotas of 40 per cent in 1983 and for the regional and local councils in 1988. This quota was never expanded to the national level.[11] The Socialist People's Party introduced quotas back in 1977 and abandoned them again in 1996. The Left Socialist Party, a party that no longer exists, introduced internal and electoral quotas in 1985.[12]

Over the years, parties have been in competition to show a public face that is sensitive to gender issues. Women have used this competition effectively to press for improved representation within their own parties. An example is the general election of 1991 in Sweden, when the numbers of women elected to parliament dropped from 37.5 per cent to 33 per cent. Women then began seriously to

---

[9] D. Dahlerup, 'Using Quotas to Increase Women's Political Representation', in A. Karam (ed.), *Women in Parliament: Beyond Numbers*, Stockholm, IDEA, 1998, p. 101.

[10] D. Dahlerup and L. Freidenvall, 'Quotas as a fast track to equal political representation for women. Why Scandinavian is no longer the model', paper presented at the 19th International Political Science Association World Congress, Durban, June 2003, p. 17.

[11] D. Dahlerup, 1998, p. 100.

[12] See www.idea.int/quota.

Chapter 2

question party selection processes. Voter surveys indicated sizeable support for a woman's party. In response to this potential electoral challenge, practically all parties paid renewed attention to enforcing equal representation for women and men on candidate lists.[13]

The Scandinavian case thus illustrates that it takes more than a PR electoral system to guarantee an advance in women's political representation. Other conditions were necessary to bring about this goal, including the mobilisation of women in political organisations and the willingness of parties to respond positively to women's representational demands. The determination of successive governments, for example by passing Acts on equality legislation and by providing an equality infrastructure in the three countries, has also been of great importance. The result has been that, these days, the goal of equal distribution of power between women and men is no longer questioned in the culture of Scandinavian politics, as can be seen in 2003 in Finland which was for a short time ruled by a woman Head of State together with a woman prime minister. In the 2000 presidential elections, of the seven candidates joining the race, four were women. After two rounds of voting Tarja Halonen, a cabinet minister, won the election and became the first woman president of Finland.

Table 2.3: Representation of women in parliament and in government.[14]

	% Women MPs			% Women Ministers		
	1980	*1988-89*	*2002-03*	*1980*	*1988-89*	*2000-03*
Denmark	24	29	38	16	21	28
Finland	26	32	37	18	22	39
Sweden	26	31	45	24	29	45

---

[13] D. Sainsbury, 'The Politics of the Increased Women's Representation: the Swedish Case', in J. Lovenduski and P. Norris (eds.), *Gender and Party Politics*, London, Sage, 1993, pp. 282-285.

[14] For all tables on the participation of women in parliament and government the source for the figures of 1980 and 1990 is: M. Janova and M Sineau, 'Women's Participation in Political

Greece, Italy, Portugal and Spain

These are four countries located in southern Europe, of which two had an extremely low representation of women in parliament in 2002. What are the common elements for explaining the (lack of) power of women in these countries?

Parliamentary democracy re-emerged in Greece in 1975 after a seven-year period of military rule. In Portugal and Spain democracy was installed, respectively, in 1974 and 1975. Voting rights for women arrived rather late in all four countries. In Spain women were allowed to vote and become candidates for office in 1931. However, there were no democratic elections during the Franco regime so it took until 1977 before women could enjoy their democratic rights again. Italian women gained the vote in 1945, Greek women were granted this right in 1952, while *all* adult women in Portugal could vote for the first time in the parliamentary elections of 1976.

We find list-PR systems in three of the four countries. In Italy a mixed system is used at the national level: 75 per cent of deputies are elected in single-member constituencies and 25 per cent through a list-PR system. The mixed system was introduced in 1993. Before then, Italy too used a very proportional type of PR system. Italy, Spain and Portugal have in common that preferential voting, for example for a woman candidate, is not allowed in parliamentary elections (in Italy only for the 25 per cent of the seats that are elected through PR).[15] Parties decide on the order of the list of candidates and voters cast their vote for a party. In Greece, voters express a preference for party lists and, within each list, for individual candidates. Constituency size is another factor. Both in Spain and in Greece, district magnitude is small and only a few candidates are elected in each district, making it more difficult for parties to balance the list according to gender. The electoral system is certainly to blame for the low representation figures, but it is clearly not

---

Power in Europe: an Essay in East-West Comparison', in *Women's Studies International Forum*, vol. 15:11, 1992, pp. 115-128; figures for 1988/1989: International Centre for Parliamentary Documentation. Series Reports and Documents, no. 14, Geneva, March 1988, pp. 10-12; figures for 2002: IPU database (www.ipu.org). Figures on the relative number of women ministers come from different sources. Since the sources often provide slightly different figures, and since it is not always clear whether junior ministers are involved in the figures as well, these data are less reliable compared to the data on women in parliaments. The percentages of women ministers in 2002 come from a research report published by the Council of Europe, *Women in Politics in the Council of Europe Member States*, December 2002.

the only factor determining the participation rate of women. Other factors minimising political participation of women have to be taken into account, especially cultural attitudes, as well as the rural geography and gate-keeping practices within political parties.

In all four countries, religion (Catholicism in Spain, Portugal and Italy and Greek Orthodoxy in Greece) has played an important role in the development of strict notions of male and female roles in society. Part of this gender ideology is that men take care of public and community affairs, while women nurture the family. In these countries, the prevailing model, supported by culture and by governmental policies, is that of the male breadwinner and the female home-maker. In Greece for example, educational standards of women are still lower than those of men and, as well as in Italy and Spain, the proportion of adult women with a paid job is less than 44 per cent.[16] Given the influence of the Church, especially in rural areas, it is not surprising therefore that there is little challenge to the dominant traditional perceptions of what are considered to be appropriate male and female interests. These views are reinforced by the acceptance by older women and rural women of their perceived inferior social status, by a lack of interest in political matters among women (particularly older women) and by a relatively higher level of interest in politics by men of all ages.[17] These perceptions of the proper roles of men and women also permeated the political parties. Guadagnini (1993) says of the Christian Democratic Party of Italy that it recognised equality for women only when this did not threaten traditional family roles. 'Thus the party supported policies of gender equality in the workplace, since women must work to help support the family, but it stopped short of encouraging women's participation in such public activities as politics'.[18] However, younger women, urban women and women with a higher than average educational level hold more egalitarian views and are more likely to develop an interest in politics.

Another factor of importance is the personalised nature of politics, especially in Greece and in Italy. Cliental voting, based on an exchange of favours, is still the

---

[15] In Italy preferential votes can be casted in the elections for the European Parliament.

[16] In Greece, the female literacy rate in 1996 was 89 per cent as against the male rate of 98 per cent.

[17] M. Pantelidou Maloutas, 'Griechenland. Frauen als Akteurinnen in der politischen Kultur Griechenlands', in B. Hoecker (ed.), 1998, p. 150.

[18] M. Guadagnini, 'A Partitocrazia Without Women: the Case of the Italian Party System', in J. Lovenduski and P. Norris (eds.), *Gender and Party Politics*, Sage Publishers, London, 1993, p. 180.

norm. Voters prefer politicians they trust to be able to return favours. Since women candidates are seen as less prestigious and less instrumental they are less favoured by the electorate.[19] Then there is the importance people attach to a personal network in the party. In order to be selected for an eligible place on the list, intense personal relations with many (local) party leaders is a necessary condition. A long party career is a prerequisite for selection. Not only are there significantly fewer women party members, but in general their party career is also much shorter. For example, in PASOK, one of Greece's main political parties, women constituted only 15 per cent of the membership in the 1990s.[20]

Political parties are a very important aspect of life in all four countries. Both in Greece and Italy they control not only the articulation and mediation of interests, but are also important providers of political and non-political jobs. It has never been easy to gain political power through working in either grass-roots or large-interest organisations. Living under an authoritarian regime caused a general lack of trust in political institutions and of course little experience with democratic rules and procedures. All of this combined with the doubts among feminists about the effectiveness of joining political parties, meant that there was no fight during the preparation of the first democratic parliamentary elections in order to demand fair representation of women. For feminists active in the 1970s and 1980s it was a difficult choice: either acquire power through participating in those institutions, political parties, to whose structures they had not contributed, or work in autonomous women's organisations. In Italy the feminist movement chose, for the most part, to 'maintain an autonomous position rather than create centres of power within parties'.[21] In Spain, too, there was much debate among feminists on whether to participate in the political parties or feminist organisations. In 1979 this led to a split of the Spanish feminist movement and this was one of the reasons why relatively few women got selected and elected in the first decade of the new democracy (only 6 per cent). However, due to pressure of feminists, a national machinery for gender equality came into place at the end of the 1970s, with a special department for gender equality based at the Ministry of Culture and the establishment of the

---

[19] *Ibid.*, p. 185.

[20] A. Cacoullos, 'Greece. Women Confronting Party Politics in Greece', in B. Nelson and N. Chowdhury (eds.), *Women and Politics Worldwide*, Yale University Press, New Haven, 1994, pp. 311-325.

[21] M. Guadagnini, 1993, p. 176.

Chapter 2

Women's Institute in 1983. All this resulted in a government plan to strengthen the social, economic and political role of women in Spain.[22]

In the 1990s, hardly any progress was made in Greece and Italy and, as a result, participation of women in the 21st century is still pitifully low. The reform of the electoral and party system in Italy should have resulted in more women politicians. After all, women politicians were not involved in the party scandals and more women in politics would have been a signal of a new politics replacing the 'old (corrupt) politics'. However the contrary was true. Replacing the list-PR system with a majority system resulted in the nomination of predominantly male candidates in the single member districts. The attempt to counter this effect, by introducing quota legislation for those seats elected by proportional representation with party lists, could not change this in the end. Finally, after the laws had been in operation for two years, the Italian Constitutional Court declared them unconstitutionally (see also chapter 8).[23]

The 21st century may also bring some real changes in Greece. In 1993, women from all parties joined together to lobby for the selection of women candidates in the 1994 European elections. This lobby was effective, with 57 women (38 per cent) out of 150 candidates contesting the election. In the event women won four (16 per cent) of the 25 Greek seats in the European Parliament. The joint effort also resulted in the foundation of the Political Association of Women, focusing on the recruitment of women into politics. Pressure from this organisation and from other, international, sources led in 2000 to the approval of the Greek parliament of an amendment to Article 4 of the Constitution in order to create the possibility to take temporary positive measures for a true implementation of the principle of equality. Given the extreme low representation figures of women in the political bodies, the lowest in the countries of the European Union, the pressure on Greek government to change the electoral laws continued. After a heated debate in March 2002, a law proposed by former Minister of the Interior Vasso Pappandreou, came into effect stating that each sex must be represented by at least one-third in local elections (see also chapter 8).

---

[22] J. Astellarra, 'Spanien. Politische Partizipation und Repräsentation von Frauen in Spanien', in B. Hoecker (ed.), 1998, p. 334.

[23] M. Guadagnini, 'Gendering the Debate on Political Representation in Italy, an Open Challenge', paper prepared for the 96th Annual Meeting of the APSA, Washington, 2000, p. 8.

Table 2.4: Representation of women in parliament and in government

	% Women MPs			% Women Ministers		
	1980	*1988-89*	*2002-03*	*1980*	*1988-89*	*2000-03*
Greece	3	4	9	0*	0	13**
Italy	8	13	10	0	3	8
Portugal	7	8	19	0	0	13
Spain	7	13	28	6	11	21***

* Melina Mercouri became Minister of Culture in 1981.
** 11 in total including 4 women ministers and junior ministers and 7 secretary generals.
***7 in total including 5 junior ministers.

Compared to Italy and Greece, there are relatively more women politicians in Portugal and in Spain. In Spain this can be explained by the victory of the Socialist Party (PSOE) in the election of 1982 and afterwards. Given their absolute majority, the party was able to introduce important reforms improving the social and economic position of women. With regard to their own party organisation in 1987 the PSOE introduced a quota of 25 per cent, which motivated many women to become affiliated. Party membership by women increased from 16 to 20 per cent of the total in 1990 and the proportion of women MPs in the PSOE increased from 7 per cent in 1986 to 19 per cent in 1989. The overall percentage of women in parliament doubled as well, from 7 to 14 per cent. Other parties have followed suit and have set quotas and this certainly has contributed to a representation figure of 28 per cent in the parliament 2000-2004.

In Portugal the representation of women increased from 13 to 19 per cent after the election of 2001. Contrary to the Spanish case this was not the result of quotas set by parties, but of an attempt by the Portuguese government to have a quota law passed. Although the law did not pass through parliament, the debate on the issue of women's political representation shook the parties awake, resulting in many more women candidates than in previous elections.

Chapter 2

In conclusion it seems that the obstacles to women's integration into the electoral process, especially in Greece and Italy, are the following. There is the dominance of strong and pervasive social attitudes affecting women's political involvement. And there appears to be little in the way of challenge to the widespread acceptance of traditional gender roles, although young and educated women are more likely to question these assumptions. In all four countries, political parties are the main gatekeepers for political positions. The closed-list systems used in Italy, Spain and Portugal provide the parties with total power over the election of women MPs. For Greek and Italian women, candidate selection and political representation is inhibited by the male-oriented and personalistic nature of politics. In Portugal and Spain women inside and outside the parties have been able to convince the party leadership to nominate more women in eligible places on the lists.

France, Belgium and Luxembourg

At first sight France and Belgium seem to have a lot in common with regard to the political empowerment of women. In France, women gained the right to vote in 1944, in Belgium in 1948, although here women were allowed to stand as candidates for parliament since 1920. In the same year Belgian women were granted voting rights for *local elections*. The Belgian socialist and liberal parties in particular successfully resisted women's suffrage at the national level, because they feared that the majority of the women's vote would go to the Catholic Party.[24] Leaping ahead to the 21st century, France and Belgium were the first two countries of the 15 under investigation with legislation concerning the political representation of women. As we see in table 2.5, introduction of legislation is understandable given the low percentages of women in both parliaments in the 1980s and 1990s. But here the similarities come to an end. The two countries differ in electoral system, in the role of the new women's movement of the 1970s, in socio-economic conditions of women and in cultural traditions concerning the recruitment of political leaders.

France elects its deputies through a single member plurality (SMP) system in two rounds. If a candidate gets an absolute majority on the first round, he or she is elected to parliament. If not, there is a second round two weeks later, in which only candidates with 12.5 per cent or more of the constituency vote are allowed to

---

[24] L. van Molle and E. Gubin, *Vrouw en Politiek in België*, Lannoo, Tielt, 1998, p. 64.

Table 2.5: Women in parliament and in government.

	% Women MPs			% Women Ministers		
	1980	1988/89	2002/03	1980	1988/89	2000/03
Belgium	7	9	34	12	12	20
France	5	6	12	14	14	26*
Luxembourg	7	17	17	0	8	28

* In total 10, 3 women ministers, 4 women junior ministers and 3 women secretaries of state.

participate. In the second round the candidate with the most votes is elected. SMP is less favourable for the election of women than is a list-PR system (see chapter 3). In France the latter system is used for the election of regional and local councillors and, consequently, we find relatively more women represented at these levels. In 2001 for example, there were 47 per cent women municipal councillors in communities larger than 3500 inhabitants.[25] In France the local political level is closely connected to national politics, mainly because of the practice of combining political mandates, the '*cumul des mandates*'. The idea is that national policy orientations should be reflected at the local level, and the easiest way to combine mandates is to be an MP who is also a mayor or a municipal councillor. This is still a very common practice: in 1997 only 7 MPs did not hold another mandate.[26] Allwood and Wadia (2000) describe how the *cumul des mandats* works negatively for women. First, it has created 'a self-perpetuating, narrow circle of elites which monopolises

---

[25] F. Gaspard, 'Assessment. Women Elected Representatives in French Municipalities', CEMR, *Men and Women in European Municipalities,* Paris, 1998, pp. 35-42. This relative high percentage is of course also a direct effect of the application of the quota law (see chapter 8).

[26] J-P. Dubois (1997), cited in G. Allwood and K. Wadia, *Women and Politics in France, 1958-2000*, Routledge, London, 2000, p. 150.

power and privileges at a number of different levels and which is reluctant to admit newcomers'. The turnover of seats is very low and the number of incumbents is very high. Secondly, it also means that the elected representative is identified with the male 'notable' who 'not only undertook political functions but also exercised a moral, father-like authority'. For women it has been very difficult to adhere to this image, since most often they cannot afford to fulfil all these (unpaid) local functions, either because they do not have the right jobs to do so or their other (caring) responsibilities are an obstacle.[27] Local politics is clearly a common route to parliament and, although there are more women municipal councillors than there are MPs, competition at this level is fierce and not many women are willing to perform several political functions at the same time. But the fact that, in 2001, almost half of all councillors in cities larger than 3500 inhabitants were women (47 per cent) will definitely have a positive impact on women's future representation in the national parliament.

Another feature of French politics is the recruitment through the so-called *Grand Ecoles*, of which the *Ecole Nationale d'Administration* (ENA) is the most prestigious. Women have always been under-represented at these schools and their catching up in educational level and professional experience has not changed this. As we see in other European countries as well, there is no longer a gender difference in educational achievement, but women are still under-represented in the schools and disciplines that lead to political office. The same is true for the entrance of many more women into the labour market. One does not find women in decision-making positions and it is precisely these kinds of jobs that introduce them to the right networks, and thereby ultimately into political office. In short, political parties have been 'masculine coteries' for a very long time, able to neglect women as candidates for elective office.

What about women in the political parties? In the 1960s and 1970s, French feminists chose en masse for a separatist strategy: women's rights were not to be gained by working together with traditional, male-dominated, political institutions like political parties. This attitude weakened the position of the women's factions and allowed parties to continue to be closed to women. In the 1980s however, as a result of internal debates over ideology and strategy, large groups of feminists became interested in working through the formal political institutions. At the same time, women started to improve their educational and professional status and became more active in society. Further, in 1981 the first Minister of Women's Affairs

---

[27] G. Allwood and K. Wadia, 2000, p. 150.

was appointed and she has put the issue of gender and politics on the agenda. All this made parties more aware of the existence of women voters and one way of showing this was to declare adhesion to gender equality in politics. In the 1980s and 1990s, female membership of parties rose to 26 per cent in the Socialist Party, 30 per cent in the Green Party, 35 per cent in the Communist Party and to 40 per cent in the more conservative party RPR.[28]

But the continued extremely low rate of representation in party leaderships and in the parliamentary parties caused frustration among active women both inside and outside the parties. They put even more pressure on the parties to take positive action and, by the end of the 1990s, almost all parties adhered to the concept of parity: numerical equality between men and women. This broad support led to legislation in 1999 requiring that parties include 50 per cent women on their lists of candidates, both in (local and European) elections using PR as well as in national elections. So far the law has not resulted in a gender-balanced representation in parliament, as is shown in table 2.5. Chapter 8 describes the details of this law, including the explanation why it has worked at the local and regional level and failed so far at the parliamentary level.

This table makes it also clear that it was easier for women in France to gain political power through nomination, for example to a ministerial post, than it was through election. According to Kleszcz-Wagner (1998), this is due to the powerful role the president of France plays in the nomination of government members. Several presidents have personally used this influence to bring women into the cabinets.[29]

Belgium is the other country in Europe where legislation, already in place by 1994, required parties to guarantee seats for both sexes. Several women politicians, like the then Minister of Women's Affairs, Miet Smet, together with women representatives in the Senate and in the Chamber of Deputies, fought hard to get this law passed.

The issue of getting more women into politics reached the agenda in the mid-1970s, when for the first time parties addressed the social, economic and legal position of women in their election campaigns. For the parliamentary election of

---

[28] *Ibid.*, pp. 55-62.

[29] A. Kleszcz-Wagner, 'Frankreich. Frauen in Frankreich: heiss geliebt und politisch kaltgestellt', in B. Hoecker (ed.), 1998, p. 136.

1974, women already active in the parties, together with women's organisations, set up a large 'Vote for a Woman Candidate' campaign, while a Feminist Party submitted an all-women list in a few constituencies. All this resulted in an increase of the number of women MPs from 4 to 7 per cent. But despite a lot of activity by the parties' women's sections, a substantial increase was not achieved until 2003.

Belgium elects its representatives through a list-PR system. Two features of the Belgian electoral system are interesting from a gender point of view: the co-optation system and the use of successors. Of the 71 senators, 30 are co-opted: 20 by provincial representatives and 10 nationally by all other senators together. Generally, co-optation is not favourable to newcomers (women), because it facilitates the re-selection of a small (male) party elite. It is often used to appoint prominent party leaders who do not want to go through an election campaign (and risk non-election) and to pick up those party leaders who have not been elected regionally. In Belgium, however, the co-optation system has also been used to compensate for the under-representation of women. In 1995, 20 per cent of nationally co-opted senators were women and 14 per cent of regionally co-opted senators.[30] Co-optation was also used to guarantee representation of candidates belonging to certain strata: the working class, farmers, and the self-employed. The large traditional parties, the Socialist Party and the Christian People's Party reserved seats on their list for these candidates and the related social organisations were asked to nominate potential candidates. Because active, autonomous women's organisations operated within each stratum, these were used as a recruitment pool when local and regional party branches were searching for working class, farming or self-employed candidates. Many women MPs found their way into parliament through these women's organisations.[31] In general the traditional women's organisations in Belgium, who have always been numerous and large, have been instrumental in mobilising and socialising women for politics. Many women politicians have their roots in the Christian Workers Women's Movement (*Kristelijke Arbeiders Vrouwenbeweging*, KAV) or in the National Socialist Women's Movement (*Nationale Socialistische Vrouwenbeweging*, NSV).

Another important aspect of the Belgian electoral system is the fact that there is a list of so-called 'alternates', who take the seat when a MP leaves parliament for whatever reason. This system can work to neutralise the advantages of the list-PR

---

[30] L. van Molle and E. Gubin, 1998, p. 75.
[31] *Ibid.*, p. 327.

system for women, because first-placed male alternates will replace the leaving MPs instead of the number two on the list, which is often a woman candidate.

Apart from these institutional barriers, the (until 2003) rather low representation of women in Belgian politics can be traced back, as in the southern countries, to the dominant ideology of gender roles: women take care of the family and men of public life. Politics remains culturally a man's job and it has been extremely difficult for women to break into this male bastion. The centralised selection of candidates and the system of alternates make it possible for male party leaders to keep women away from eligible places on the lists of candidates. Even the relatively high participation of women in traditional women's organisations, combined with active women's factions within the parties, could not prevent this.

It is understandable therefore, given this lack of progress in the 1980s and 1990s, that politically active women formed the opinion that the only solution would be a law on gender representation. This law passed parliament in 1994 and since then the number of women in the representative bodies has been increasing gradually. Chapter 8 discusses the content of this law. Belgium is also the first EU country with a gender quota regulation for its executive bodies. In 2002 the Belgian parliament accepted a change in the Constitution stating that in each executive body (national government, local and regional governments, but also governing bodies of large social welfare councils) at least one member has to be a woman. One obvious reason why these quota laws have been more readily accepted in Belgium than elsewhere is the familiarity of the Belgian people, given the country's social structure, with language and regional quotas. In the past, however, the existence of deep social cleavages (language, religion, class) were an obstacle to women's political participation since they stopped women from uniting on the issue of gender representation and as such the cleavages worked against the forming of a culture of gender equality.[32]

Contrary to the situation in Belgium and France, women in Luxembourg were granted the right to vote back in 1919. But the fact that such voting rights were granted 30 years earlier did not result in a much higher representation of women

---

[32] A. Woodward, 'Belgien. Politische Partizipation in Belgien: Die gespaltene Frau', in B. Hoecker (ed.), 1998, p. 31.

[33] R. Wagener, 'Luxemburg. Luxemburg: Verspäteter politischer Einsteig der Frauen', in B. Hoecker (ed.), 1998, p. 341.

Chapter 2

in parliament: until 1968, either one woman was represented in the Luxembourg parliament, or none at all.[33] Once again the electoral system may be partly blamed. In Luxembourg voters can either vote for a list or cast personal votes. Voters have as many votes as there are MPs to be elected for that region, with a maximum of two votes per candidate. With personal voting, the voter can choose between candidates on any party list. As in Finland, this system favours well-known candidates, and parties do their utmost to select popular candidates, bypassing newcomers, including women candidates. Another important factor is the more general social role of women in Luxembourg: their participation in the labour market has always been low and cultural pressure on women to become housewives and mothers was very strong. Until 1993, only 37 per cent of adult women participated in the labour market. Furthermore, women themselves have not been very keen to strengthen their political power. Women's organisations in the 1970s and 1980s were not very interested in the representation of women in politics. Even women active in the parties were more concerned with their parties' view on women's issues than on representation. Only under the influence of the quota debate that took place in Germany in the mid-1980s, did the issue of the under-representation of women reach the agenda of parties. Since then data on women politicians have been gathered and published and, as a result of consequent public interest in the issue, parties have been more willing to nominate women for office.[34] The Social Democratic Party decided in 2002 to adopt a new party statute including an article on equal opportunities. They also set a quota of 50 per cent for internal party bodies and one-third on electoral lists. The Socialist Party also modified the party regulations in 2002, adopting a quota of one third for the internal party boards. Finally, the Green Party uses a quota of 50 per cent. Their women's section organises training for prospective women candidates.

Britain and Ireland

Britain and Ireland are, like Belgium and France, not at the forefront in involving women in decision-making. In Britain, until the elections of 1997 around 6 per cent of members of the Lower House were women. In the Irish Dáil, the proportion of women was never higher than 15 per cent. Despite the fact that both countries had women in top political positions – Prime Minister Margaret Thatcher (from

---

[34] *Ibid.*, p. 237.

1979 to 1990) and Presidents Mary Robinson (1990-1997) and Mary McAleese (1997–), few women functioned as cabinet ministers. Of Thatcher it is explicitly known that she made no effort to promote other women politicians.[35]

In Ireland, an important explanation of the low representation of women in politics is the success of the Catholic Church in 'keeping women at home'. A large majority of Irish voters are Catholic and there still is a strong (though weakening) tradition of religious practice. The participation rate of women in the labour market has always lagged behind the rates of other European countries. Until the 1980s, married women stayed at home to take care of their children. Compared to the other countries in this study, Irish women are more likely to leave education earlier, have larger families, stay away from work longer and have no great desire to return to the labour market.[36] A second factor is the masculine nature of politics related to the historical importance of nationalism in the Irish party system. The main historical split on which the differences between the two largest parties, Fine Gael and Fianna Fáil, are based is nationalism. This ideology tends toward hierarchical, authoritarian and absolutist structures, which is more the domain of men than of women. As Gardiner and Leyenaar (1997) point out, when nationalism coexists with a dominant religion sharing many similar values, the result is intense resistance to power-sharing with women.[37] Evidence of this is found in the view of party leadership that women party members are there to provide the support services for the election of male candidates. The reluctance of men to treat women as equal is, according to Galligan, one of the main causes for the large absence of women from power.[38]

The third factor is the electoral system. The use of single transferable vote (STV) is associated with the very personalised nature of Irish politics. Under STV every personal vote counts, meaning that personal campaigns by the candidates are necessary. Fewer women than men can afford these costly undertakings, not least because the majority of women have traditionally not been in paid employment.

---

[35] B. Campbell, *The Iron Ladies,* London, Virago, 1987.

[36] F. Gardiner and M. Leyenaar, 'The Timid and the Bold. Analysis of the 'Women-friendly State' in Ireland and in the Netherlands', in F. Gardiner (ed.) *Sex Equality Policy in Western Europe,* Routledge, London, 1997, p. 74.

[37] *Ibid.*, p. 78.

[38] Y. Galligan, 'Party Politics and Gender in the Republic of Ireland', in J. Lovenduski and P. Norris (eds.), 1993, p. 161.

A positive effect of STV, however, is that a woman candidate can run on a so-called 'woman's ticket' and appeal to (women) voters to vote for her. However this does not happen very often. Another result of the personalistic nature of Irish politics is the continuing importance of family connections in determining the chances for selection as a candidate and the electoral success. Galligan shows that, between 1981 and 1992, twice as many women as men MPs had family ties with previous political incumbents.[39]

Like France, Ireland used to recognise the 'dual mandate' – the accumulation of political functions. Women's groups have criticised this practice, because it makes it difficult for newcomers and in 2003 this practice was abolished.

So far the main political parties, Fianna Fáil and Fine Gael, which have traditionally attracted around 80 per cent of the vote, have not been very active in promoting women in their midst. Only after Mary Robinson, nominated by the relatively small and social democratic Labour Party, was elected as president in 1990, beating a prominent male contender from the largest party, Fianna Fáil, was gender equality taken more seriously. The result was that in 1992 a Minister for Equality and Law Reform was nominated. The leftist (smaller) parties have tried to incorporate more women, which resulted in a greater representation of women in the parliament. But given the electoral strength of the other two parties, the efforts of the smaller parties had little overall effect.[40]

The cultural climate, however, seems to be changing. For several years now, the right-wing Progressive Democrats have had a woman leader and she has been Deputy Prime Minister continuously since 1997. Also worth noting is that in the 1997 presidential elections, all the main parties nominated women candidates, including a radical Catholic fundamentalist woman who went on to become a Member of the European Parliament (MEP). The fact that now, on average, Irish women have higher levels of education than men, will of course affect the participation rate of women in politics in the near future.

Two women's organisations have been instrumental to getting more women elected to the legislature. In 1971, the Women's Political Association was founded and launched many campaigns mobilising women to become involved in politics and vote for women candidates. In 1973, the Council for the Status of Women

---

[39] *Ibid.*, p. 149.

[40] Y. Galligan, 'Irland. Die politischen Repräsentation von Frauen in der Republik Irland', in B. Hoecker (ed.), 1998, p. 200

Table 2.6: Women in parliament and in government.

	% Women MPs			% Women Ministers		
	1980	1988-89	2002-03	1980	1988-89	2000-03
Britain	3	6	18	*	*	30
Ireland	4	4	8	4	19	13

* In the cabinets headed by Margaret Thatcher for 11 years, there was no other woman minister besides herself. Between 1993 and 1997 two women ministers joined the cabinet of John Major, Thatcher's successor in 1990. The Labour Prime Minister Tony Blair appointed 18 women to his cabinet, starting in 1997.[41]

(later renamed in the National Women's Council of Ireland) started its fight for gender equality. They monitor the (lack of) progress of women in decision-making and since 2002 have given priority to lobbying for change on this issue. In addition, the Irish government has taken extra measures to support women's political opportunities through funding gender equality officers in the major political parties.

Traditionally, British parties have been highly resistant to the promotion of women in politics, particularly electoral politics. While women have been allowed to stand for parliament since 1918, between then and 1987 less than five per cent of all MPs were women. The 1987 election saw a rise in the number of women MPs from 23 to 41 (6 per cent), with a further jump to 60 (9 per cent) in 1992. Until the mid-1970s the proportion of women candidates also remained fairly static. Only after 1974 did the numbers of women fielded as candidates triple: in the election of

---

[41] J. Lovenduski, 'Grossbritannien. Grossbritanniens sexistische Demokratie: Frauen, Männer und die Politik im Parteienstaat', in B. Hoecker (ed.), 1998, p. 4.

Chapter 2

1992 women represented 21 per cent of all candidates. Since then the major parties, Conservative and Labour, have been increasing the proportion of women candidates nominated to contest parliamentary seats: the Conservatives have doubled their number of women candidates, while Labour women enjoyed an even stronger increase. [42]

The electoral system and the selection procedures this involves have always been looked upon as a main cause for the extremely low participation of women in the British parliament.[43] Lovenduski (1994) points to the 'social closure practiced by the male elite as part of British class politics' as the main source. The traditional recruitment practices

> involve lengthy, continuous apprenticeships, with considerable weight given to seniority in key institutions such as the judiciary, the civil service, the universities and the trade union hierarchies; ...; implicit qualification criteria that, in practice, are male oriented; and a tradition of official secrecy, including the widespread practice of nominating through undisclosed channels ... Such devices, which might be called the 'chap' strategy, mean that promotion panels, search committees, and nomination bodies are able to recruit in their own image – a predominantly male, upper-middle class, and white image.[44]

These observations are in keeping with the finding that, contrary to other European countries, membership of women in the two main parties, the Conservative Party and the Labour Party, has always been relatively high. In the Conservative Party women members equalled men and they fulfilled important roles as local party leaders and during campaigns. In the Labour Party women's presence has been around 40 per cent since the 1970s.[45] However, having a large pool of women

---

[42] This text on Britain has been published before in: M. Leyenaar, B. Niemöller, M. Laver and Y. Galligan, 1999.

[43] See for example A. Karam (ed.), *Women in Parliament: Beyond Numbers*, IDEA, Stockholm, 1998.

[44] J. Lovenduski, 'Great Britain. The Rules of the Political Game: Feminism and Politics in Great Britain', in B. Nelson and N. Chowdhury (eds.), 1994, p. 300.

[45] P. Norris and J. Lovenduski, 'Gender and party politics in Britain', in J. Lovenduski and P. Norris (eds.), 1993, pp. 40-42.

at their disposal did not lead automatically to the same percentages of candidates and elected women.

The British electoral system, the single-member plurality system (SMP), involves first-past-the-post contests in 659 single-seat constituencies throughout the United Kingdom. Local party branches in each of the 659 constituencies decide upon the candidate for election. In both parties the selection of candidates is a very intense undertaking, consisting of hopefuls applying to selecting constituencies, going through several interviews and presenting themselves to large gatherings of party members. The local party branch in the constituency, of course, wants the candidate with the highest possible chance of winning the election. If the party holds the seat already, then it wants to keep it. If it does not, then it will choose an attractive candidate to lure voters away from the other parties' candidates. For a long time, women candidates were seen as being less attractive to the voters than males, regardless of other characteristics. For that reason alone, local party leaderships preferred male candidates for office. Prejudices about the unsuitability of women candidates meant that in Britain, for example, women candidates ran significantly more often than male candidates in constituencies where the party had very little chance of winning the seat.[46]

Especially in the Labour Party, women have been very active in convincing the party leadership to adopt affirmative action guaranteeing a larger share of women in the parliamentary party. Their lobby succeeded, when in the course to the election of 1997 the Labour Party decided that 100 constituencies must have all-women shortlists (see for more details chapter 8). The effectiveness of the all-woman shortlist, in conjunction with the strategy of placing women in winnable seats, was shown in the election results. All of the women candidates chosen in this way were elected to parliament and the proportion of women MPs raised to 18 per cent.[47] In the 2001 parliamentary elections the number of women MPs went down again by one, from 120 to 119. Altogether 18.1 per cent of UK MPs are women, meaning that more than four out of five MPs are men. The number of women elected is clearly related to the number of women selected by the parties as candidates. At the 2001 general election the Labour Party fielded 149 women candidates, compared with the Conservatives' 92. The fall in Labour women MPs is due to the

---

[46] M. Charlot, 'Women and Elections in Britain', in H.R. Penniman (ed.) *Britain at the Polls 1997,* Washington, American Enterprise Institute, 1981, p. 253.

[47] J. Lovenduski, 'Grossbritanien', in B. Hoecker (ed.), 1998, pp. 167-188.

Chapter 2

Table 2.7: Distribution of seats in the House of Commons after the election of 2001.

Party	Total no. of seats	No. of women MPs	% Women MPs
Labour	412	95	23.1
Conservative	166	14	8.4
Liberal Democrat	52	5	11.5
Other	29	4	13.8
Total	659	118	18.1

Source: website www.Labour.org.

small number of women selected in 'inheritor' seats; only four out of 42 candidates selected to replace retiring MPs were women.[48] Labour leadership compensated for this deficit, however, by appointing a record of 31 women ministers (7 of them members of the inner cabinet) in the Labour government.

The example of the Labour Party shows that setting quotas by parties operating in a SMP system is possible, but the consequences, women replacing men as candidates, are much more visible than when a certain percentage of a list is reserved for women. The resistance of male potential candidates will therefore be even more forceful. To avoid this, the Labour Party in Scotland and Wales, where new parliaments were installed in 1999, used a different method to ensure the election of women in SMP districts: twinning (see chapter 8). Due to this system of twinning as well as the fact that in both regions a mixed (AMS) system is used, the

---

[48] See www.labour.uk. Reference to Rachel McCollin, National Women's Officer, The Labour Party, Millbank Tower, Millbank, London SW1P 4GT (June 2001).

representation of women in the Scottish parliament is 37 per cent and in the Welsh parliament 50 per cent after the 2003 elections.[49]

Germany and Austria

In both Germany and Austria women's presence in the Bundestag has increased quite steadily over the last 20 years. In 1980, only 9 per cent women participated in the German Bundestag, while the first election after the unification of Eastern Germany and Western Germany in 1990 brought 21 per cent women to parliament. Unification had the effect, however, of producing a simultaneous decrease in women's political representation in the former East Germany: 33 per cent women had been represented in the former Eastern German parliament. This however was due to the system of reserved seats: a certain number of seats in parliament were assigned to the Women's Federation. But according to Lemke (1994), however, despite women's formal numerical representation, their de facto power was negligent.

> The state's prime concerns were economic modernisation and political stability, as well as fertility of women because the birth rate had declined sharply in the late 1960s and 1970s. Thus the state provided for women in a paternalistic manner, and women themselves remained politically powerless. So, paradoxically, women formally enjoyed equal rights and generous welfare benefits, especially as mothers, but politics continued to be dominated by men; women literally had no voice.[50]

Women in the Federal Republic of Germany have, like women in France, Italy and Greece struggled with the question of whether to join the parties or form new, autonomous (women's) organisations. In the 1970s and beginning of the 1980s the '*autonome Frauenbewegung*' (autonomous women's movement) was quite popular among well-educated women. They concentrated on grass-roots activities and established a world for women: women's health centres, summer universities for women, bookstores and cafés for women. The establishment in 1979 of a political

---

[49] P. Chaney, 'Increased Rights and Representation: Women and the Post-devolution Equality Agenda in Wales' in A. Dobrowolsky and V. Hart, 2003, p. 175. See also in the same volume, F. Mackay, F. Myers and A. Brown, 'Towards a New Politics? Women and the Constitutional Change in Scotland', pp. 84-98.

[50] C. Lemke, 'Women and Politics: the New Federal Republic of Germany', in B. Nelson and N. Chowdhury (eds.), 1994, p. 270.

Chapter 2

Table 2.8: Women in government and in parliament in Austria and in Germany.

	% Women MPs			% Women Ministers		
	1980	1988-89	2002-03	1980	1988-89	2000-03
Austria	10	11	28	15*	15*	25**
Germany	9	21	32	7*	21*	43

* Estimate.
** In total 4 women, including 2 women ministers and 2 women junior ministers.

party from a leftist movement in which many feminists were active, the Green Party, changed the anti-party approach somewhat. Right from the beginning, the Green Party put gender equality on the agenda and applied a 50 per cent quota and the 'zipper' system to both its internal party positions and its representative positions.

The parliamentary elections of 2002 in Germany returned 32 per cent women to parliament. This is largely the result of the activities of the women's factions inside the parties, especially in the Socialist Party (SPD) and in the Green Party who have lobbied intensely since the 1970s for a better representation of women in politics. Women's factions in the Christian Democratic Union (CDU) and in the SPD were established after the Second World War and committed themselves during the early years of these parties to mobilising and educating women party members. In the SPD they became more radical at the beginning of the 1970s and since 1973 the women's faction became a 'vociferous and tenacious pressure group for women's equality in the SPD'.[51] Slowly the party started to listen to their demands. Women's voting behaviour helped to convince parties to change their

---

[51] E. Kolinsky, 'Party change and women's representation in unified Germany', in J. Lovenduski and P. Norris (eds.), 1993, p. 128.

masculine image. In the 1980s, polls showed that young women and women in their 30s and 40s expressed a deep frustration with the large, traditional parties. Women turned away from these parties, no longer believing party politics would ensure gender equality. Many of these women became interested and active in the Green Party as well as in small citizens' groups.[52] As mentioned before, it was the Green Party who first adopted a 50 per cent quota for women parliamentary candidates in 1985, using the 'zipper' system. For them, gender equality was part of the ideology and, except for the very top positions in government, the Green Party has been more or less able to meet these quota requirements.[53]

Competition between the two leftist parties for the participation and votes of younger, well-educated women left the SPD no other choice than to embrace quotas as well. At a 1988 party congress it was decided that, by 1994, women should hold no less than 40 per cent of all party offices and, by 1998, no less than 40 per cent of parliamentary seats. Quotas will be used only until 2013, since by then equal participation of men and women in the party should be 'normal'.[54] To remain attractive to young women voters, the CDU did not opt for quotas but instead modernised its views on the family and women's traditional roles. It stressed the need for benefits for child-rearing and for facilitating the combination of paid employment and care for children. Although a few prominent CDU women have filled high-level political jobs such as 'speaker of the House', cabinet ministers and candidate for party leader, the overall representation of women is still much lower than in the SPD or in the Green Party.

Germany uses a mixed system to elect its MPs, the Additional Member System (AMS). Voters have two ballots: one is used to vote for a party list and determines the total number of seats for a party through PR; the other ballot is used in the constituency to vote for a candidate by use of the SMP system. Half of the seats are allocated on the basis of first-past-the-post elections to single-member constituencies. The remaining seats are allocated on the basis of a national list-PR election. Thus, if one party were to win, say, 50 seats in the single-seat elections, and be due, say, 60 seats on the basis of overall national proportionality, then the list-PR allocation would give that party another 10 seats. The AMS system has found

---

[52] A. Seeland, 'Germany', in *Expert Network Women in Decision-Making*, Panorama Strategies, 1993.

[53] See www.db-decision.de.

[54] E. Kolinsky, in J. Lovenduski and P. Norris (eds.), 1993, p. 130.

Chapter 2

Table 2.9: Distribution of seats in the German Bundestag after the election of 2002.

Party	Total no. of seats	No. of women MPs	% Women MPs
SPD	251	95	38
CDU	190	44	23
CSU	58	12	21
Green Party	55	32	58
FDP	47	10	21
PDS	2	2	100
Total	603	195	32

Source: Website www.db-decision.de.

favour in recent times because it can deliver high levels of national proportional representation from the list-PR element (depending upon the threshold used), and at the same time accommodate the single-seat constituencies believed to keep national representatives close to the people they represent. In terms of impact on the representation of women, women's chances of getting elected to a German single-member district are much less than those of getting elected through the list-PR vote. For example, in the 1990 parliamentary elections of the 331 members elected via party lists, 93 (28 per cent) were women. Of the 331 members of parliament elected directly through the constituencies, only 31 (12 per cent) were women.[55] Given these differences in success rates, women candidates prefer to run for a ticket on the list rather than present themselves as candidates in the single-member districts. In the 2002 elections, the majority of candidates opted for the so-called 'Doppelkandidaturen' (to be a candidate on the list as well as in a district). Of the

---

[55] *Ibid.*, p. 142.

Table 2.10: Participation of women in the German government after the election of 2002.

	Ministers			Junior Ministers		
	Total	No. women	% Women	Total	No. women	% Women
SPD	11	5	46	18	6	33
Green Party	3	1	33	7	5	71
Total	14	6	43	25	11	44

Source: Website db-decision.de

438 candidates who only stood for election in the constituencies only 51 (11 per cent) were women. The majority of them (37) were candidates for the Green Party.[56]

Although the SPD and the Green Party won only a very slender majority (51 per cent) of seats, the two parties decided to continue their coalition government. The composition of the new government shows us that gender equality is really taken seriously by these two parties. Table 2.9 provides the number and percentages of women cabinet ministers and women junior ministers in the government of Gerhard Schröder.

In Austria women have been entering parliament at a very slow pace. Women got the vote in 1918 and until mid-1970s, not more than 7 women (13 per cent) were represented in parliament. Since then, this percentage has increased to one quarter of parliamentary seats.[57] Parties are the gatekeepers for all political func-

---

[56] See www.db-decision.de.

[57] B. Steiniger, 'Österreich. Zwischen Konflikt und Konsens: Frauen im politischen System Österreichs', in B. Hoecker (ed.), 1998, pp. 276-286.

tions, elected as well as appointed, and a long and active party career is still the main vehicle to political power. Since World War II, women's party membership has been about one-third in the two large parties, the Socialist Party (SPÖ) and the Austrian People's Party (ÖVP), but less women performed executive jobs within the parties. In both parties, a women's section has been very active and, in the SPÖ, this section has fought for gender quotas. The increase of women's participation is in large part due to the Green Party, with 50 per cent women MPs in their parliamentary party.

An important explanation for the under-representation of women is the strong corporatist nature of Austrian politics. Interest groups and political parties are very much interrelated and form a closed network that is difficult to access. Political posts have been divided among the members of these close-knit networks. In a clear division of gender roles, men performed the public roles and women the private, resulting in low levels of political interest on the part of women. This changed in the 1980s, when the Green Party was founded and more and more young Austrians started to criticise traditional party politics.[58] During the 1990s, more and more voters turned their back on the traditional large parties which had been in power for a long time, the SPÖ and the ÖVP. Interestingly enough, male renegades went to the Freedom Party Austria (FPÖ), while more women connected with the Green Party and the Liberal Forum. In the 1990s one can speak of a gender gap in voting behaviour. In the 1995 and 1999 elections the gender gap widened to a difference of 21 percentage points.[59]

EUROPEAN UNION

The EU Member States are sovereign and it is up to national governments and parliaments to introduce legislation guaranteeing the political representation of women, to convince political parties to select more women for eligible places on their lists, or to take no action at all. This does not mean, however, that the European Union, as an institution with supranational and intergovernmental characteristics, cannot fulfil a role in creating a climate of gender equality in all spheres, including politics. The EU has issued several binding directives on equality. Examples are the following directives: in 1975 on equal pay, in 1976 on equal

---

[58] *Ibid.*, 1998, p. 288.

[59] See www.zap.or.at 'Gender and Generation Realignment'.

opportunities in the labour market, in 1978 on equal treatment with regard to social security, in 1992 on pregnancy leave, in 1996 on parental leave and in 1997 on part-time work.[60] In some countries, this meant radical adaptation of national legislation.[61] The issue of equal participation in decision-making has not been the subject of a directive, probably because the organisation of politics is viewed too much of a national issue and European interference in this matter would not be appreciated by national governments. But several non-binding resolutions were passed in the 1990s and other activities have been organised to enhance the political decision-making of women.

In 1994, the European Parliament passed a resolution calling upon the Member States to improve the political role of women.[62] The Council of Ministers adopted a similar resolution on 27 March 1995:

> The Council confirms that balanced participation in decision-making, in all spheres of life, is a condition of equality between men and women. It is essential to do everything possible to effect changes of attitude and of structures essential to real equality of access to decision-making posts between women and men in political, economical and social domains.

In 1996 this text was converted into a recommendation for all Member States

> [to] adopt a comprehensive, integrated strategy designed to promote balanced participation of women and men in the decision-making process and develop or introduce the appropriate measures to achieve this, such as, where necessary, legislative and/or regulatory measures and/or incentives.[63]

Apart from resolutions and recommendations, the EU has undertaken several other stimulating activities. Within the context of the third and fourth medium-term Community Action Programmes on equal opportunities for women and men, many initiatives have been carried out in the Member States regarding the

---

[60] See www.europa.eu.int.

[61] A. van der Vleuten, *Dure Vrouwen, Dwarse Staten. Een institutioneel-realistische visie op de totstandkoming en implementatie van Europees beleid*, Nijmegen, Nijmegen University Press, 2001, pp. 267-269.

[62] Reference of the resolution is: A3-0035/94, EP 179.623.

[63] Council Recommendation of 2 December 1996.

empowerment of women. In 1993 the topic was the European elections; in 1994 participation of women in regional and local decision-making; and in 1995 facilitating networking of women in decision-making posts. Another EU-financed project was the European expert network 'Women in Decision-Making'. The European Commission set this up in 1992 and its main task was to examine the hurdles that kept women from attaining decision-making positions and to devise strategies and instruments to achieve higher levels of participation. One expert in each Member State functioned in the network and, in its five years of existence, many publications on the issue and many activities have resulted.[64]

Concerning its own decision-making institutions, the European Parliament and the European Commission, the EU has achieved better results than most of its Member States. In 10 out of the 15 countries more than one-third of the Members of the European Parliament (MEPs) are women. For some countries, such as France, Belgium, Greece, Ireland and the United Kingdom, the deviance with the representation at the national level is striking. Right from the beginning women have participated substantially in the European Parliament. Women were allowed to participate, since it was a new institution so no male incumbents had to step back, and the EP was founded at a time when the nomination of women into political offices was high on the agendas of political parties. The European Parliament has always been a more 'woman-friendly' parliament than that of most of the Member States. Already by 1984, a permanent standing parliamentary committee on women's rights had been formed and this committee, according to many women researchers, has done a lot of work to improve conditions of European women and to introduce gender equality.[65] Given the greater presence of women and the apparent influence of women MEPs on policy-making, the European Parliament is also a more attractive place to work. To this can be added the fact that the *modus operandi* of the European Parliament is not formed by long-standing values and traditions developed by male politicians. Vallance and Davies (1986), in their study on women MEPs, cite a British woman MEP who remarked that 'the European Parliament is not constructed like the Westminster Parliament as a men's club with

---

[64] See for example M.H. Leyenaar, *How to Create a Gender Balance in Political Decision-Making*, European Commission, 1997. This guide has been translated in 11 languages.

[65] See E. Valence and E. Davies, *Women of Europe: Women MEPs and Equality Policy*, Cambridge University Press, 1986; C. Hoskyns and S. Rai, 'Gender, Class and Representation: India and the EU', *European Journal of Women's Studies*, 1998, no. 5, pp. 345-365.

Table 2.11: Percentage of women MEPs by country.

Country	1979	1984	1989	1994	1999
Austria					38
Belgium	8	17	17	32	32
Denmark	31	38	38	44	38
Finland					44
France	22	21	22	31	40
Germany	15	20	31	34	36
Greece		8	4	16	16
Ireland	13	13	7	27	33
Italy	14	9	10	11	12
Luxembourg	33	50	50	50	0
Netherlands	24	28	28	32	36
Portugal			13	12	20
Spain			15	33	34
Sweden					41
United Kingdom	14	15	14	17	24
Total % women	16	16	20	26	30
Total MEPs	410	518	518	518	626

places that are "holy of holies" where women aren't suppose to go'.[66] And Barbara Castle, another female British politician who left national politics for a seat in the European Parliament commented on the fact that there was no government-versus-opposition battle going on.[67] The EU has succeeded in radiating a woman-

---

[66] E. Valence and E. Davies, 1986, p. 10.

[67] B. Castle, *Fighting All the Way*, London, Macmillan, 1993, p. 519.

friendly image and this too has had an effect on the nomination processes in the Member States. Parties have felt the need to nominate women to the EP at a much higher rate than at the national level.[68]

Reaching a gender balance in the composition of the European Commission has proven to be more difficult, since each Member State can only nominate one or two commissioners. In the European Commission that was installed in 1989 out of 17 commissioners two were women (12 per cent), one female commissioner was appointed by France and one by Greece. In both 1994 and in 1999 five women have been appointed out of 20 Commissioners (25 per cent). In 1994, Denmark, Sweden, Italy, France and Germany delegated a female commissioner. In 1999 this was done by Spain, Luxembourg, Germany, Sweden and Greece.

So far, no binding directives have been issued forcing the 15-25 national states to implement gender equality in political representation. What has been done in the fields of income, education and access to the labour market, has not been dared in the field of politics. In the near future, the EU faces at least two challenges in this area, where it can show a strong commitment to a gender balance in political decision-making. The first crucial challenge is the introduction of a European Constitution, drafted by the European Convention and especially the articles on the functioning of the institutions. In Part III of the Draft Constitution, Title VI, Article III-232 Article a provision is made for the future election of the European Parliament, namely that the elections to the European Parliament should be conducted according to a common electoral system. At present each country organises its own election for the Members of the European Parliament and each party runs its own process of candidate selection. The introduction of a common electoral system provides an excellent opportunity to take a serious look at electoral procedures from the perspective of best practice policies on gender balance (see chapter 9). The second challenge is the enlargement of the European Union with 10 new Member States in 2004. Given the low figures of representation in some of the 'old' Member States, such as Greece, Italy and Ireland, it was not possible to use a minimum representation figure as a condition for entry. But, given all of its policies on gender equality, the EU should, right from the initial accession of new Member States, point to the significance of a balanced political representation. Table 2.12 shows the figures on women's political representation in the 10 countries that joined the EU in 2004.

---

[68] J. Freedman, 'Women in the European Parliament', in K. Ross (ed.), 2002, pp. 180-182.

Table 2.12: Women in parliaments of the accession countries, 2001.

Country	% Women MPs 2003	% Women Ministers 2002
Cyprus	11	0
Czech Republic	17	0
Estonia	19	29
Hungary	9	6
Latvia	21	5
Lithuania	11	23
Malta	8	7
Poland	20	21
Slovakia	19	0
Slovenia	12	20

Source: Women MPs, October 2003, IPU; Women Ministers, 2002, Council of Europe

EVALUATING EUROPE

As we have seen in this chapter, Europe is a melting pot. The 15 countries in this study differ in almost every aspect that we have discussed here. Not only does each country use different methods to elect its members to parliament, but they also differ with regard to the social-economic position of women and in the acknowledgement of gender equality as a basic human right that should be implemented in each field of society. This short overview of women's empowerment in the 15 countries has shown that many different factors can have an impact. Years of socialisation, for example by the church, proclaiming that women and men should fulfil different roles in society and that operating in public life is a valued role only for men, have caused a severe backlog in women's representation in countries such as Greece, Italy and Ireland. It has been tougher there for women to break into the traditional male bastion, in contrast to countries with a more flexible ideology on gender roles.

Although the electoral system does have an impact on the access of newcomers to parliament, it is certainly not the only factor explaining the low representation of women. In Greece, which uses a list-PR system, there are hardly any women in parliament. Here the personal character of the elections is viewed as an important cause for the lack of women. However, in Finland where, because of the importance of preferential votes, the elections also revolve around persons, we find one of the highest percentages of women in parliament. What is important, though, is that in list-PR systems it is easier to apply quotas. And quotas have proven to be the best guarantee for a higher representation of women, as we have seen for example in Germany. As was shown by the British case, it is not impossible to use quotas in a simple plurality system, but neither is it easy. So far in countries where parties adopted quotas in the 1970s, 1980s and 1990s, more women have shown up in the political arena.

The women's factions of political parties have been very instrumental in getting more women into parliament. Their existence was re-energised by the emergence of the new women's movement at the end of the 1960s. In those countries where (feminist) women decided to work in and with political parties, as they did in the Scandinavian countries, in order to improve women's status, we find a more receptive attitude towards gender equality in politics. In the Scandinavian countries and the Netherlands, a real increase in women's parliamentary participation occurred at the end of the 1970s, in most of the other countries in the 1980s. From that time on, a higher proportion of women can be found in the representative bodies with almost every election. Looking at participation in the labour market and in higher education, women in general have improved their status. They have caught up with men in higher education and the majority of women have paid jobs in the workforce. In several countries, child-care facilities have been greatly improved and institutional experiments are being carried out to combine care and paid employment. Strangely enough, this recent change in the gender division of political resources has not resulted in a similar increase in women's *political* participation. It seems that politics itself carries obstacles for newcomers, especially women. The nature of politics is that it is about power, which is not something incumbents want to share with too many others. We have seen in the brief overview that women as activists, as party members, as politicians had to bulldoze party leaderships into selecting more women to internal party and external representative offices. Men give up their power base neither quickly nor voluntarily. This is one of the reasons why we find more women in newly established political bodies such as the European Parliament, or the recently created parliaments of Scotland and Wales. When there are no incumbents with traditional claims on seats, it is easier to 'allow' newcomers in as well. In Scandinavia, women party activists have used this strat-

Political Representation of Women in Fifteen European Countries

egy to gain access to the party offices: the total number of party offices was extended so that every other place could be taken by a woman, while no men lost their seats. Politics is also about fierce competition, about pushing oneself forward to gain attention and – in the end – about selection and election. There are indications that in general fewer women than men want to expose themselves to these competitive aspects of politics.

The main conclusion of this chapter is thus that there is a wide variety of factors explaining the (lack of) progress in women's parliamentary participation in Europe. In the next chapter an attempt is made to structure this broad overview, presenting an explanatory framework of the barriers and opportunities facing women along the path to a seat in the legislature.

CHAPTER 3

AN EXPLANATORY FRAMEWORK FOR WOMEN'S POLITICAL REPRESENTATION

The previous chapter demonstrated that every society and every political system in Europe has its own values, rules and procedures that affect positively and negatively the chances for women to become involved in parliamentary politics. But, despite the uniqueness of each case, it is still possible to present a framework of factors that help or hinder women in gaining access to political functions.[1] The overview that follows is based on empirical research carried out to study the limited political participation of women.[2]

The framework makes a distinction between five stages of political participation: voting, recruitment, selection, election and representation. *Voting* is the first step. The right to vote, and to be eligible, is of course a necessary condition for political participation. *Recruitment* is the process by which people get involved in political and party activities, leading eventually to actual candidacy. Recruitment of women depends largely on the cultural background of a country and its social and economic development. The process of *selection* determines which citizens, from the pool of those who are active in politics, are eventually seen as being qualified for political office. The *election* provides the final decision as to which candidates will become members of the political body. After being elected into political office, politicians should *represent* the citizens and defend their interests. Here we are interested particularly in factors that determine whether women politicians remain in office or leave after one term.

---

[1]   Parts of these texts have been published previously in M.H. Leyenaar, 1997 and in M. Leyenaar, B. Niemöller, M. Laver and Y. Galligan: *Electoral Systems in Europe: a Gender Impact Assessment*, 1999.

[2]   See the bibliography in this book.

An Explanatory Framework for Women's Political Representation

Figure 3.1. Explanatory framework: pathway to politics.

(Eligible) citizens → Pool of potential candidates → Pool of candidates → Political elite

VOTING → **RECRUITMENT** → **SELECTION** → **ELECTION** → **REPRESENTATION**

Institutional factors

VOTING	RECRUITMENT	SELECTION	ELECTION	REPRESENTATION
Suffrage	Social climate (religion)	Electoral system	Voting procedures (preferential voting)	Support structure
Civic education	Cultural climate (machismo)	Selection process		Women (mother) friendly working conditions
	Gender division of labour (child-care facilities)	Selection criteria		Culture of politics
	Gender equality	Affirmative action		
	Civil society	Women's sections		
	Corporatism	Party system		
		Party competition		

Individual factors

Political interest	Structural	Political and civic experience	Electoral attractiveness	Rewards (influence)
	Situational	Quality of life	Financial resources	
	Psychological			
	Family background			

In each step in this process, voting, recruitment, selection, election and representation, both *individual* and *institutional* factors affect the chances of women to become involved in political decision-making. The first category addresses the extent to which individual characteristics favour political participation. For example, high levels of educational and professional experience, or coming from a 'politicised' family are advantages when pursuing a political career. On the other hand having small children is a disadvantage to women who are striving to achieve a representative position. Institutional factors relate to the organisation of society, its norms and values, as well as to the political system itself. In the previous chapter we have already mentioned the impact of the electoral and party system on the parliamentary representation of women.

Following women's footsteps in politics over time, it becomes clear that the relative weight of the different factors changes over time. In the early 20th century, legal obstacles, like the ban on women's suffrage or of mothers in paid employment, were of great importance. Before and immediately after World War II, religion and the existing traditional gender ideology, as well as individual barriers such as the lack of educational and professional background, stopped women from gaining political power.

In the 1990s and at the beginning of the 21st century, the selection process and selection criteria are the main obstacles, as well as a culture of politics that results in a personal choice of many women not to pursue a political career. Figure 3.1 shows the five different stages of political participation and state the relevant factors that affect women's chances to become a political representative. The next paragraphs discuss the separate factors more extensively.

VOTING

Voting is one of the easiest acts of political participation and it can be viewed as a kind of precondition to candidacy for political office. Electoral studies of the past show that women tended to vote less often than men.[3] Duverger (1955) explained this by pointing to the negative attitude of men, referring to the problematic introduction of women's suffrage and to women's lower levels of political interest,

---

[3] H. Tingsten, *Political Behaviour: Studies in Election Statistics*. London, P.S. King & Son, 1937; M. Duverger, *The Political Role of Women*, Paris, UNESCO, 1955.

which were mainly caused by their dependent social and economic position. He sums it up like this:

> The man – husband, fiancé, lover or myth – is the mediator between them and the political world. 'When things go wrong, women blame their husbands, men blame the government' is a fairly apt summing up of this basic attitude.[4]

Since the 1980s, significant gender differences in turnout have become much smaller in the 15 European countries with women voting almost as much as men do. Since there are no data measuring actual voting behaviour, we turn to survey data, such as the Eurobarometer. Table 3.1 describes the voting intentions over the years and shows the percentages of European citizens who answer that they are *not going to vote* in the next elections, or answer that they *do not know it yet* or *give no answer at all*. The latter two categories are included, because they can be viewed as strong indicators for non-voting behaviour.

The table provides data for four different years. The last column shows the average for the period between 1977 and 1999 and is based on data from many additional years. Looking at these averages we see that the average gender difference is about 3 per cent: women tend to vote less often than men. Denmark, Greece, Italy and Portugal show a gender gap of six per cent, while the gap is smallest (2 per cent) in Belgium. Another finding is the increase over time in the percentage of European men and women with a non-voting intention. The only exception to this finding is Denmark: here fewer citizens intend *not* to vote in 1999 compared to 1973. In all other countries the percentages of non-voters has increased, in Italy and Luxembourg the most.

In general in Western Europe, voting now offers few obstacles for women on the path towards political office. There are no constitutional barriers for women concerning the right to vote or to be elected. Strangely enough however, political parties can still ban women from membership and thus from candidacy for political office, as is the case of the Dutch Reformed Party (*Staatkundig Gereformeerde Partij*). Female adherents of this party have brought this to court on the grounds of sex discrimination, but so far the Dutch courts have ruled in favour of the party, ranking the fundamental right of freedom of organisation higher than discrimination against women.

---

[4] M. Duverger, 1955, p.129.

Chapter 3

Table 3.1: Voting intentions: percentages that answer that they are not going to vote, that they do not know yet or who give no answer.

	1970		1980		1990		1999		1970-1999	
	M	*F*	*M*	*F*	*M*	*F*	*M*	*F*	*M*	*F*
Austria					38+	43+	42	38	37	40
Belgium	27	37	49	61	40	36	34	41	41	43
Denmark	28*	33*	25	35	23	29	17	23	21	27
Finland					64+	64+	24	26	43	45
France	24	30	31	39	34	38	36	47	28	32
Germany	20	24	12	15	22	27	34	39	23	26
Greece			41	52	31	33	48	60	39	45
Ireland	30*	31*	32	37	31	27	33	40	31	34
Italy	30	35	22	31	40	49	55	65	36	42
Luxb'rg	36*	32*	29	24	34	42	49	53	36	40
Nethrl'ds	16	23	17	17	12	14	19	23	17	20
Portugal			44¶	48¶	39	50	33	48	37	43
Spain			45¶	48¶	39	41	51	51	43	46
Sweden					28+	30+	31	32	29	33
UK	22*	19*	18	21	22	24	27	37	19	22

* 1973   ¶ 1985   + 1995

Source: Eurobarometers, 1970-1999.

Knowing the rules of the political game is a precondition for participation in politics. Access to civic education stimulates the development of political interest and the act of voting. In the 15 countries in our study, women in general have the same access to civic education as men, but not the same level of political interest.

An Explanatory Framework for Women's Political Representation

Table 3.2: Political discussion: percentages that answer 'often'.

	1970 M	1970 F	1980 M	1980 F	1990 M	1990 F	1999 M	1999 F	1970-1999 M	1970-1999 F
Austria					23⁹	13⁹	20	9	22	11
Belgium	11	4	11	7	13	6	11	8	13	6
Denmark	26	15	18	12	20	15	23	18	22	15
Finland					18⁹	14⁹	14	12	16	12
France	18	8	15	10	15	12	12	7	19	13
Germany	29	15	16	14	22	14	19	11	21	11
Greece			34	17	53	39	37	14	44	24
Ireland	22	9	15	10	15	10	15	7	17	9
Italy	24	6	27	7	24	10	23	11	24	11
Luxb'rg	51	7	30	16	27	13	21	12	24	14
Nethrl'ds	13	9	20	14	19	13	15	9	19	14
Portugal										
Spain			10*	5*	11	5	9	6	10	6
Sweden					17⁹	15⁹	16	14	15	13
UK	19	8	20	13	20	15	13	10	18	12

* 1985 ⁹ 1995
Source: Eurobarometers, 1970-1999.

Women still talk about politics less frequently than men do. Table 3.2 shows again some data from the Eurobarometer, this time the percentages of men and women who discuss politics *often*.

The gender gap in table 3.2 is much wider than for voting intentions. Analysing the figures in the final column, showing the average percentages for the 1973-1999 period, it is clear that fewer women than men discuss politics often. In Greece the gender gap is 20 per cent, in Italy 13 per cent, in Austria 11 per cent and in

Chapter 3

Germany and Luxembourg 10 per cent. In Sweden, Finland, Portugal and Spain gender differences are less than 5 per cent. Comparing the figures from 1973 with those from 1999 there is not such a clear trend as there was in table 3.1. In Belgium, Denmark, Italy, Luxembourg and the UK, the percentage of women discussing politics increased somewhat, but in France, Germany and Ireland it decreased.[5]

RECRUITMENT

Why, as we saw in the previous chapter, do some countries show a much larger involvement of women in political and party activities than other countries? And why do more men than women become engaged in politics?

Social and Cultural Climate

Starting with the institutional factors, it seems that the political participation of women depends heavily on the more general social and cultural climate of a country. With regard to the social climate, the predominant religion within a country strongly affects the level of women's parliamentary representation. Certain religious practices encourage and strengthen the inequality of women in society. Religious practices are an important factor in the development of a traditional sex-role ideology that includes strict notions of male and female roles in society. Based on biological differences in reproductive functions, relatively coherent and complex patterns of ideas, practices and cultural experiences for each sex have been constructed (a so-called gender ideology). Part of this gender ideology is that men take care of public and community affairs, while women nurture the family. We have seen in the short overviews of women's empowerment in the 15 countries in

---

[5] The validity of these results on gender differences in political discussion are more and more questioned because, when people are asked about the frequency with which they discuss *concrete* political issues, then gender differences tend to disappear. Politics as an abstract concept is less entertaining for women than for men. But, when it refers to child-care facilities, the combination paid employment and caring, unemployment, poverty or gender equality, then men and women tend to be equally interested. See for example M.J. Koopman and M. Leyenaar, 'Het Vergeten Electoraat: Vrouwen en Verkiezingen', in C. van der Eijk and B. Niemöller (ed.) *In het Spoor van de Kiezer. Aspecten van 10 jaar Kiesgedrag*, Meppel, Boom, 1984; See also J.Mossuz-Laveau (1995), cited in G. Allwood and K. Wadia, 2000, pp. 120-121.

chapter 2, that, for example in those countries where Catholicism is still a relevant factor in people's lives (Ireland, Italy), women are having more difficulties entering politics in substantial numbers than in countries where the effect of Catholicism has waned over the years and in secular countries. Parts of this cultural climate are the patriarchal values and norms that still operate, most prominently in the Southern European countries. Taking care of the public cause is seen as a male privilege. Greece is a country where in the beginning of the 21st century women's social role is still defined by home and family. Greek society remains imbued with strong traditional attitudes towards social institutions, including politics, while political matters and political participation are seen as the prerogative of men.[6]

Gender Division of Labour and Gender Equality

These social and cultural factors naturally affect women's economic position in a country as well as the level of gender equality. In the past, the strict division of labour between men and women left little scope for women to get involved in public affairs – since there were hardly any nurseries, part-time work was not allowed and tax laws inhibited women's employment. In most countries in the 21st century, the majority of adult women combine child rearing with paid employment (see chapter 2, table 2.2), which means that a political office should be also possible. In those countries, like Italy, Greece and Spain where less than 45 per cent of women participate in the labour market, society is less well geared for the independent economic and political position of women.

Thanks to EU legislation, the Member States are quite similar with regard to the adoption of constitutional provisions or laws to promote equality between women and men. Legally, women can rely on equal treatment with male colleagues and have the right to inherit, own and manage property. European women also have the right to enter freely into marriage, equal rights in divorce and other aspects of family law. The 15 countries differ, however, in the implementation of these laws and in the level of incorporation of gender equality in society. The Nordic countries are an example of countries where gender equality is a widely accepted norm that has permeated almost every aspect of society, including politics.

---

[6] A. Calcoullos, 'Greece. Women Confronting Party Politics in Greece', in B. Nelson and N. Chodorow (eds.), 1994, pp. 312-322.

Chapter 3

Civil Society and Corporatism

The state of the civil society in a country also has an effect on women's political representation. Women often participate in the life of society, not through political organisations, but through community associations and a wide variety of other groups and organisations. Not only do these experiences provide women with political interest, skills and a network, in some countries, such as Belgium, political parties turn to these social organisations when searching for potential candidates for elective office. Social organisations are used as a recruitment pool for candidates and participation in these groups helps women gain access to politics. On the other hand too much interest representation may have a negative impact on women's political participation, as we have seen in the description of the empowerment of women in Austria. When the state mediates among social interests and communicates formally with designated interests (corporatism) there is little or no representation for advocates of gender equality. Corporatism institutionalises group access, for example to parliament. Many groups have 'gender profiles', with women in humanitarian and men in economic and professional organisations, of which the latter are supposed to be more relevant for representation. Unions are notorious for having a predominantly male leadership, no matter how large the number of women members. A generally low level of representation in the corporate system leads consequently to low representation of women in politics.[7]

Structural Factors

There is of course a strong link between the opportunities a society provides and the development of individual women. At the individual level, different explanations of women's disadvantaged political position can be distinguished into *structural factors*, *situational factors* and *psychological factors*. Most of these explanations can be traced to the existing gender division of labour.[8] Structural explanations – that is explanations based on a group's place in the social structure – emphasise differential access to political resources. Many social scientists see

---

[7] H. Hernes and K. Voje, 'Women in the Corporate Channel: a Process of Natural Exclusion?', *Scandinavian Political Studies*, vol. 3:2, 1980, pp. 163-186.

[8] S. Welch, 'Women as Political Animals? A Test of Some Explanations for Male-Female Political Participation Differences', in *American Journal of Political Science*, vol. 21:4, 1977, pp. 712-716.

the persistence of women's lack of political power as a predictable outcome of the ways in which advantages are distributed in society.[9] Structural factors refer to educational level, professional experience and level of income. Education is one of the greatest forces for change in women's lives. Education influences a woman's chances for paid employment, her age at marriage, her control over childbearing, her exercise of legal and political rights and her ability to achieve political power. A high level of education appears to be a necessary condition for becoming involved in political activities. In each country, the majority of MPs are university educated.[10] Another important political resource is occupational status. Research has shown that women's participation in political life depends largely on their access to employment, which gives them not only material independence, but also certain professional skills. However, women often occupy an unfavourable situation in the labour market. First, there are still many women who do not perform any paid labour at all. Secondly, when they do, they often focus their education and career development on the so-called nurturing professions. Besides the fact that these experiences are less valued by those recruiting political leaders, it is also true that women are often concentrated in occupations with little autonomy to decide on leaves of absence and working hours. Very often women lack the advantages of 'professional convergence', the fact that holding certain professions qualify for a political position. The third political resource, the level of income, is mainly relevant in political systems where a certain amount of money is needed, for campaigning for example, as is the case in electoral systems where the vote is personalised, such as Finland and Ireland.

Situational Factors

Situational factors refer to the circumstances of the majority of women, in particular their role as home-makers. It used to be that being married was a disadvantage for women seeking to enter high-level political positions. The political elite held the opinion that wives were unfit to perform in a legislative position. At present however, it is not so much being married that is the barrier, but having young children. With some exceptions, the political rights given to women were not matched with societal adjustment to accommodate this public role of women. Due

---

[9] J. Lovenduski, *Women and European Politics*, Harveston Press, Brighton, 1986, p. 129.

[10] See the country chapters in J. Borchert and J. Zeiss (eds.), *The Political Class in Advanced Democracies,* Oxford, Oxford University Press, 2003.

Chapter 3

to the absence of a supportive system of child-care facilities, flexible working hours etc., the combination of being a mother of small children and being a politician is difficult to carry out. Mothers are often not able to control the allocation of their time, while the hours of a politician are often unpredictable. Derived from the fact that women are the main child minders is the concept of guilt. From interviews with women politicians it becomes clear that many of them have a continuous feeling of failing their families.[11] Anticipating these feelings of guilt can influence a potential female candidate, as well as candidate selectors, in a negative way. A final example of the family circumstances of most women is support from the partner. Women politicians admit to the importance of (psychological) support from their husbands. In many cases the partners of women politicians are active in politics as well.[12]

Psychological Factors

The third group of individual characteristics of importance in the process of recruitment are the psychological effects of sex-role socialisation and more specifically political socialisation. Political socialisation is the process by which politically relevant values – feelings, knowledge, personal characteristics and capacities – are imbued.[13] The distinction between the private and the public domain, related ideas about the social roles of men and women (sex-role socialisation) and the definition of politics as belonging to the public domain, typically allow a lesser transformation of political values and attitudes for girls and women than for boys and men.[14] Immediately after World War II, when this ideology was still very prominent in each of the 15 countries, almost all women who got involved in politics came from a political background, for example with parents who were also politically

---

[11] R.B. Mandel, *In the Running. The New Woman Candidate*. New Haven, Ticknor and Fields, 1981, p. 91; see also A. Woodward and D. Lyon, 'Gendered Time and Women's Access to Power', in M. Vianello and G. Moore (eds.), *Gendering Elites, Economic and Political Leadership in 27 Industrialised Societies*, Basingstoke, Macmillan, 2000, p. 102.

[12] S.J. Carroll and W.S. Strimling, *Women's Routes to Elective Office. A Comparison with Men's*, Rutgers, Center for the American Womand and Politics, 1985, p. 16; see also J. Neale, 'Family Characteristics', in M. Vianello and G. Moore (eds.), 2000, p. 160.

[13] F. Greenstein, *Children and Politics*, Yale, Yale University Press, 1965, p. 4.

[14] R.M. Kelly and M. Boutilier, *The Making of Political Women. A Study of Socialisation and Conflict*, Chicago, Nelson-Hall, 1978, pp. 173-183.

active.[15] These days it is only in those countries or parts of countries where these values are still practiced, such as rural Greece and Italy, that women may lack confidence in their own political capabilities.

In general the impact of these structural, situational and psychological factors on the chances of women being recruited into a political career is less than it was 20 years ago. The gender ideology that organises women's and men's lives in a very strict way, has lost its strength in the majority of the 15 countries. Many more women are highly educated and participate in the labour market. More and more young men are willing to share some of the caring and household duties. Discriminatory tax and social security laws have disappeared and the availability of child-care facilities is also expanding. Overall, therefore, the impact of individual factors on women's political recruitment is declining.

SELECTION

The next stage in the process under investigation is the selection process carried out by political parties. What determines whether someone ends up at a good place on the list of candidates, or as their parties' sole candidate in the district? How this selection is carried out is very much dependent on the electoral system of a country. When we compared the 15 countries in the previous chapter, the electoral system was mentioned as being very important for women's representation in politics. Political parties and not voters are the main 'gatekeepers' to political office in almost all democratic political systems. Party decisions on the fate of would-be politicians are taken within a framework of formal rules, supplemented by informal practices that constrain the choices made and shape the eventual selection. As might be expected there is great variation on these matters between parties, even within the same country, arising from differences in party organisation, ideology and power structure.

Over the years, voters have indicated that they are not opposed to, and are indeed often inclined to support, women candidates. Thus, parties have responded by including women among their lists because it makes electoral sense to do so. However, some parties have gone further and recognised that it is not enough to put women on the party slate, but that it is necessary to have women in parliament.

---

[15] M.H. Leyenaar, *De Geschade Heerlijkheid*, Den Haag, SDU, 1989, p. 313.

Chapter 3

The extent to which the candidate selection systems encourage or inhibit women's opportunities for political representation is the subject of this section.

Electoral System

Considering the electoral systems used in the 15 states, the main distinction is between single-member plurality systems (SMP) and list-PR systems. SMP is mainly confined to Britain and, in a two round-system, to France. In Germany and Italy it is found in combination with the list-PR system. The mechanics of SMP could not be simpler. The country is divided into single-seat constituencies. Candidates are nominated in these constituencies, and voters cast a ballot by marking an 'x' beside the name of their most preferred candidate. The candidate with more votes than any other is declared the winner.

In the other countries, votes are transformed into seats through a system of proportional representation. The basic principles of list-PR electoral systems are also very simple. Within a given electoral area, parties nominate lists of candidates, ranked in order. In the simplest version of list-PR, each voter votes for one of these party lists. The proportions of votes for each party list are calculated. Seats are allocated to each party in proportion to the share of votes that the party list received in the election. The particular candidates to be elected are chosen in rank order from the party list. In other words, if a party is due ten seats on the basis of the popular vote, then the top ten candidates on the list are elected. The countries that use list-PR systems differ however, in several important respects such as whether voters have any say over the ordering of candidates on a party list (preferential voting), the size of the constituencies (number of MPs elected in a constituency) that are used in the election and whether there is an electoral threshold below which a party is allowed no seats at all.

What is the impact of different electoral systems on the representation of women? Let us compare the two main types of system from the perspective of the candidate, the party and the voter. In a first-past-the-post system with single-member districts, individual candidates need to fight for their seat in several arenas. First, they have to fight within their party, where they have to convince the party leadership of their suitability as candidates for the constituency in question. If they are successful here, they then have to fight during the election campaign against competitors from other parties. Although the party machine backs its own candidates, they still play a major role in the campaign. Candidates in SMP systems are expected to engage in door-to-door campaigning, to participate in rallies, to mobilise voters at markets and shopping malls. Generally speaking women are less inclined than men to put themselves forward in this way. They are less convinced about their own suitability, less inclined to fight and to show aggressive behaviour. All this results in lower numbers of women even presenting themselves as candidates in the first place. Another reason why women are at a disadvantage in SMP-systems is that it is only in the last ten years or so that women have come forward as candidates. Thus, in many single-member constituencies, male candidates have been active for a long time. Given the well-documented electoral advantage of incumbents (those who are running for election for the second or third time) women, as relative newcomers, may find it difficult to gain access, since parties are typically very reluctant to deselect incumbent candidates. Candidate selectors in SMP systems – typically local party branches – have thus always been more reluctant to select women candidates. The change in the overall attitude towards women's role in society that occurred during the 1970s in Western Europe, including their role in politics, did not change these views. Only in the 1990s, after some high-profile women had shown that women could perform well in politics, did prejudices about electoral appeal of women begin to disappear.

The mechanisms leading to election operate very differently in countries using list-PR systems. In closed-list systems, where voters vote for a party and cannot change the order of the list of candidates, the chances for women candidates to be elected depend totally on their place on the party list. In these cases, it is political parties and the criteria they use that decide how many women represent the party in the parliament. However, dealing with a *list* of candidates instead with having to nominate only *one* candidate, makes it easier for the party to take several criteria into account, including gender. When a party expects to win several seats, it is possible for parties to balance their party ticket and divide winning slots on the party list among various internal party interests, including the women's section of the party. Another reason to place women on the lists is to appeal to gender-sensitive voters. There is some evidence that, when a party starts paying attention to its women, it becomes more attractive to women voters. For example, the German SPD gained female membership after it introduced a quota for women party members.[16]

In list-PR systems, political parties are the major players in the election campaign and the candidates play a less aggressive role. Typically, only the person heading the list is obliged to appear on television and to take part in debates with

---

[16] E. Kolinsky, 'Party Change and Women's Representation in Unified Germany', in J. Lovenduski and P. Norris (eds.), 1993, p. 130.

other party leaders. Active party members often handle the door-to-door campaigning and rallies, while the candidates must merely be seen to be present at these meetings. This means that the main hurdles for both male and female candidates in a list system are to present themselves as candidates and to convince their respective party leaderships that they deserve a high place on the list. With regard to the effects of incumbency, it is much easier with a list-PR system to make room on the list for newcomers, often women.

A party list system may also facilitate the entry of women into parliament through the process of replacing MPs who retire or die during their period of office. In contrast to SMP systems in which by-elections have to be organised in this event, the next candidate on the party list replaces the outgoing MP. Frequently, these replacements have been women. Women, after all, often occupy slots in the grey zone on a party list where it is not clear whether the seats are winnable or not. In many countries with list-PR systems, the number of women in the parliament is higher at the end of a parliamentary term than at the beginning, especially in systems where ministers have to give up their seat in parliament before joining the cabinet.[17]

Other aspects of the electoral system also matter, such as the size of the electoral district and the presence of electoral thresholds. In countries using list-PR systems, the size of the constituencies vary significantly. In Greece there are constituencies with only one or two representatives, while in the Netherlands the whole country is viewed as a single 150-member constituency. The size of the constituency not only affects the proportionality of the election result, it also influences the chances of women being elected. The reason is that parties may make their strategies for selecting and ranking candidates dependent on the size of the district. Parties nominate as many or more candidates as there are seats to win in a constituency. When the size of the district increases, there is a higher chance that a party will win more than one seat. Parties may then be more willing to balance their tickets for the reasons discussed above – to satisfy different internal party sections and to attract as many different groups of voters as possible. This is a matter of simple arithmetic. If a party with 10 per cent of the vote in a given constituency is to elect both a man and a woman representative, then it must win at least two seats,

---

[17] D. Sainsbury, 'The Politics of Increased Women's Representation', in J. Lovenduski and P. Norris (eds.), 1993, p. 267.

which implies a minimum constituency size of 20 members. For a party with only 5 per cent of the vote to elect both a man and a woman candidate, by the same logic, the minimum constituency size must be 40. Small constituency sizes, of 12 or less, simply make it very difficult for all but the largest parties to elect both men and women candidates. A related issue is that the size of the district affects the turnover of candidates. The more seats in the same constituency, the higher the turnover rate, which increases the electoral chances of women by reducing the incumbency effect.

The main reason for establishing an electoral threshold is to avoid having too many small parties in parliament which would make the formation of government coalitions somewhat harder. Although higher thresholds do generate less proportional election results, they may paradoxically have a positive effect on the chances for women to be elected. This is because high thresholds favour larger parties, which, because of the number of representatives that they elect, may well find it easier to put forward gender-balanced lists of candidates. This is once more related to the ranking of candidates on the party list. Male party leaders often take the top slots on the list and women candidates tend to show up farther down the list when the party is taking the balancing of the party ticket into account. Small parties, therefore, with only two or three seats, are often represented by male candidates only. And it is these smaller parties that are likely to be excluded by having higher electoral thresholds.

In the previous chapter we have seen that the simple distinction between SMP and list-PR system is not sufficient to explain differences in women's representation. Not only are other aspects of an electoral system important, it is the selection process that ultimately determines in the end the chances for women to get involved in politics.

Selection Process

The first step in candidate selection involves the design and implementation of the selection process. Important aspects concern how long before the election each party begins the recruitment of candidates, whether a specific selection committee is formed and whether a profile of the ideal candidate or list of candidates is used. The sooner parties start with the recruitment of candidates, the better this is for women. Women aspirants, after all, are less likely than males to be readily available. Fewer women are party members or perform party activities. Since most selectors are male, their networks also mostly consist of males. When looking for women or minority aspirants, selectors therefore need time because they must look beyond their own turf. The use of a formal selection committee is favourable for women, because it can often act more impartially than the local party leadership and is therefore easier for newcomers (often women) to approach. Especially when the selection process is decentralised, the existence of a profile is a way to structure the selection process and make local selectors aware of the need for a balanced list.

The second step in the selection process is the actual putting forward of names of potential candidates. These names come from a pool of serious contenders for political office and this brings us to one of the core problems: the supply of women contenders. The most common methods of recruitment involve approaching members at party meetings, by mail or by a personal visit. Since women are typically a minority among party members and at party meetings, however, it is necessary to search for candidates outside the party and to use other methods of recruitment. This of course means that parties have to encourage contenders who are not yet members of the party. A very successful method to increase the number of women aspirants is to place advertisements in newspapers asking women (and men) to send in their applications. The Labour Party in the Netherlands did this for the parliamentary elections of 1998 and 2002 and received so many applications from women that it was possible for the selection committee to nominate 45 per cent women candidates.

The third step is the screening, ranking and shortlisting of nominees. The inclusion, as part of their selection, of assessment talks with aspiring candidates, works out positively for women. If these talks include the incumbents as well, then this provides the selectors with an opportunity to assess the performance of the politicians in a more objective way, making reselection less automatic. It appears that the more professional and transparent the organisation of the selection process, the higher the chances are for women to be selected. It is also important to find ways to increase the number of women aspirants, and one way of doing this is to look for women not only inside parties, but to inform women in general of the possibility of applying for candidacy.

The final step in the process is the adoption of the party list or candidate. Depending on the system of selection, it may be possible to organise lobbies aiming at selecting a specific candidate or to take care that a certain candidate is placed high on the list. There are many examples of women's sections within parties, which lobby, either at national party conferences or in local constituency meetings, to get their own candidates selected.

Parties also differ in the extent to which the selection process is centralised or decentralised. Do national party elites, local party branches or party members ultimately determine which candidate represents the party in a constituency or, in list-PR systems, the rank order of the candidates? And does this make a difference

An Explanatory Framework for Women's Political Representation

to the chances of women candidates? The selection of parliamentary candidates in the Labour Party of Britain is a good example of a decentralised process. The adoption of Labour parliamentary candidates is largely the prerogative of the local constituency party and the National Executive Committee intervenes only at the end of the process, when the candidate has to be endorsed.[18] The selection of parliamentary candidates in the Dutch Labour Party, the PvdA, is on the other hand very centralised. The national party leadership selects a committee to supervise the application process and the conducting of interviews with potential candidates and the preliminary ranking of the candidates. The Party Congress, consisting of delegates from the local party branches, formally decides on the final ranking, but in practice at this stage rarely changes it. As of 2002 a referendum among party members is organised to select the number one of the list, the so-called list-puller, but the remainder of the list is selected centrally.

In general, a decentralised selection process, in which local branches or individual party members have the last say in the selection of candidates, has tended to result in the selection of fewer women. This appears to be because national party leaders are more concerned about male-female balance than local or regional party branches. Separate women's sections exist in many parties, whose main objective is to get as many women candidates selected as possible. National party leaders are confronted much more forcefully with these demands and have responsibility for keeping different internal party groups satisfied. National party leaders also tend to balance the list to please as many different groups of voters as possible, including women voters. Local party branches are clearly less concerned with these matters since women party members tend to organise themselves only at the national level.

Selection Criteria

Regardless of who is making the selection, selectors must always use some set of criteria for making their ultimate choice. Often these are formal criteria published by the party, but all kinds of informal criteria may also be used. How do these formal and informal selection criteria affect the selection of women candidates? Parties do obviously differ in the selection criteria that they use, but it is possible to identify criteria that are used by almost every party. In the past, high educational

---

[18] P. Norris and J. Lovenduski (eds.), *Political Recruitment. Gender, Race and Class in the British Parliament*, Cambridge University Press, 1995.

levels as well as a professional background that converged with politics (lawyer, civil servant) were important assets. These criteria had a negative impact on the selection of women since in many countries women had participated less fully than men in the labour market. These days, political resources such as education and professional background still matter, but with less impact on women's selection, since there are enough women with similar educational and professional backgrounds to those of men. What is typically valued most is to be well-known within the party. A long party career brings the necessary reputation, as well as being valued as a sign of strong party affiliation, indicating that the candidate will be a trustworthy party representative. The most common route to a high-level position is through previous political positions. All parties view demonstrated political experience as the most crucial requirement for a potential candidate. Such a selection criterion has a negative effect on women's chances of being selected. Taking into account the length of membership and the number of activities carried out by women within the parties, women often still have less experience than men. A good example can be found in the selection of mayors in the Netherlands. A committee is formed consisting of the leaders of the parties represented in the council of the community in question. The main selection criterion put forward by these committees is political experience of the candidate. This is then translated into 'serving as mayor in another local community' or 'at least four years of experience as a local alderman'. At first sight this seems to be a gender-neutral criterion. However, it obviously lowers the chances of women contenders, since in 2002 only 20 per cent of mayors and only 17 per cent of aldermen were women (see chapter 5).

Given the fact that previous political experience is valued so much by selectors, it is understandable that incumbency is the most important asset for a candidate. In every country or party incumbents have the highest chance of being (re)selected as candidates. In SMP systems, they form the safest bet to win the seat again. In list-PR systems they have a lot of support, which they can mobilise for getting a high place on the party list.

Another important criterion is organisational experience. Chairing a local or national interest organisation is viewed as an asset for a political career. The contender has learned the necessary skills – such as negotiating, chairing meetings and communicating with members – and can offer the political support of the organisation in question. Large women's organisations have often served as an intensive training ground for women politicians as well as being a recruitment pool when parties started explicitly looking for women candidates. In the mid-1980s, for example, 80 per cent of women MPs in Sweden and 81 per cent of men had been active in a party and/or in a organisation before their selection as MPs.

Half of these women had been active in a women's organisation.[19] When women's organisations are viewed as having an important functional role, then they are important recruitment pools. When selectors look for people with ties to trade unions, employer's organisations and large consumer or environmental organisations, then women are at a disadvantage, since they are found in smaller numbers in these organisations and are less likely to be in leadership positions.

Affirmative Action

Being a woman can also be a selection criterion in itself. As a result of the continuous pressure of women activists both within and outside political parties, and because of the parties' concern to attract the female vote, the attitudes of parties towards the political participation of women shifted in the 1980s. Gender became an explicit issue for many political parties and many of them adopted special policies to improve the position of women in the selection process.

First, parties have adopted policies aiming to enlarge the number of women *aspirants*, those who want to become candidates for political office. Most large parties offer training programmes for their women members and cadres, programmes that are specially designed to train women to stand for parliament and deal with campaigning skills, presentation and negotiation techniques and media training. Secondly, parties have introduced quotas. Gender quotas imply that women must constitute a certain number or percentage of the members of a body, whether this is a list of candidates, a national parliament or local council, a government or an advisory committee. In the previous chapter we referred to the use of quotas as one of the explanations for why relatively large numbers of women can be found in the parliaments of the Scandinavian countries. In chapter 8 when discussing future developments on the empowerment of women, the issue of quotas will come up again.

Women's Factions

The use of quotas has often been put on the agenda by the women's sections of political parties. Their existence has helped women gain political power. In many of the traditional political parties in the 15 countries, women party members have organised themselves. Often this happened at the same time that the new women's

---

[19] D. Sainsbury, in J. Lovenduski and P. Norris (eds.), 1993, p. 279.

movement emerged in Europe, but there are also examples of women's factions established before World War II. In the Netherlands, for example, women in the Social Democratic Party founded their 'Women's Clubs' back in 1905 and the liberal women joint efforts in 1921.

Women's sections differ in appearance and in degree of organisation. Often there are parallel structures, with the women's sections holding their own party conferences and defining their own policy programmes. Sometimes they operate as a network, as in the British Labour Party where women were organised loosely in sections, councils and conferences.[20] In other cases there is a centrally organised women's section, like in the German SPD and CDU. It is also possible that no women's section formally exist, but that there are close ties with an autonomous women's association. Both in Italy and in the Netherlands, the Communist Parties did not have a women's section, but in practice the Dutch Women's Council and the Italian Women's Union acted as support organisations for these parties.[21] Another example is the Federation of Progressive Women that has always been very close to the Spanish Socialist party, the PSOE.[22] There are also women's political associations that are not associated to one party, but represent in a way all women party members and are very active in the drive for more women parliamentarians. The Women's Political Association in Ireland was founded in 1971 and they have been the prime mover in getting more women in parliament. They have organised both training sessions and awareness-raising campaigns, as well as practical support for women candidates.[23]

The women's sections within parties gained more influence with the large influx of women party members in the 1970s and 1980s. Due to an increase in the level of political interest by women, the number of women members of political parties grew significantly and these women expected to play a prominent role in the party, equal to that of men. The focus on education and mobilisation by

---

[20] P. Norris and J. Lovenduski, 'Gender and Party Politics in Britain', in Lovenduski and Norris, 1993 (eds.), p. 54.

[21] M. Guadagnini, 'A *Partitocrazia* Without Women: the Case of the Italian Party System', in J. Lovenduski and P. Norris (eds.), 1993, p. 176.

[22] C. Bustelo, 'Spain, Analytical Statement', in European Network 'Women in Decision-Making', *Panorama*, 1994, p. 96.

[23] F. Gardiner, 'Ireland, Analytical Statement', in European Network 'Women in Decision-Making', *Panorama*, 1994, p. 107.

women's sections disappeared and an active lobby for equal representation came into place.

Women's factions have had a positive impact in several ways. First, they have lowered the entry barriers for women by providing a training ground for newcomers. Women moving into a male-dominated environment needed to be part of a wider network of women from which they could draw advice and support. Secondly, women's organisations can be considered as a recruitment pool. Leadership positions in the women's faction of a political party often led to a representative post in the parliamentary party. Miet Smet, cabinet minister in Belgium from 1992 to 1999 founded the organisation Woman and Society, the women's division of the Christian People's Party. Yvette Roudy, an activist for women's representation in the Socialist Party of France became a Minister of Women's Rights from 1981-1986.

Party System/Party Competition

Women's representation is in general larger in the parliamentary groups of left-wing parties than of right-wing parties. Conservative ideology glorifies female participation in the family rather than politics, while socialist ideology contains specific commitments to female emancipation. Parties with a centre to left orientation on the ideological spectrum have a track record of high female representation. Further, the smaller left-wing parties (especially the so-called green or ecological parties) have a relatively greater number of women in their parliamentary party than the large social democratic parties do. An explanation can be found in the social composition of the membership: relatively young, well-educated people, with free time on their hands, with sufficient women willing and able to stand for election. A second reason may be that these parties challenge not only the established economic and social order, but also the traditional division of tasks and roles between women and men. By nominating at least 50 per cent women as candidates, they show their willingness to break with the existing gender ideology. A party system consisting of one or more left-wing parties will have a positive impact on women's empowerment.

The same is true when there is a healthy competition between the parties. Parties compete for the support of voters at election time and now that the ideological distinctiveness of parties has decreased all over Europe, parties have to use other criteria to appeal to the voters. One of these is the parties' attitude to gender equality and women's political representation. As discussed in the previous chapter, one of the reasons why the German Christian Democratic Party and the German Socialist Party debated the introduction of gender quotas was the discovery that young women expressed a deep frustration with the large, traditional parties not longer believing in changes favourable to women. They had turned away from these parties and became involved in the Green Party.

Political and Civic Expertise

Concerning the individual aspects that help or hinder women in the selection process, we already pointed to length of party membership and political expertise as useful qualities. Also viewed as positive by the selectors is a strong and lengthy involvement in non-political organisations. Women often have a long history of participation in community, school and religious organisations, where they develop political skills and build up a network. Involvement in these organisations often means encouragement to run for office, because parties view the support a candidate can rely on from these organisations as an attractive asset.

As was mentioned before, support from a husband or other family members is also very useful, even more so when members of the family are also active in politics and have a large network at their disposal.

Quality of Life

We have yet to discuss the motives of people who want to go into politics, given that it is hard work with long hours, often in the evenings and on weekends. Common motives include the desire to influence decision-making, sympathy with a particular party, and family traditions of political activity. It is still true that, given the traditional division of labour in the family, the gender segregation of the labour market and the fact that many women have been socialised to take care of the family while men occupy themselves with public and community affairs, women not only often have lower resources of time and money, but also of political interest, confidence and ambition. Even when active in a political party, many women will neither put themselves forward as candidates nor consent to a candidacy when asked.

In the 21st century, many women have overcome the barriers of the traditional gender ideology, but will nonetheless refuse to be selected for a political position. High-level political positions impose heavy demands: long days, 24-hour availability, the necessity for total dedication and the need for mobility. Meetings are an important part of the representative job and dependence on voluntary supporters mean that meetings have to be scheduled in the evenings and during weekends. In general, being flexible can be problematic for women, since strict planning is the only way to combine work, care and politics. For women, there are also other spheres of interest, besides a political career, which are seen as being just as important.[24] These include family, friends and local community, and the attention of women is often divided between these spheres, more so than for men. Socialisation of men over 45 years old has caused a narrower orientation towards work and career, and a lesser interest for these other spheres.[25] The fact that women divide their time and attention between a career, family, friends and community stands in the way of a traditional linear career pattern. Research shows that men and women differ in the importance they attach to a high salary and power (for men these are more important) and to relevant and interesting work (more important for women).[26] Women are less inclined to make sacrifices in order to reach the top of the political ladder. It is not true that these women lack ambition or commitment, but more that they do not possess a clear career plan that includes spending time on politics. Women see themselves as having more alternative possibilities at their disposal, and therefore will not set everything aside for a political career. In politics and especially for the leadership positions, one has to fight to get on, and strong women candidates often give in to pressure by the party leadership to step down in favour of a male candidate. This was the case in the leadership fight in 2002 in the German Christian Democratic Party, where Angela Merkl voluntary retreated in favour of Edmund Stoïber. In the Netherlands, in the campaign for the parliamentary elections of 2002, the second candidates on the lists of PvdA and VVD, both women, gave way to men placed lower on the lists. These men were thought by the party leadership to be more electoral attractive and they were given a prominent role in the campaign when the number one candidates of both parties (both men) were attacked by the media (see chapter 7).

ELECTION

In countries using a non-preferential list-PR system, the selection process determines in effect who is elected to the legislature. After they have been ranked,

---

[24] D. de Gilder, N. Ellemers, H. van de Heuvel and G. Blijleven, 'Arbeidssatisfactie, Committment en Uitstroom. Overeenkomsten en Verschillen tussen Mannen en Vrouwen'. in *Gedrag en Organisaties*, vol.11, 1998, pp. 25-35.

[25] See N. Chodorow, *The Reproduction of Mothering*, Berkely, University of California Press, 1978; C. Gilligan, *In a Different Voice*, Cambridge, Harvard University Press, 1982.

[26] V. Valian, *Why So Slow. The Advancement of Women*, Cambridge, MIT Press, 1998.

Chapter 3

candidates know, given opinion poll results, more or less what their chances are of being elected to parliament. Voters only decide on the precise number of MPs for each party. In both SMP systems and preferential (open-list) systems used in Austria, Denmark and Finland, elections are decisive. Here voters can influence the choice of candidates who are actually elected. Depending on the number of preferential votes a candidate needs, it is possible for a candidate placed low on the party list to be elected to parliament.

Preferential Voting and Electoral Attractiveness

For a long time, women candidates were seen as being less attractive to voters than males, regardless of other characteristics. For that reason alone, local party leaderships preferred male candidates. Especially in SMP systems, the local party branch wanted the candidate with the highest chance of winning. The opinion that women were not the best candidates for winning votes did have some basis in reality. Data from surveys in Europe held in the 1970s and 1980s show that both men and women voters had more confidence in a male than a female politician. While, by 1983, a clear majority of both men and women (60 and 61 per cent) told survey researchers that they had as much confidence in male as female representatives, the equivalent figures in previous surveys were lower. In 1975, 42 per cent of male respondents and 50 per cent of the women said this; in 1977 the numbers were 46 and 44 per cent respectively.

These days, however, there is no clear indication of prejudice against women candidates on the part of voters. Recent parliamentary election results in Ireland, the Netherlands and Britain were analysed by comparing votes received by men and women candidates of the same party, holding constant as many factors as possible.[27] At first sight the results from the parliamentary elections in 1997 in Ireland showed fewer votes for women candidates than for their male party colleagues. However, the effect of gender on voting was not statistically significant, once account was taken of whether or not the candidate was an incumbent. This clearly implies that women candidates got fewer votes than men did, not because they were women, but because women were less likely to be incumbent and thus to benefit from the significant incumbency bonus. The 1998 parliamentary elections in the Netherlands showed that here too incumbent candidates received

---

[27] This was done for the already mentioned study on *Electoral Systems in Europe: a Gender-Impact Assessment*, 1999 (see note 1).

significantly more votes than challengers. When controlling for incumbency, women candidates did not receive significantly fewer votes than their male counterparts. In the parliamentary election of 2003 women candidates received relatively even more preferential votes. Analysis of the 1992 and 1997 national elections in Britain showed no measurable gender effects in voting patterns for the three main parties. Women candidates do just as well, on average, as their male party colleagues.[28]

REPRESENTATION

The last stage in the process of women's empowerment is representation or staying in office. After recruitment, selection and election, one is seated in parliament. If a woman stays in position there is a high chance that she will be reselected and re-elected, regardless of the electoral system or the selection process that is used. Having more women incumbents together with a fair percentage women candidates on the lists or a fair number of women challengers in an SMP system, will eventually lead to a gender balanced composition of the 15 parliaments. In the previous sections we noticed that still not enough women candidates are placed on eligible places on the lists or nominated as challengers. But it is also true that a larger share of women politicians leave office sooner than their male colleagues do.[29] Especially in those countries were women MPs still constitute a large minority, working conditions in parliament may well not have been adapted to the circumstances of (many) mothers. Parliamentary meetings often start or continue into the evenings, which makes permanent child care necessary. In most countries there are no regulations for pregnant MPs. Women MPs who belong to a small parliamentary party cannot therefore afford to become pregnant while in office.

---

[28] For Britain see also P. Norris, E. Vallance and J. Lovenduski, 'Do Candidates Make a Difference', in *Parliamentary Affairs*, 45, 1992, pp. 496-517 and P. Norris, 'Introduction: Theories of Recruitment', in P. Norris (ed.) *Passages to Power: Legislative Recruitment in Advanced Democracies*, Cambridge University Press, 1997.

[29] P. Castenmiller, M. Leyenaar, B. Niemöller and H. Tjalma, *Afscheid van de Raad*, Ministerie van Sociale Zaken, 2002.

Chapter 3

Culture of Politics

What may be an obstacle to women continuing as public representatives once they have achieved this position, is that the culture of political parties and representative bodies, the shared values, ideas and practices, does not coincide with the cultural norms and values of the women MPs. Research has shown that in many organisations, values such as independence, control, competition, rationality and objectivity are dominant, while there is less room for values and practices related to caring, emotionality and closeness. Men and women differ in attitudes to decision-making: women are more focused on consensus and balance in communication and more democratically oriented, while men are more focused on competition and have a more autocratic orientation.[30] Women politicians may often not feel at home and isolated in the world of politics, also because they operate in other networks. Apart from the time factor, this is often a reason for women to leave their political positions after a single term, while men are more often inclined to stay on for further terms.

Another reason to abandon political office is finding out that one's overall influence on decision-making is actually very small. Given the necessary sacrifices, finding out that one has not much power as a woman MP, often creates disappointment. This is especially true for women MPs who regard themselves as feminists and whose intention is to articulate and defend women's interests.

CONCLUSION

There are many obstacles along the path to representation in the legislature. Some of these barriers are the same for both men and women, but there are also many that particularly hinder women in acquiring political power. Countries differ, for example, in the opportunities for women to get access to education and to the labour market. In those countries where traditional views on women's roles are still valued, women are confronted with another political socialisation, which may result in a lower level of political interest, political efficacy and political knowledge than men have.

Enlarging the recruitment pool is therefore to further gender equality in the 15 countries. In those countries, such as Ireland, Greece and Italy, where religion still

---

[30] A. van Vianen and A. Fischer, 1998, pp. 249-264.

plays a dominant role and the gendered division of roles is persistent, participation of women in politics is hardly increasing. Politics remains viewed as men's domain, not suitable for women. But gender equality is permeating European societies more and more: women have caught up with men in educational level and more women than ever are joining the labour market. What lags behind, however, is a similar equalising of caring tasks. In all 15 countries, it is predominantly women who take care of children and the elderly. For many women the combination of paid employment, caring for children *and* playing an active role in a political party is simply not feasible. Politics itself is also not well-adjusted to the working hours of mothers with meetings in the evenings and no replacement arrangements for pregnant parliamentarians.

However, since the 1970s women have, in the majority of the countries in our study, caught up with men in education and occupational status. But a greater access for women to political resources has not resulted in a similar increase in the number of women in the representative bodies. This reveals the importance of barriers within the selection, such as the selection procedures and criteria of political parties. Many of these are biased in ways that promote the continued tenure of groups and individuals, predominantly men, who are already in positions of power. Given our knowledge of the gender impact of electoral systems and candidate selection procedures it is possible to define new rules and procedures guaranteeing a more balanced participation of men and women. In chapter 9 these best-practice policies on gender representation will be discussed extensively, as well as an example of an electoral system that is friendly to women and other newcomers to politics.

Another matter is whether enough women will, in the future, be *willing* to take on a representative or governing position. Noting the trend that capable women are increasingly deciding not to accept high-level management or political positions because of the demands of the job in question, it may become more difficult to find enough qualified women willing to set their private lives aside for a while. Therefore, not only do selection procedures have to be scrutinised in order to get more women nominated, a gender assessment of the working conditions of the institutions seems also to be necessary.

On the other hand, the total number of high-level representative and governing functions in a country is not very high, probably meaning that enough women will be ready to do these jobs when asked. Compared to 20 years ago, many women who now enter politics, especially at the national level, make a conscious decision to do so. In the brief description in the previous chapter of the empowerment of women in 15 European countries, we saw that in the majority of countries political parties are now actively searching for women candidates. They are responding to

Chapter 3

an electorate that wants to be able to vote for a women candidate and to the demands of women's sections for a more 'mature' democracy.

In the second part of this book we present a case study of the Netherlands. In its four chapters, the political empowerment of women is described and analysed, which enables us to concretise many of the factors we discussed in this chapter that help or hinder women's political participation.

PART II:
THE CASE OF THE NETHERLANDS

CHAPTER 4

THE NETHERLANDS: POLITICAL RIGHTS FOR WOMEN

Foreigners often typify the Dutch people as '*nuchter*', while having some difficulty in pronouncing this word correctly. '*Nuchter*' means cool, not easy emotionally aroused and it refers to rational behaviour. This attitude is reflected in the political system. Dutch politics can be characterised as extremely proportionate – meaning that even very small parties can be represented in parliament and that every interest group can have its say – as well as being very compromise seeking, since no party ever has a majority.

In the previous chapter an overview was presented of the barriers that influence the chances for women to get elected to representative bodies. In our description of the empowerment of women in the Netherlands we will discuss several of these aspects such as the impact of the electoral system and that of the party system. The political system in the Netherlands settled into its current shape in 1917. At that time the electoral system was changed from a majority system into a system of proportional representation, census suffrage was replaced by general suffrage for men, a party system had developed with strong Catholic, Protestant, liberal and socialist parties, and the now famous '*poldermodel*' of negotiation and compromise among the representatives of the different sectors of society became common practice. By the time women were granted the right to be elected (1917) and the right to vote (1919), the struggle for women's suffrage had taken about 35 years. The overall view at that time, was that women's proper role was in the family and therefore not in politics.

In this chapter I describe the main characteristics of the Dutch political system in terms of its consequences for political participation of women, following this with a brief historical sketch of the main parties' attitudes towards the integration of women. But we start our narrative of the empowerment of Dutch women with the story of Aletta Jacobs, the first woman to challenge the authorities on the question of the right to vote.

Chapter 4

'NO GENDER BARRIER AT THE POLLING BOOTH'

Until 1887 there was no explicit constitutional prohibition barring women from the vote. The existing law (since 1848) allowed only people with a certain income, and older than 25 years of age, to vote. Financial well-being decided whether one could cast a vote or not. This meant for example that in 1853 only 2.7 per cent of the total population was eligible, about 11 per cent of the male population of 23 years and older. Increasing prosperity expanded the percentage of voters: from 4 per cent in 1880 to 12 per cent in 1904. Aletta Jacobs pointed out the discrepancy between the Constitution and the actual practice. Being well-off herself (she was the first woman allowed to go to university and was, subsequently, a medical practitioner), she used the parliamentary elections of 1883 in an attempt to assert her rights.

> When the lists with the names of the voters were published in 1883, I looked at whether my name was included. Of course I knew my name would not be there, but I wanted to do everything right. When I did not find my name on the list, I sent a letter dated 22 March 1883 to the Mayor of Amsterdam, requesting to be placed on the voters' list, since I answered all conditions for eligibility. I included written proof of this. The Mayor and aldermen thought my letter to be very entertaining. To great laughter my letter was read out loud and nobody really understood the meaning of its content.[1]

Her request was denied, since:

> the author may refer to the Law, but according to the Spirit of our Political Institutions, women do not have the right to vote. And even, if one denounces the Spirit of our Laws, one should question whether women should possess all the rights of citizenship. Looking at civil laws, women are barred from custody with the exception of the custody of their children.[2]

Appeal to the Higher Court did not help. The Higher Court ruled that, when the Constitution refers to an 'Inhabitant of the Netherlands' it is referring to men, since 'otherwise this would have been explicitly stated'. Moreover, it was argued

---

[1] A. Jacobs, *Herinneringen*, Nijmegen, Sun reprint, 1978/1924. p. 94, translation Monique Leyenaar.

[2] *Ibid.*, p. 95

that since it is the husband and father who pays taxes for his wife and children, it is logical that women should not be allowed to vote. Rather conveniently those women who also paid taxes, such as widows and unmarried women, were not taken into account. The result of Jacobs's action was that, in 1887 when the Constitution was renewed, the word 'male' was added to 'inhabitant of the Netherlands'.

The publicity around this case raised interest in the issue of suffrage for women, and led to the establishment of the Organisation for Women's Suffrage (*Vereeniging voor Vrouwenkiesrecht*, VvVK) in 1894, which was chaired by Aletta Jacobs for a few years. The majority of women engaged in the VvVK were, just like Aletta Jacobs, well-to-do. Until 1913 the VvVK held the opinion that restricted suffrage for women was better than no suffrage at all. After 1913 they also supported the demand for general suffrage. Around 1900 the VvVK had around 20,000 members and arranged many different propaganda activities. They sent an appeal to the Queen, and organised large demonstrations and a women's vigil at the parliament in The Hague when it was discussing the Constitutional changes in 1913 and in 1916.

The activities of the VvVK and many other organisations resulted in the removal of the qualification 'male' from the Election Law in 1917. Two years later in 1919, women in the Netherlands acquired the right to cast their votes at elections.

POLITICAL SYSTEM

Which aspects of a political system have an impact on the political participation of women? First, as we have seen, the choice for an *electoral system* is important. Who is allowed to vote and has the right to be elected is of course the main question. But it also matters greatly, as we saw in chapter 3, whether a majority system or a system of proportional representation is in place or whether an electoral threshold is being used. Secondly, the *party system* influences the political participation of women, most importantly the attitude of the dominant parties towards the integration of women in their midst. But the number and size of political parties (party fragmentation) also plays a role as do the procedures used by the parties for selecting candidates for political office. Two other typical Dutch characteristics of the political system are relevant as well. There is the fact that Dutch society was strongly socially as well as politically segregated along the lines of religion and class.[3]

---

[3] A. Lijphart, 1968, chapter 2.

Chapter 4

Consociationalism and pillarisation (*verzuiling*) are relevant in understanding women's political empowerment. The strong religious pillars denounced an active role for women in politics. In addition, the pillars have often agreed on gender and family policies in a bid to create consensus across an otherwise divided society.[4] Examples are the political consensus on only granting men suffrage, and the 1930s consensus on the legal ban for married women to be employed by the government.

ELECTORAL SYSTEM

The constitutional monarchy was established in the Netherlands in 1814 with a monarch as formal Head of State and a prime minister as head of government. In the Constitution of 1848, political power of the monarch was strongly reduced and parliamentary democracy was a fact. From that time on, an executive responsible to a bicameral parliament governed the Netherlands. After every election, the leader of the largest party is asked to form a cabinet together with other parties to reach a majority within the parliament. The parliament controls the activities and decisions of the cabinet. The members of the provincial councils elect the 75 representatives of the first chamber indirectly. The 150 members of the Second Chamber are directly elected, as are the members of the provincial and local councils. All the other political offices, such as the mayors or state governors, are filled by appointment.[5]

From 1848 until 1917, delegates to the parliament were elected in districts, using a majority system. Each district elected two members and, since half of the members of parliament stepped down every two years, elections took place every two years to elect one of the MPs. Not all citizens had voting rights, since only those men could vote who were being taxed for property. In the second half of the 19th century this amounted to about 10 per cent of the male population.[6] As we have seen from the story of Aletta Jacobs, it was not until 1887 that women were

---

[4] J. Bussemaker and R. Voet, 'Introduction', in J. Bussemaker and R. Voet (eds.) *Gender, Participation and Citizenship in the Netherlands*, Aldershot, Ashgate, 1998, p. 6.

[5] In 2004 parliament is discussing a cabinet proposal for a constitutional change stating that from 2006 onwards mayors will be directly elected by the citizens.

[6] P.J. Oud en J. Bosmans, *Honderd Jaren. Een Eeuw van Staatkundige Vormgeving in Nederland, 1840-1940*, Assen, van Gorcum, 1982, pp. 1-49.

explicitly excluded from voting rights in the Constitution of 1848. In theory those women who met the taxation criteria were legally allowed to vote.

The introduction of general suffrage for men and the replacement of the majority system in 1917 by a system of proportional representation with lists instead of individual candidates was the outcome of a deal between the confessional parties on the one hand and the liberals and socialists on the other. The dominant issues at the end of the 19th century, reflecting the religious and class cleavages in Dutch society, centred around government funding for private (religiously oriented) schools and the introduction of universal suffrage. These issues were resolved in 1917 in a major compromise between the political parties that had been formed by that time. The socialist and liberal parties accepted equal public funding for private and public schools and the religious parties approved the extension of suffrage. With this so-called 'pacification' of 1917, when universal suffrage for men and the right for women to be elected was established, the door to universal suffrage for women had been opened.[7] Since then the electoral system has changed little, with the exception of changes in the voting age and the abolition of compulsory voting in 1970. Currently, all citizens of 18 years and older are eligible to vote. Voters do not have to register because the Netherlands provides for a universal registration system. The voter casts a single preferential vote for any candidate on one of the lists presented by parties. For all practical purposes the country as a whole forms one constituency. The ballot contains the names of all candidates competing for seats, grouped by party. Although citizens may vote for any candidate on the ballot, the majority cast their vote for the first person on a party list.[8]

It was argued in chapter three that two aspects of the electoral system are decisive for the number of women in parliament: the method of turning votes into seats and the size of the constituency. A system of proportional representation is more advantageous for women and other newcomers to politics than a majority system, especially when political parties put forward lists of candidates. When a party expects to win several seats it can balance its list of candidates in terms of several criteria, including gender. Apart from the electoral formula being used, we have seen that women have a better chance of being elected in larger than in smaller constituencies. The electoral system of the Netherlands, in this sense, has the

---

[7] *Ibid.*, p. 221.

[8] In the parliamentary elections of 2003, 80 per cent of all voters voted for a list by giving their vote to the first candidate on the list.

largest possible constituency. Seats are distributed by a system of proportional representation and district magnitude is 150, which equals the total number of legislators.[9]

Since 1919, the electoral system has not put up a formal barrier for the election of women. However, neither the Dutch parliament, the government, the local and provincial councils, nor the offices of mayor or State Commissioner have come to reflect the gender balance in the electorate. The causes of this may be found in features of the Dutch party system.

PARTY SYSTEM

In list-PR systems where voters vote for a party and cannot change the order of the list of candidates, the chances of women candidates being elected depend fully on their place on the party list. In these cases, it is political parties and the criteria they use that decide how many women represent the party in the parliament. The attitude of the parties towards integration of women in politics is thus very important. Two orientations seem to be relevant when discussing the integration of women in the political parties: religious orientation and ideological orientation in terms of left and right.

The main dimensions of the Dutch party system are rooted in the social splits that dominated Dutch politics during the last quarter of the 19th century and the first half of the 20th: religion and class. There still are many parties whose origins are to be found in these social cleavages. There is the Christian Democratic Party (*Christen Democratisch Appel*, CDA), a merger of three parties based upon religious persuasion – the Catholic Peoples Party (*Katholieke Volkspartij*, KVP), the Anti-Revolutionary Party (*Anti Revolutionaire Partij*, ARP) and the Christian Historical Union (*Christelijk Historische Unie*, CHU). They formally merged into the CDA in 1980. Another large party is the Labour Party (*Partij van de Arbeid*, PvdA). A third large party is the People's Party for Freedom and Democracy (*Volkspartij voor Vrijheid en Democratie*, VVD), a party with strong conservative overtones. Owing to their size, these parties have dominated parliamentary politics and

---

[9] In 2003, the government submitted to parliament a bill concerning the reform of the electoral system. The draft bill suggests a mixed system. Half of the seats (75) are elected through the list-PR system with one single constituency and the other half are elected through multi-member constituencies.

coalition formation in the entire post-war period. Until 1994, the Christian Democrats were the pivot of Dutch parliamentary politics – between 1946 and 1994 the Christian Democrats or one or two of the former religious parties always formed a government with either the PvdA or the VVD. In the parliamentary elections of 2002 a new (and at that time large) party entered the stage, List Pim Fortuyn (LPF) named after its leader Pim Fortuyn who was murdered nine days before the election of May 2002. This new, populist, party challenged the lack of transparency of decision-making and the lack of decisiveness of the government as well as the inability of the cabinet in office to solve problems such as waiting lists for hospital operations and increasing figures on criminality. Further, the LPF placed the issue of the presence of immigrants and especially the question of their lack of integration in Dutch society high on the political agenda. Founded in February 2002, the LPF received 17 per cent of the total vote in the elections held in the same year. They were also represented in the government formed after this election. However, this cabinet dissolved after 79 days in office and in the parliamentary elections held in January 2003 the LPF received 6 per cent (8 seats).

Medium-sized parties include D66, or Democrats 66, a progressive liberal party that was founded in 1966 with the ambition to renew the functioning of democracy. They have always stressed issues such as the direct election of mayors and the legal introduction of a referendum. Other current middle-sized parties (with 7-12 seats) are Green Left (*Groen Links*, GL) and the Socialist Party (*Socialistische Partij*, SP). GL is a left-wing party, formed in 1989 out of a merger between the Communist Party and two other radical parties. The SP, another left-wing party, was represented in parliament for the first time in 1994, but was already active at the local level before this. In addition to these parties, which are all potential coalition partners for a cabinet, a number of 'minor' parties have been represented in parliament. Some of these have occupied seats since long before the war, and some of them have sprung up since the late 1950s. On the right we find, for example, two small religious parties: the Christian Union (*Christen Unie*, CU) (a merger between two Calvinist parties) and the Political Reformed Party (*Staatkundig Gereformeerde Partij*, SGP).

The orientations of parties in terms of class and religion have an impact on their stance towards gender equality. In the Netherlands too, the religious parties traditionally criticised women's participation in the public sphere more so than non-religious parties. As was mentioned in chapter 3, in general the practice of religion strengthened the inequality of women in the family and society by promoting the idea that a woman's proper place is in the home. More directly, women's

Chapter 4

political participation was negatively influenced by the fact that the religious parties did not welcome women in their midst. For example it took the Calvinist ARP until 1953 to allow its women members to stand for election. Even now, we find fewer women parliamentary representatives of religious parties than of the other party groups, as is shown in table 4.1. The small religious parties, RPF, GPV and SGP, have not delegated any women. Only the CU, the merger of RPF and GPV, had one woman MP elected in 2002 and in 2003, who was elected with preferential votes (see chapter 7). Most of the time KVP, ARP and CHU had only one woman in their parliamentary party. Their successor, the CDA, began nominating a substantial number of women MPs in the 1990s.

A similar pattern holds for the distinction between left and right-wing parties, albeit in the 1970s and after. Before and immediately following World War II, women were active in all main parties, they formed women's sections and demanded representation. Gender equality as such, however, was more an issue of the liberal and the left-wing parties than of the confessional parties. But in the 1970s, after the issue became more incorporated in the left-wing parties, women party members were more active within socialist and social-democratic parties than in the liberal or conservative parties. Distinguishing the Dutch parties from the left through to the right, we see in table 4.1 that women's representation in later periods is higher in the more leftist parties.

A final feature of the party system we discuss here is the impact of party fragmentation on the number of women in politics. Due to the characteristics of the electoral system, it is rather easy for Dutch parties to gain a seat in the parliament: a party needs just 0.67 per cent of the total valid vote to do this. Owing to this low threshold for gaining representation, there has always been a relatively large number of parties winning seats in parliament. As we described in detail in chapter 3, the smaller the representational basis of a party in parliament, the fewer women delegates we will find. This has to do with the higher competition inside the party, a struggle often lost by potential women candidates. In the period between 1956 and 2003 there were many small parties with no women representatives (not shown in table 4.1).

There are several smaller parties mentioned in table 4.1. that have not been discussed so far. Right of centre are the General Assocation for the Elderly (*Algemeen Ouderenverbond*, AOV), Democratic Socialists 70 (*Democratisch-Socialisten 1970*, DS'70) and the Centre Democrats (*Centrum Democraten*, CD). The AOV gained six seats in the elections of 1994, mainly because the previous cabinet threatened to cut old-age benefits. The turbulence around this issue gained the party a lot of attention and consequently six seats. A woman, Jet Nijpels, headed the AOV and she represented the party with one other woman. In the election of

Table 4.1: Percentage of women in the parliamentary party of Dutch parties with women representatives, 1956-2003.

	1956	1953	1963	1967	1971	1972	1977	1981	1982	1986	1989	1994	1998	2002	2003
SP												0	20	44	44
GL											50	60	55	60	63
CPN	14	0	0	0	0	0	0	33	67						
PSP		0	0	0	0	0	0	33	33	100					
PPR					0	0	33	33	50	50					
EVP									100						
PvdA	12	10	11	8	10	14	15	23	17	19	31	38	49	48	48
D66				14	9	17	25	24	50	11	33	50	43	43	33
DS'70					12	17	0								
CDA							10	15	13	20	22	27	32	40	32
KVP	5	8	8	7	6	7									
CHU	8	8	8	17	10	0									
ARP	0	0	8	7	8	7									
VVD	23	21	25	12	13	14	18	12	19	22	18	26	26	25	29
LPF														15	13
AOV												33			
CU													0	25	33
RPF	0	0	0	0	0	0	0	0	0	0	0	0	0		
GPV	0	0	0	0	0	0	0	0	0	0	0	0	0		
CD											0	33			

Chapter 4

1998 there were no seats for the AOV, due to several splits within the parliamentary party among other things. DS'70 was a split from the PvdA entering parliament in 1971 with eight seats, of which one was for a woman. In 1972 they gained six seats and the same woman, Sophia van Veenendaal van Meggelen, stayed on as MP. The CD was an ultra right-wing party gaining seats mainly on the issue of the unwanted presence of immigrants. In 1989 they gained one seat and three in the elections of 1994 of which one was for a woman, the wife of the party leader.

To the left of the spectrum we find the Progressive Radical Party (*Progressieve Partij Radicalen*, PPR), founded by progressive ex-members of the Catholic Party, the Pacifist Socialist Party (*Pacifistische Socialistische Partij*, PSP) and the Evangelical Party (*Evangelische Volkspartij*, EVP), a progressive Christian party. The PPR and EVP produced the first woman parliamentary leaders in 1982. PPR and PSP, together with the Communist Party merged into Green Left and entered parliament in 1989 with six MPs, of which three, including the parliamentary leader, were women.

Table 4.1 shows that until the 1970s the main parties did not differ very much in the number of women they delegated to the parliament. Each of them embraced the odd women to fulfil the 'quality seats' reserved for women. In the 1980s the small left-wing parties had always one or two women (out of three MPs) in the parliamentary party and in the 1990s the PvdA started to take women's representation seriously as well with 31 per cent women in 1989 and 48 per cent in 2003. Although in the 1950s and 1960s, the liberal party VVD had relatively many more women representatives than the KVP, ARP and CHU, in the years after both CDA and VVD stay somewhat behind with a quarter to one third women MPs.

Pillarisation

The various emancipatory movements not only gave rise to political parties, but also to a wide array of other social institutions, organised along denominational and class lines. Political, social, cultural and some economic organisations were to a large extent based on the same cleavages in the population, resulting in the formation of relatively cohesive segments of society or subcultures for Catholic (the most numerous), Protestant, Socialist, and 'Neutral' (secular, liberal) groups. Born as a Catholic, one went to a Catholic church, and attended a Catholic school. When ill, one was hospitalised in a Catholic hospital. One joined the Catholic youth organisation and the Catholic trade union and one listened to the Catholic broadcasting organisation. And of course one voted for the Catholic party. This process, which is generally known as *verzuiling* or the pillarisation of Dutch society, began to break down in the 1960s as religion became less important for individual citizens.[10]

Another important characteristic of Dutch political development is the extension of neo-corporatism after the Second World War. In the 1950s and 1960s a highly institutionalised network of interest groups was formed, the majority of these oriented towards ministries, such as the Ministry of Social Affairs, Internal Affairs, Culture, Education and Agriculture. A defining characteristic of the neo-corporatist structure of the Dutch political system was defending group interests by representation in all kind of advisory boards.[11]

These characteristics of Dutch society, *verzuiling* and *neo-corporatism*, are important in explaining women's political involvement in the Netherlands. As mentioned before, strong religious overtones diminish the possibilities for women to participate. During the *verzuiling* the norms and values of the Catholic and Protestant churches prevailed. Another characteristic of the pillarised political system was the cooperation of the political elites and the passiveness of citizens.[12] Citizens did not question the leadership of the party elites and accepted decisions without hesitation. In this climate, women did not question their subjugated role in society.

In the 1960s the system of *verzuiling* began breaking down when religion was getting less important. At the beginning of the decade some 82 per cent of the population was religious and more than 70 per cent of these voters supported their respective religious parties. In the 1980s however, the electorate contained considerably fewer religious voters (63 per cent) who were also less likely to vote for religious parties (41 per cent of them did so in 1982) than for secular parties (48 per cent in 1982).[13] Many people at that time were demanding more influence on political decision-making. Women began recognising gender discrimination and were demanding changes in society.

Another consequence of *verzuiling* was the pillarisation of women's organisations. Prior to the new women's movement of the 1960s, women were organised in

---

[10] A. Lijphart, 1968; R. Andeweg and G. Irwin, *Governance and Politics of the Netherlands*, New York, Palgrave, 2002.

[11] R. Andeweg and G. Irwin, 2002, pp. 140, 141

[12] A. Lijphart, 1968, pp. 144-160.

[13] R. Andeweg and G. Irwin, 2002, p. 35.

Chapter 4

so-called 'traditional' women's organisations. Examples of these traditional organisations include the Catholic Women's Club (*Katholiek Vrouwen Dispuut*), Dutch Organisation of Housewives (*Nederlandse Vereniging van Huisvrouwen*), Dutch Organisation of Farmers Wives *(Nederlandse Bond voor Boerinnen)* and the Dutch Catholic Organisation of Farmers Wives (*Nederlandse Katholieke Boerinnenbond*). Most of the traditional women's organisations viewed themselves as politically neutral and they were not bothered with the questions of gender inequality or the oppression of women. The lobby for more women in political decision-making bodies was left to the women's factions in parties and trade unions.

The system of neo-corporatism had also some drawbacks with regard to women's political involvement. Swiebel and Outshoorn (1991) point out that, for newcomers to the political arena such as the organisations of the women's movement, it was hard to get into the system of close-knit policy networks, often formally institutionalised in official advisory bodies.[14] Moreover, economic interests heavily dominated the corporatist network, while women's interests tended to be ignored.[15] It is in this context of a pillarised and corporatist political structure that women had to fight hard for their political rights.

PARTIES' ATTITUDE TOWARDS THE INTEGRATION OF WOMEN IN POLITICS[16]

In 1917, when women gained the right to be elected, the electoral system was changed from a majority system with several districts into a system of proportional representation with party lists. The extension of the electorate in 1919 and

---

[14] J. Swiebel and J. Outshoorn, 'Feminism and the State, the Case of the Netherlands', paper presented at the Annual Meeting of the Dutch Political Science Association, Twente, June 1991, p. 6.

[15] See for example H. Hernes and E.Hänninen-Salmelin, 'Women in the Corporate System', in E. Haavio-Mannila *et al.* (eds.), 1985, p. 122; J. Lovenduski, 1986, p. 166; J. Oldersma, *De Vrouw die Vanzelf Spreekt*, Leiden, DSWO Press, 1996.

[16] This part is based on the extensive research of Hella van de Velde on women in the political parties. We presented a paper together at the Joint Sessions of the ECPR, Essex on 23-27 March 1991: 'Women's Access to Political Parties, the Netherlands'. In 1994, Hella van de Velde published an extensive study in Dutch about the role of women in Dutch parties titled: *Vrouwen van de Partij. De integratie van vrouwen in politieke partijen in Nederland, 1919-1990*, Leiden, DSWO Press, 1994.

the transformation of the electoral system meant a strengthening of the role of political parties. The parties dominated the selection process and formed a bridge between the representatives and the electorate. From that time the political representation of women became entirely dependent of the parties' attitude towards political involvement of women. First I shall look at the opinion and behaviour of parties with regard to the issue of women's suffrage. Then I shall describe what happened in the parties after women gained the right to vote. What exactly did the parties do to involve women in politics? After World War II the traditional parties modernised and in the 1960s and 1970s new parties entered the stage. Whether this influenced the party attitudes towards the political integration of women is also described below.

Women's Suffrage

Debate in the parties and parliament at the beginning of the 20th century was fierce. The extension of voting rights, including suffrage for women, was a hot issue on which the political parties were strongly divided. Outside the parties too, many organisations were demanding general suffrage for men, for women or for both groups. All of these organisations stood for the principle that none should be excluded from exercising their political rights. However the criteria for exclusion were different for men and women. For the male part of the population, income decided whether or not they were allowed to vote. This barrier disappeared with time as more men were starting to earn a decent income and pay taxes. The reasons to exclude women from voting were more ideological. Opposition to the enfranchisement of women was based mainly on the idea that women and politics did not mix, that a woman's proper place was with the family. The arguments used in one of the parliamentary debates in 1916 on the granting of women's suffrage are illustrative:

> The man carries authority: the – caring – task of the woman is within her family. It is not her vocation to participate in politics;

> The man represents his family, including his wife;

> Women are too emotional and not capable of judging objectively. It appears from every historic tale that they lack this capacity;

> Women dealing with politics – '*cette sale besogne*' – will lose their femininity. She enters a field which God has not created for her, where her inner life will be damaged, her grace blemished and her honour hurt;

Chapter 4

> Women already influence decision-making indirectly. There is no need to give them direct influence.[17]

Traditionally the religious parties criticised women's participation in the public sphere more than the other large parties. Over the course of the debate however, differences between the confessional parties became manifest. The Calvinist Anti-Revolutionary Party was the most adamant in its rejection of the idea of women's suffrage. On the basis of its interpretation of the Bible, it opposed all activity of women outside the home and the family.[18] The party opposed general suffrage, which proclaimed the right of every citizen to vote. According to its view, the smallest entity in society was the family and not the individual. For this reason the ARP introduced the idea of a form of suffrage in which the head of the family, the man, with his vote would also represent the other members of his family. Unmarried men were to be treated as the head of a family, while on the other hand, unmarried women were not. Catholic politicians were the first to support the concept of family suffrage.[19] However, the question of women's suffrage was not of decisive importance to them. In fact, for their constituency it was barely a point of discussion, especially since Catholic women did not participate in the debate on voting rights for women. Consequently, when suffrage rights were extended to both men and women, they quickly renounced their opposition.[20]

---

[17] J.C. Schokking, *De Vrouw in de Nederlandse* Politiek, Assen, Van Gorkum, 1958, pp. 29, 30. Translation Monique Leyenaar.

[18] The ARP frequently referred to the following bible texts:

'Then the Lord God said, it is not good for the man to be alone; I shall make a partner suited to him' (*Genesis*, 2:18);

'To the woman He said, I shall give you great labour in childbearing, with labour you will bear children. You will desire your husband; but he will be your master'(*Genesis*, 3:16);

'[And to the man He said:] and only by the sweat of your brow will you win your bread until you return to the earth' (*Genesis*, 3:19);

'Wives be subject to your husband as though to the Lord' (*Ephesians*, 5:22);

'For the man is the head of the woman, just as Christ is head of the church' (*Ephesians*, 5:23).

[19] A Catholic national party organisation was not established until 1926 when the Roomsch-Katholieke Staatspartij (RKSP), the Roman-Catholic State Party, was founded. Earlier however an association of local Catholic branches had existed.

[20] J.C. Schoking, 1958, p. 151.

The Protestant Christian Historical Union was the most divided over the issue of women's suffrage. Their parliamentary leader was against the introduction of the right for women to be elected to parliament. In a parliamentary debate in 1916, he argued this by expressing his fear of the seductive influence of women MPs on the voting behaviour of their male colleagues. If women entered parliament, the possibility existed that male MPs would ground their voting not on the basis of the issue at hand, but on the basis of their (intimate) feelings towards the women in the Chamber. Another source of conflict was the possibility of suffrage for married women. Some delegates expressed their fear that voting rights for married women would cause women to neglect their families. The argument was that attending political meetings and reading the newspapers would absorb too much time.[21] Those within the party who advocated general women's suffrage argued that women were instinctively experts on issues such as education, marital laws, child care and the problems caused by excessive drinking.[22] Those in favour also held the opinion that Christians should permit women a place in society equal to that of men.

In the final parliamentary debate in 1919, seven MPs from the ARP voted in favour and six MPs against the Marchant-bill introducing women's suffrage. However, four out of six MPs from the CHU and *all* Catholic MPs supported its introduction.

The fact that all Catholic MPs and a majority of the Protestant parliamentarians voted in favour of the Marchant bill, was largely due to a deal that was made with the socialists and liberals. The proposed changes in the Constitution also meant a favourable settlement of their fight for the establishment of independent and government-funded Christian schools.

Another reason to grant women the vote was the fear of the majority in parliament of a possible revolution by socialist and communist groups, as had occurred in 1918 in Germany. Since women were thought to be more conservative in their voting behaviour, the participation of women in politics would be a stabilising factor. A third reason for the religious parties to support the change in the Constitution was the conviction that women were more likely to vote for the religious parties than for the liberal or socialist parties.

---

[21] *Handelingen der Staten Generaal 1916/1917*, Tweede Kamer, p. 153.

[22] H. van Spanning, *De Christelijk Historische Unie. Enige Hoofdlijnen van Haar Geschiedenis*, dissertatie RUL, Leiden, 1988, p. 181.

In contrast to the religious parties, both of the main liberal parties of this period, the Liberal State Party (*Liberale Staatspartij*, LSP) and the Liberal Democratic League (*Vrijzinnig-Democratische Bond*, VDB), supported the concept of women's suffrage. In fact, the bill establishing women's suffrage rights was introduced in 1919 by a liberal member of parliament, Marchant (VDB). By then, many of the leading women in the Dutch women's suffrage movement had already joined one of the liberal parties. In 1901, for example, the then president of the Association for Women's Suffrage (*Vereeniging voor Vrouwenkiesrecht*), became a member of the national executive of the VDB.[23]

The Social Democratic Workers' Party (*Sociaal-Democratische Arbeiderspartij*, SDAP) first mentioned the aim of general suffrage for men and women in their party manifesto of 1895. In practice, however, suffrage for women was not of equal importance to the party as compared to general suffrage for men. Despite the statement in the party manifesto, the SDAP introduced a bill in the Second Chamber in 1903 proposing general suffrage only for men. When the Socialist International accepted a resolution in 1907 declaring that general suffrage for men and women was of equal importance, party policy of the SDAP was reformulated in accordance with this. However, although it was agreed within the party that its leader Troelstra would undertake an initiative to introduce women's suffrage at the same time as the general franchise for men, he withdraw his amendment to the bill calling only for general suffrage for men out of fear the bill would not be passed.[24] Instead, it was the liberal MP Marchant who introduced the bill. Some of the reluctance to introduce suffrage for women came also from the perception that women's votes would weaken the socialist movement, for women were imagined to be more conservative in their political preferences.

After 1919: the Confessional Parties

The first national ballot in which Dutch women participated took place in 1922. At that time the religious parties had to convince their potential female constituents to overcome their (religious) reservations and to use their vote. The message was that Christian women should use their vote to protect society, marriage and the family from those forces, which threatened traditional values – liberalism and socialism.

---

[23] J.C. Schokking, 1958, p. 113.

[24] J. Outshoorn, *Vrouwenemancipatie en Socialisme, een Onderzoek naar de Houding van de SDAP ten Aanzien van het Vrouwenvraagstuk tussen 1894 en 1919*, Nijmegen, 1973, p. 88.

After the introduction of women's suffrage, the Catholic party and the CHU placed no restrictions on the participation of women in their respective parties. The CHU started to recruit women members, they produced special information about politics meant for female citizens and they selected a woman for the national executive of the party, the lawyer Frida Katz. In 1921, Katz became the first female CHU representative in a municipal council. From 1922 until 1941 she was the only female MP for her party. The Catholic party nominated a woman MP in 1922, Sophie Bronsveld-Vitringa. She was a member of the Second Chamber for only three years, but was succeeded in 1924 by another Catholic woman MP.

On the other hand, the third religious party, the ARP, did not take the participation of women in politics for granted. In 1921 the party decided that the ARP would not nominate women for representative bodies. According to the party, the political participation of women was contrary to women's duties to the family and clashed with the submissive behaviour demanded of women as stated in the Bible.[25]

In all the confessional parties, membership of women was rather low. During the period of pillarisation, party membership of the head of the family was sufficient to consider the entire family as (unregistered) party members. However, a small number of women were very active right from the start. This was even true for the ARP, which explicitly forbade the active participation of women. I refer here to those women who were active members of Christian or Catholic women's organisations and who were involved in voluntary social work. They felt that women should participate in society, including politics, 'as women', 'by representing maternal virtues like caring and emotional attention'.[26] Notions of gender equality did not fit into this view and therefore the restrictions their party had placed upon them were not seen as unjust.[27] Catholic women were in a similar position since the Episcopacy had prohibited their Roman Catholic Women's Organisation (*Roomsch Katholieke Vrouwen Bond*) from engaging in politics. Regardless of these policies, there have always been strong ties between these Catholic women's organisations and the Catholic party. Prominent women from the ranks of these organisations

---

[25] Rapport van de A.R. commissie-inzake – Het Passieve Vrouwenkiesrecht, 1921, pp. 27-28.

[26] J.C. Schokking, 1958, p. 441.

[27] H.S.S. Kuyper, 'De Anti-Revolutionaire vrouw en het staatkundig leven', in J. Kampen (ed.), *Schrift en Historie, Gedenkboek bij het 50-Jarig Bestaan der Georganiseerde ARP 1878-1928*, 1928, p. 446.

Chapter 4

were in direct contact with the leadership of the party. Because of these contacts, a Catholic woman was immediately eligible for the Second Chamber in 1922.

The CHU was the first Dutch confessional party in which female members organised themselves independently. Soon after the introduction of women's suffrage, female adherents of the CHU met informally in local groups to discuss political and social issues. In 1935 these groups united in the Centre for Christian-Historical Women's Groups (*Centrale van Christelijk-Historische Vrouwengroepen*). The main goals of the organisation were the political education of women and the dissemination of party literature among women. In 1940 the Centre had approximately 800 members active in 22 local groups.[28] During the first years of the existence of the Centre, the national executive of the CHU took an ambivalent stance towards the women's organisation. It approved of the initiative, but only on the condition that two male representatives of the national executive were present at the national meetings of the organisation and that Frida Katz, the CHU MP, would be the president of the women's section.[29]

After 1919: the Liberal and Socialist Parties

As described earlier, both main liberal parties, the Liberal State Party (LSP) and the Liberal Democratic League (VDB) supported women's suffrage and many of the prominent women from the suffrage movement joined the liberal parties. Female membership of the VDB is estimated to have been around 25 per cent in 1938.[30] Before World War II, the VDB had delegated two women as representatives to the Second Chamber. In the other pre-war liberal party, the LSP, several women participated in its national executive and two women were represented in the parliamentary party. Both the LSP and the VDB supported equal rights for men and women. In the 1920s feminist demands such as the revision of legislation concerning marriage and the family, formed part of the party manifestos.[31] In the 1930s, however, the liberal attitude towards gender equality

---

[28] Annual report of the CHU, 1940.

[29] G. Veldhuijzen, Wat *bezielde die vrouwen? Vijfenveertig jaar Centrale can CH-vrouwen*, De Meern, Centrale van CH-vrouwen, 1979.

[30] J.C. Schokking, 1958, p. 113.

[31] In an article in its Program of Principles the LSP formulated one of its purposes as: 'The complete political, judicial and economic equalisation of men and women' (*Beginselprogramma LSP*, 1921, Art. 6). The VDB included comparable statements in several successive political programs.

changed somewhat. From 1933 until 1937, the VDB and the LSP participated in two successive coalition cabinets with the confessional parties, headed by the popular ARP leader H. Colijn. As a result of this coalition and their own crumbling electoral support, the liberal parties compromised with conservative principles. Issues concerning gender equality disappeared from their respective agendas. For example, the liberal cabinet members cooperated with their colleagues to introduce legislation banning married women from the civil service.[32]

Both the LSP and the VDB had a women's section within their organisational structure. The Women's Caucus (*Vrouwengroep*) of the LSP was established in 1921 when the party was founded. The women's section of the VDB, the Liberal Democratic Women's Club (*Vrijzinnig-Democratische Vrouwen Club*) was established in 1917. In the LSP, all female party members were considered to be members of the women's section. Since 1930 this was also true for the VDB. Nevertheless, very few women seem to have been active in the two organisations. The objective of these women's sections was mainly to encourage women to participate in party politics, chiefly by means of education and propaganda. The women's section of the LSP also officially intended to look after women's interests. Clearly, however, these efforts did not stop the liberal parties from compromising on issues regarding the status of women.

The VDB and the LSP women's sections both tried to support female candidates for political office. But the women's section could not prevent a situation in which the party leadership of the LSP did not select a woman candidate for the parliamentary party in 1933. The national executive of the LSP justified this by pointing to the lack of interest of women members in party activities.[33]

It appeared that the relationship between the women's sections and the party leadership was rather strained. The party needed the women's sections to mobilise women as party members and to educate women politically. On the other hand, they feared that the organisations would become too independent. Furthermore, opinions dissenting from the official party position were viewed as a threat to party unity. In the VDB in particular, the general opinion was that, in a liberal party, a separate women's organisation was superfluous because gender equality

---

[32] The VDB cabinet minister Marchant, the same person who presented the bill which established women's suffrage 20 years earlier, introduced several bills to restrict the participation of women in the labour force.

[33] Minutes of the executive of The Women's Caucus of the LSP, 18 June 1937.

Chapter 4

is inherent to liberal ideology. Specific women's activities were therefore not necessary.[34]

When, after 1917, women became eligible for political office, one woman for the socialist SDAP entered parliament, In 1918, Suze Groeneweg became the first woman in the Dutch parliament. During the first years of its existence, very few women participated in the SDAP. In 1900 the first woman was appointed to the national executive. Later on more women became members of the party: from 1910 until 1940 the share of women in the party membership increased from 11 per cent to 33 per cent.[35] This increase was mainly due to the activities of the League of Social-Democratic Women's Clubs (*Bond van Sociaal-Democratische Vrouwenclubs*, BSDVC). The BSDVC was founded in 1908, and in 1914 it consisted of 28 groups with approximately 1000 members, in 1920 there were 90 groups with approximately 5000 members and in 1939 there were 208 clubs with 13,800 members.[36] The main goal of these women's groups was to recruit women as SDAP-members and educate them into active party membership. A woman who signed up for a women's group was simultaneously required to become a party member. In order to inform and educate women, the women's league distributed its own periodical, the *Proletarian Woman* (*De Proletarische Vrouw*). Socialist women also gathered in reading-clubs where they discussed political matters and together read articles and books published by the socialist press. Some time passed before the SDAP officially recognised the BSDVC as part of its formal organisation. The desirability of a separate organisation for women was repeatedly questioned and, as a result, the decision on whether or not to recognise the women's league was delayed time after time. Finally, in 1914, the party congress of the SDAP acknowledged the BSDVC. On that occasion the BSDVC was granted its own delegates in the party congress and two in the party council. In addition to recruiting, informing and educating female party members, the women's league concerned itself with political issues affecting the position of women. Before 1919 it devoted itself to women's suffrage. In the 1930s the issue of women's

---

[34] Minutes of the national executive of the VDB, 1926, no date (in the archive of the women's club of the VDB, IIAV).

[35] U. Jansz, *Vrouwen Ontwaakt!*, Amsterdam, Bert Bakker, 1983, pp. 209-210.

[36] See, for 1914 and 1920, *Arbeidersjaarboekje 1914*, p. 31 and *Arbeidersjaarboekje 1920*, p. 151; and for 1939, U. Jansz, 1983, p. 210.

employment became a priority. The right of married women to paid jobs was often questioned during this period because of increasing unemployment. The BSDVC protested strongly against every limitation of that right. In principle the SDAP supported the interests of women in this matter. As the recession continued, however, male SDAP representatives sometimes supported proposals in the parliament to limit this right. Another important issue for the BSDVC was disarmament. For a long time it shared its anti-militaristic views with the party as a whole. However, halfway through the 1930s the SDAP, in response to increasing international tensions, began to favour a strengthening of the national defence system. The women's section nevertheless held on to its pacifist views. The expression of its dissenting opinion on this issue leaded to a strained relationship between the BSDVC and the party leadership.[37]

After 1945

The Second World War produced a turn in the tide for Catholic and ARP women. Housewives and mothers had been forced by the special circumstances of the war to leave their private homes and enter public life. Women had to replace those men who were forced to join the German army or to work in German industry and had to meet daily needs for their families, something that became more difficult over time. Some women were also engaged in illegal activities in the Resistance. As a result the Catholic Church changed its attitude towards the role of women in society. Pius XII, the pope at that time, declared that women also had duties to fulfil outside their homes.[38] Catholic women all over the world referred to these papal declarations when demanding for their share in public life.

As a consequence of these developments, more women than before manifested themselves in the new KVP that was established in 1946. A small group of active women, including the first woman cabinet minister to be, Marga Klompé (she was appointed as minister in 1956) pleaded with party officials to increase the participation of women in representative bodies and party offices. As a result of their efforts the party congress of the KVP declared in 1949 that as many women as possible should be members of the representative and party bodies.[39] However

---

[37] For a comprehensive history of the women's organisation of the SDAP and the PvdA, see U. Jansz, 1983.

[38] J.C. Schokking, 1958, cites from quotations of pope Pius XII concerning this issue, p. 152.

[39] J.C. Schokking, 1958, p. 154.

Chapter 4

these intentions were not formalised. In 1958 only four of the 48 members of the party's national executive were women. Nineteen of the 255 members of the regional executives were women and, at the local level, 640 of approximately 5000 members of branch executives were women. The share of KVP women in representative bodies was even lower.[40]

In 1956, the size of the Second Chamber was increased from 100 to 150 members. When the number of women MPs did not increase as a result, women party members of the KVP demanded action. The national leadership of the KVP installed a committee to study the integration of women within the party. In its report, the committee recommended dissemination of political information to both male and female party members, the introduction of a family membership subscription and a revision of the party rules to fix a minimum number of women in party committees.[41] A permanent party committee, called Woman and Party (*Vrouw en Partij*) was further established to implement the proposals. This committee lasted until 1980 when the KVP merged into the Christian Democratic Party (CDA). Overall, its results have been very meagre, since a quota was never set and it always maintained the status of an advisory committee.

In the ARP, the ban on the active participation of women in politics was again put on the agenda by some female members and by local party branches. Here too a committee was established to study the issue. This committee concluded in 1949 that women should be allowed to participate in public life under certain conditions.[42] The party executive, however, repeatedly postponed the publication and discussion of the committee's report even though, within the ranks of the party, support for the exclusion of women had diminished.[43] Finally, in 1953, the party congress decided that the party could nominate women, although in this resolution the political participation of women was still defined as an exceptional situation. In 1963 the first ARP woman, the lawyer Jacqueline Rutgers, was elected to the Second Chamber.

---

[40] J.C. Schokking, 1958, p. 158.

[41] Rapport Nolte, 10 July 1957.

[42] Rapport van de A.R. Commissie Donner, 1949, p. 18.

[43] An example is the popularity of the book *Man and Woman in Public Life* (*Man én vrouw in het volle leven*) written by a woman party member F.T. Diemer-Lindeboom and published in 1949. The book was praised by the party leadership and the press. Party members organised meetings to study and discuss the book. In her book Diemer-Lindeboom argued convincingly in favour of an unrestricted participation of women in politics.

During the 1940s and 1950s ARP-women organised themselves in separate groups at local level. The main aim of these groups was political education of women and the recruitment of female party members. In 1959 the AR Women's Group (*AR-Vrouwencontact*) was set up, a body that was meant to co-ordinate and stimulate the activities of the local groups. But the AR Women's Group had only an advisory status within the party and was never formally acknowledged by the party leadership. Immediately after its establishment, local women's groups became very active and the number of female party members increased rapidly. From 1955 to 1966 their share of the party membership grew from 2 to 10 per cent.[44]

For women in the CHU, World War II served more as an interruption than a turning-point. Lady Christine Wittewaal van Stoetwegen succeeded Frida Katz in the parliamentary party and she would be the only woman there until 1967. The number of CHU women in lower-level representative bodies increased slowly during the post-war period. The activities of women in the party were mainly concentrated in the women's organisation, the Centre of Christian-Historical Women's Groups. The Centre was officially represented in several party bodies like the national executive and the party council. In 1960, the Centre had about 1200 members, half of the total number of women party members.[45] The main goal of the local groups was the political education of women, but from the 1950s onwards the Centre also devoted its energy to establishing support for the nomination of women for political offices. During each national election, the organisation lobbied for the nomination of other eligible women. However, it was not until 1967 that the second CHU woman was elected to the Second Chamber, and both of them lost their seats again after the 1972 elections. The lack of success caused some irritation among the members of the Centre. A more activist approach caused a conflict between the Centre and the national party leadership. At the same time other groups within the party started to question the hierarchical structures in the party, and more specifically the highly decentralised candidate selection process. To meet all these demands the party council, consisting of delegates from the local branches, in order to guarantee the representation of women and young people, submitted a proposal in 1973 to an advisory committee of the party formed to revise the party regulations. It proposed to reserve at least one fifth of all seats in

---

[44] F.T. Diemer-Lindeboom, 'Honderd Jaar ARP en de Vrouw', in C. Bremmer (ed.), *Personen en Momenten, uit de Geschiedenis van de ARP*, Franeker Wever, 1980, p. 191.

[45] G. Veldhuijzen, 1979.

Chapter 4

party bodies for women and the same percentage for young party members. These seats would stay empty until a qualified female or young candidate was found. The revision committee, however, rejected these proposals immediately and, as a result, the selection procedures in the CHU remained unchanged until 1980 when the CHU merged with the other two confessional parties and formed the CDA.

The liberal party group returned in the post-war period as the People's Party for Freedom and Democracy (VVD), founded in 1948. Since then, one or more women were always included in both the party's national executive and parliamentary party. In the period 1965-1975 the party rules even guaranteed the participation of a minimum of four women in the 27-member national executive. In 1969 the VVD became the first Dutch political party to elect a woman as chair of the party.

The women's section of the party Organisation of Women in the VVD (*Organisatie Vrouwen in de VVD*) has been part of the party structure since 1948. It has continually emphasised its interest in increasing the number of women in representative and party offices. For example in 1956, when the number of seats in the Second Chamber was increased, it pleaded for the election of a second woman to the liberal parliamentary party. It repeatedly tried to recruit women from its ranks for representative and party offices.

In the first years of its existence, the organisation focussed primarily on the need to educate and inform women. From the second half of the 1970s, it also tried to contribute to party policy, particularly regarding women's issues. The women's section promoted a type of liberal feminism, in which notions such as 'free choice for everyone' and 'equal opportunities' were central. Formal linkages between the party and its women's organisation existed at several different levels in the party organisation. From 1953 onwards seats were reserved for delegates from the women's section in the party council and national executive.

The Labour Party (PvdA) was founded in 1946. Since the beginning, women have been present in the national executive and in the parliamentary party of the PvdA, but always as a minority. Until the 1970s the number of women in the national executive remained fairly constant: three out of a total of 21 to 25 individuals. In 1948 four per cent of the party's MPs were women. In 1957 the share of women MPs had increased to 14 per cent, but shortly after this the percentage decreased again. The low participation rate of women in representative and party offices became an issue in the PvdA during the second half of the 1970s. After a strong lobby by the party's women's organisation in 1977, the party congress accepted a quota of 25 per cent for the party boards and representative bodies.

The women's organisation of the PvdA played a significant role in putting the low representation of women on the party's agenda. Until the 1960s the Women's League of the PvdA (*Vrouwenbond in de PvdA*), like the pre-war BSDVC, had as its main objective the education of female party members.[46] The League organised congresses and training courses for women. The organisation was not supposed to express opinions that were in disagreement with the general line of thinking of the party. Nevertheless, within their own ranks the women dealt with many issues. Their activities as well as their name changed in the 1960s together with a reorganisation of the whole party. Over that period the number of party members decreased rapidly and the party failed to establish contact with the newly emerging social movements. Young women were also not attracted by the work of the League. During the reorganisation of the party in the 1960s, the party committee that prepared the reorganisation questioned the existence of a separate women's organisation. The argument was that the League was an old-fashioned phenomenon, which did not appeal to young and emancipated women. The committee recommended that women should be full-fledged party members and that the local women's organisations should be integrated in the local party branches. These steps, they argued, would encourage the selection of women for representative bodies. Instead of following this advice, some women party members decided in 1969 to rename the central women's organisation as Women's Contact in the PvdA (*Vrouwencontact in the PvdA*). Along with the change in name, the women's section lost its provision for a paid general secretary and its guaranteed representation in the national executive of the party.

Paradoxically during this same period, the interest of women party members for gender equality was growing. This development influenced the activities of Women's Contact. It began to make political statements on women's issues such as the legalisation of abortion. Often PvdA women protested in public against discrimination of women and on these occasions the PvdA women acted under the banner Red Women. In practice, two sorts of women's groups existed side by side in the PvdA during the 1970s. Women's Contact groups consisted mainly of older female party members, while the Red Women were younger and well-educated. Steadily, Women's Contact groups disappeared. In 1975, Red Women became the official women's organisation of the PvdA. The political activism of the organisation resulted in several clashes with party leadership. The national executive wanted

---

[46] For a comprehensive history of women's organisations in the PvdA, see U. Jansz, 1983.

Chapter 4

the Red Women to consult with them before undertaking any action or before making any political statements. At a certain moment the formal links between the women's section and the party were abolished, but reinstated again in 1977.

As with the end of World War II, the 1970s also form a kind of turning-point, as we will see in the next chapter. It is in 1977 that, for the first time *four* women took part in government and the number of women in parliament exceeded the 10 per cent. In chapter 6, when explaining this turning-point, the description of the attitude of the main political parties towards women in the 1970s and later will be continued.

Here we finish our analysis of the impact of the party system on women with another Dutch phenomenon, women's parties.

WOMEN'S PARTIES[47]

Around the time of the introduction of women's suffrage, quite a few women articulated doubts about the willingness of parties to nominate women as their candidates. They opted for a different strategy of empowerment, the founding of separate women's parties. A strategy that can be successful as was proven by the women's party in Iceland, Kvennalistinn, which won 10 per cent of the total vote in the general elections of 1987. This strategy has also been undertaken in the Netherlands. Between 1917 and 1990, nine different women's parties participated in local or national elections. The first two women's lists emerged at the time of the parliamentary debate on women's suffrage. The seven other attempts to get women represented in political bodies by way of a women's list occurred after World War II. Of all these women's parties, five were nationally organised and four acted only at the local level. Table 4.2 summarises the nine parties, their year of foundation, the electoral success and their main objectives and ideologies.

A first attempt to establish a women's party occurred in 1917, within the ranks of the Association for Women's Suffrage (VvVK). In the year that women were granted to stand for election, but not yet granted the right to vote, Aletta Jacobs initiated a debate on the issue of separatism, because she had little trust in the willingness of the existing parties to nominate women to eligible places on their

---

[47] See M. Leyenaar and H. van de Velde, 'Belangenbehartiging door vrouwen. Vrouwenpartijen', in *Acta Politica*, XXIV, no. 1, 1989, pp. 3-29.

Table 4.2: Women's parties in the Netherlands

Party	Year founded	Electoral success	Objectives			
			Representation of women	Representation of interests	Feminist ideology	Criticism of political culture
Feminist Party	1918	No	Yes	Yes	Yes	Yes
General Dutch Women's Organisation	1919	No	Yes	Yes	Yes	No
Pragmatic Policy	1946	No	Yes	Yes	Yes	Yes
Dutch Women's Party	1972	No	Yes	Yes	No	No
Women's Party	1985	No	Yes	Yes	Yes	Yes
Local parties						
Catholic Women's List Venlo	1958	Yes	Yes	No	No	No
Women's List of Leerbroek	1978	No	Yes	No	No	Yes
Women's Action Party Amstelveen	1982	No	Yes	Yes	No	Yes
Women's Party Landgraaf	1985	Yes	Yes	No	No	Yes

lists of candidates. She pleaded for separate women's parties as a strategy to get women elected. However, the majority of the VvVK rejected Jacobs' proposal to take part in the election with a women's list. Jacobs then joined an existing party, the VDB and here she was selected as a candidate. Her place on the list, however, appeared unlikely to result in her election.

At that time two women's parties emerged – The Feminist Party (*Feministische Partij*, FP) established in December 1918 and the General Dutch Women's Organisation (*Algemeene Nederlandsche Vrouwen Organisatie*, ANVO) in February 1919. Around 1920 the FP had about 200 members and the ANVO around 1500 members divided over 15 branches. The ANVO participated in the municipal elections in Amsterdam in 1920, but did not gain a seat.

The two women's parties differed somewhat in ideology. The founding mothers had been active in the suffrage movement, but came from different organisations. The FP presented itself as a feminist *and* socialist party. The ANVO emphasised its neutral stance with regard to political ideology. The two parties shared a moralistic view of politics. Both the FP and the ANVO believed that women had a special vocation to 'heal' a disordered and violent world. The cruelties and chaos due to the First World War was proof for these parties that men were not fit to rule. Both parties emphasised pacifism and the need for social reform. The FP and ANVO designed an ideology consisting of a special feminine view on politics and society, based on general notions on women's nature. Women were supposed to be more peaceful and caring than men. The FP stated in its platform:

> As women we want to build up and protest, instead of destroy. Women have kept their feminine and maternal talents too exclusively for the family and have not dared to speak in society the language that shows their own views and judgements.[48]

In an ANVO pamphlet a similar argument is written:

> Based on the work women have been doing for centuries, we have to reconstruct politics and society, starting with the family as a cell out of which society is formed. That is why our manifesto concentrates on the liberation of women and the elevation of the family.[49]

---

[48] Evolutie, no. 26, 1919.

[49] Pamphlet, 'Reedenen van bestaan van de ANVO', 1919.

The liberation of women was presented as a *sine qua non* for women to fulfil their task in society. Notwithstanding their idealistic principles, both parties addressed concrete issues in their manifestos such as equal rights for women and men, better housing, social legislation, improved education and equal working conditions for women and men. The FP also dealt with issues such as tax reform, independence for the overseas colonies, taxes on capital goods, equal pay for equal work by women and men, reform of the marriage laws and accessibility of all professions for women. Clearly the FP was more radical than the ANVO.

The two parties merged in 1921 and took part in the parliamentary elections of 1922, the first national elections in which women were allowed to vote. The programme they presented concentrated on equal rights for men and women and on pacifism. The party gained 6000 votes whereas it needed 30,000 votes to win a seat in parliament. In 1924 the party was disbanded.

Immediately after World War II, a former prisoner of the Nazi prisoners' camp at Ravensbruck founded another women's party, Pragmatic Policy (*Practisch Beleid*, PB), with branches in at least five different towns. The branch in Amsterdam boasted 100 members. This party was very similar to the parties in the 1920s. PB stressed the supposed different nature of women and it addressed the female voters as mothers and housewives. It argued that the qualities attached to these roles, such as care, harmony, ethics and a down-to-earth approach to life, needed to be heard in politics and in society as a whole. PB participated in several municipalities in the local election of 1946 with the following appeal:

> We want to look after the interests of the inhabitants of our municipality as practical women and as good mothers; our general line of action is to advance general welfare and joy of living; we stand for true Dutch virtues of justice, honesty, decency and sense of duty.[50]

The party did not gain any seats and dissolved after the election.

Another women's party emerged at the time of the (new) women's movement in 1972. The three main objectives of the Dutch Women's Party (*Nederlandse Vrouwen Partij*, NVP) were equal representation of women in all political bodies, abolition

---

[50] Pamphlet of *Practisch Beleid*, 1946.

Chapter 4

of all legislation discriminating against women and the abolition of biased information coming from the government.[51]

The NVP manifesto concentrated on women' issues such as the legalisation of abortion, more paid jobs for women and safe public spaces, but it also contained issues such as the abolition of military service and the introduction of laws to stop abuse against animals. The NVP participated in the regional elections of 1973 and, when it did not gain a seat, disappeared from the scene.

The Women's Party (*Vrouwenpartij*, VP) was founded in 1985 and participated in the parliamentary elections of 1989, but it received only 12,095 votes, not enough for a seat. Women from different women's organisations established it and their objective was twofold: emancipation of women and feminisation of society.

> Emancipation of women means equal rights for women and men as autonomous individuals and all possibilities to use these rights. This also means breaking through the traditional sex roles. Feminisation means a structural change of our society. The present standards and values must be adjusted to the opinions women have.[52]

With the concept of feminisation the VP too introduced an ideology of special 'feminine' views on politics and society. The difference with the ideology of the parties in the 1920s was that the VP did not derive 'feminine' values and views from women's nature, but from cultural notions and socialisation:

> It is true that women had to train themselves for 4000 years or more in taking care, being nice, intuitive understanding, organising, being creative, etc. That is why they developed the talents that are necessary to reform our tough, logical and businesslike society into a healthy and human society.[53]

Like the women's parties in the 1920s the VP assumed a special vocation for women in society and demanded the abolition of military service and the improvement of the environment. They also focussed on women's issues, such as economic independence for women, a more justified division between men and women of paid work and care, equal representation in politics and introduction of legislation against sexual violence.

---

[51] *Opzij*, January 1972.

[52] Party manifesto, 1987.

[53] Internal report VP, 1985.

But the VP did not win enough votes to enter parliament so it was unable to articulate these interests.

The other parties mentioned in table 4.1 are parties that only existed in one municipality. Contrary to the nationally oriented parties, they did not develop an overall view on politics and society and the role of women in it. These parties only concentrated on the representation of women on the municipal council. Not surprisingly, three of them emerged in rural municipalities where there had never been a woman councillor. Moreover, a woman had never been placed on a candidate list of one of the parties. Two of them had electoral success. The Catholic Women's List (*Katholieke Vrouwenlijst*) in Venlo won four of the 31 seats in the local elections of 1958, and three seats in 1962, while Women's Party (*Vrouwenappel*) won three seats out of 29 in the local election of 1986 in Landgraaf. Since then this party has been represented in the council. In the local election of 2002 it again gained two (out of 27) seats.

It is clear that important reasons to found a separate women's party are dissatisfaction with the existing parties for not selecting enough women on their lists of candidates and the fact that the male-dominated parties do not represent women's interests. Looking at the five nationally oriented parties, it is remarkable that three of them explicitly tried to develop a party ideology centred on 'feminine' qualities such as caring, pacifism and cooperative behaviour.

CONCLUSION

This chapter described part of the political context of the empowerment of women in the Netherlands by focussing on the main vehicles to political power, the political parties. When the electoral system changed from a majority system to a list-PR system, women with the ambition to become MPs had to choose between becoming active in the main political parties or founding their own parties.

The struggle for suffrage was fierce and women had to overcome many prejudices to succeed. The confessional parties in particular questioned the moral right of women to become engaged in politics, '*cette sale besogne*'. One of the Protestant parties, the ARP, prohibited its female members from presenting themselves as candidates for political office until 1953. The relatively low participation of women in politics in the Netherlands may thus be partly traced back to the dominance of the religious parties in Dutch politics, to the relative high level of party fragmentation and to the fact that the more left-wing parties never really dominated the political arena. But more important are the ideas parties had with regard to the representation of women. Until the 1970s all parties embraced the concept of so-called quality seats: the parliamentary party should consist of different types of representatives such as farmers, businessmen, civil servants, military *and* women. One or two women in the parliamentary party were therefore enough. By the end of the 1970s, under the influence of the new women's movement, all this changed and the left-wing parties in particular nominated more women. Confessional and right-wing parties followed at a slower pace.

The women's sections in all parties have been instrumental in getting more women selected to run for office. Active women educated, mobilised and lobbied for changing party rules so that more women would enter representative bodies.

Given the slow pace of the parties in involving women in their midst, it is no wonder that some women decided to found their own parties. Nine women's parties have existed and two of them have had electoral success, albeit at the local level. Clearly voters who believed in their demand for representation supported these parties. After all, in both cases women first tried to convince the existing parties to select women at eligible places and only after numerous refusals did they set up a new party.

The demand for representation is one thing, but another characteristic of (some of) the women's parties is their focus on the typical qualities of women, which, in their view, were very much needed in politics. Women in politics would 'heal' a violent and emotionally cold society by being more often pacifistic, caring and sensitive. These ideas are heard in the 1920s but also in the 1970s. Later, however, the emphasis is more on the broadening of the political agenda with issues such as child care, legalisation of abortion, reduction of sexual violence, etc., and on the changing of the procedures of political decision-making. The idea was that since women politicians are supposed to be less hierarchical and less power-oriented, political decision-making would change when women entered politics in greater numbers.[54] What really happened becomes clear in the next chapter when we look into the backgrounds and activities of the women legislators.

---

[54] See J. Kool-Smit, *Hé Zus, Ze Houen ons Eronder. Een Boek voor Vrouwen en Oudere Meisjes*, Utrecht, Bruna, 1972.

CHAPTER 5

FROM TOKEN TO PLAYER

Apart from wooden shoes, coffee shops and tulips, the Netherlands is perhaps best known for having been ruled – since 1890 – by a queen. The main duties of the monarch however, are ceremonial. The real political players are the appointed and elected politicians: the cabinet ministers, the MPs, the local and provincial councillors, mayors and state-governors. In this chapter I describe the process of political empowerment of women in the Netherlands. Four periods are distinguished: the period of the *pioneers*, the women who entered parliament and other political bodies between 1917-1946. Then there are the *tokens* or *group representatives*, the women politicians from 1946 until the mid-1970s. In the third period, from 1975-1989, we find the *defenders of women's interests*, and the 1990s and beyond can be characterised by the *players*. For each period we analyse progress or lack of progress in terms of the number of women entering parliament and government. We also look at the background of these women and try to find out whether in each period different kind of women were preferred by the political parties to represent them. A third matter that we explore is the possible difference in role orientations (and as a consequence in political behaviour) of women politicians over this period. Especially interesting is the question of whether women MPs differ in their representative role orientations in the extent to which they view themselves as representatives of women.

As we have seen in the description of the ideology of women's parties, several arguments are used validating the demand for more women political representatives. The first deals with the recognition of women's rights to full citizenship and the implication that these rights must be reflected by their effective participation, at all levels, in political life. The second argument refers to differences in interests between women and men. As long as women and men are conditioned to have different social roles, positions and values, women as a group have different interests from men. The idea is that women politicians are more aware of their own needs and interests and are therefore better able to press for them. The third argument deals with the style of political decision-making. Women politicians would

Chapter 5

be more critical of the power-play, the tricks, lack of transparency and technocracy and their presence, it is argued, would change these features. Thus the first argument ties in with a feeling of justice and the demand for equality and equal treatment, while the other two arguments assume that an increased participation of women in political bodies would alter the outcome of political deliberation, in terms of both agenda and procedures. Here we are interested in the question of whether and how these three arguments are reflected in the orientations and behaviour of Dutch women MPs in each of the four periods.

This analysis focuses on the national level and on elected and appointed positions: women in parliament and in government. Further in this chapter I will discuss the other levels of political representation: the local councils and local government, the provincial councils and government and the women elected to the European Parliament.

1917-1946: PIONEERS

The first parliamentary elections in which women stood as candidates took place in 1918. Twenty-two women were placed on the lists of candidates of mainly socialist and liberal parties. Only one of them was elected, Suze Groeneweg, a candidate for the Labour Party. Born in 1875 she started her political career in 1903 when she became a member of the Labour Party. She was a teacher, actively involved in improving education facilities for lower-class children. After a few years she became a member of the party executive. Her relation to the women's organisation of the Labour Party was somewhat ambivalent. On one hand she set up a local women's organisation in Rotterdam and tried to mobilise women to become politically active, but on the other hand she strongly opposed the formal integration of the women's organisation in the Labour Party, even though acknowledgement by the party meant reserved seats in the executive and at party conferences, as well as financial support. According to Outshoorn (1973) Groeneweg was very much against separatism. She viewed an independent women's organisation as an argument that the party is not doing enough for its women members. For her, a separate party magazine for women was a demonstration of the inferiority of women. Her strongest argument against a separate women's section was that it would give the party an excuse to stop worrying about the lack of women's participation in the party.[1] When in 1914 the Labour Party finally acknowledged the women's organisation, Groeneweg stopped her activities in it. It is because of this ambivalence that many Labour women had mixed feelings about her being the first woman ever to enter parliament.

As an MP she dealt with issues on motherhood, especially pregnancy leave, on free medical care, education, alcohol abuse and military concerns. When addressing these issues, she always pointed to the role of women. Her maiden speech on 7 November 1918, elaborated on the interests of the wives of the military. Parliament had decided to establish an enquiry committee looking into the conditions in a military camp. Groeneweg criticised the one-sided composition of the committee and pleaded for the appointment of women to the committee:

> Besides expertise this committee also needs legitimacy. Women, the largest part of the Dutch population, cannot have confidence in the work of this committee, because they are not represented.[2]

Twice she submitted a proposal for a legal arrangement of pregnancy leave and child care. Further she stood up for unmarried teachers who were being discriminated against regarding their salary and she pleaded in favour of a ban on the sale of alcohol.[3]

For three years she was the only woman, but in 1921 Johanna Westerman became an MP for the Liberal Party (*Vrijheidsbond*). They were the only two women MPs elected by solely male voters. At the next parliamentary election in 1922 women could vote for the first time. These elections resulted in another five women MPs, bringing the total at seven (7 per cent since, until 1956, the total number of MPs was exactly 100). In this first period there were never more than two women MPs representing the same party and their total number was never higher than seven. Table 5.1 shows the number of women elected to the Second Chamber.

The average percentage of women in the parliamentary parties was between six and nine per cent with the lowest representation in the Catholic parties and the highest in the liberal parties. One of the two Protestant parties, the ARP, is not represented in this table since it prohibited its women members from standing as candidates.

---

[1] J. Outshoorn, 1973, p. 65.

[2] Handelingen Tweede Kamer, 1918-1919.

[3] Handelingen Tweede Kamer, 1918-1939.

Chapter 5

Table 5.1: Number of women MPs 1918-1946, grouped by party.

	1918	1922	1925	1929	1933	1937	1946
RKSP	0	1	1	1	1	0	
KVP							0
CHU	0	1	1	1	1	1	1
SDAP	1	2	2	2	2	2	
PvdA							1
LSP	0	2	1	1	0	0	
VDB	0	1	1	2	1	1	
VVD							1
CPN							1
Total*	1	7	6	7	5	4	4

* Since the total number of MPs was 100, these figures can also be interpreted as percentages of the total.

Table 5.2: Background characteristics of male and female MPs, 1918-1946.

	Men		Women	
	%	N (100%)	%	N (100%)
Social class: high (profession father)	48	295	77	13
Mother member of a political party	57	124	67	12
Mean age in years when entering	45	216	47	13
University education	45	303	54	13
Married*	–	–	50	6
With children*	–	–	17	6

* no data for male MPs

Source: Parliamentary Documentation Centre (PDC).

During this period no women were appointed to the pre-war cabinets. Until 1939 there was only one female senator from the Social Democratic Labour Party (total number of senators at that time was 50). A second female, socialist senator joined her in 1946.

Who are those pioneers in Dutch politics?

The few women in parliament at that time were very much part of an upper social echelon, often from an upper or upper-middle class family, with a university degree, unmarried, and childless. Mothers were, especially for the religious parties, not acceptable to the party elite making the nominations for parliament. The majority of women MPs were lawyers or teachers before becoming a parliamentarian. The fact that women in 1919 became important targets as potential voters did not mean that parties set up conscious policies to nominate women for political positions, despite the presence of women's factions in these parties.

Using the available information, mostly from interviews with the women MPs themselves, one can conclude that the pioneers, although unmarried themselves, took the attitude of 'housewife-politicians'. They mainly interested themselves in issues related to the family and children, as well as with educational matters.[4] Two women MPs of that time, one socialist woman MP and one from the CHU, point out that the women in parliament addressed issues that their male colleagues would not have 'touched' and they dealt with these issues using 'a feminine perspective'.[5]

The pioneers in politics had to overcome many barriers: themselves, public opinion and parties who were of the opinion that women did not belong to politics. Only unmarried and preferably lawyers or schoolteachers, were allowed to enter the male bastion. Housewives and mothers were certainly not seen as suitable people to play the political game.

1946-1975: TOKENS OR GROUP REPRESENTATIVES

The end of World War II, as we have seen, renewed the demand for a greater representation of women. Active women in the parties made it very clear that they would not accept the parties' lack of support for the participation of women.

---

[4] C. Pothuis-Smit, *Wat Deden de Vrouwen met Haar Kiesrecht? Het Algemeen Vrouwenkiesrecht in de Praktijk 1919-1940*, Arnhem, Van Loghum Slaterus, 1946, pp. 57, 58.

[5] *Ibid.*, pp. 153, 157, 158.

Women's factions were reanimated and party leaderships were pressured to appoint women to national executives and in the parliamentary parties. Now that women, during the war, had been also engaged in all kinds of public activities, the male elite could no longer appeal to arguments that a woman's proper and only place was in the home. For the first time the sharp distinction between public and private life was crumbling, and with it, previously clear-cut gender roles. But it took until the end of the 1960s before gender roles were really attacked. For example in 1955 still less than two per cent of married women were engaged in paid labour.[6]

Especially in the confessional parties, the near-exclusion of women from political office became a source of embarrassment and parties felt increasingly obliged to nominate at least one woman not only to the parliamentary parties but also as government ministers. The practice of appointing a *token* woman became very apparent in the cabinets of the time. Table 5.3 shows the number of women in the different governments from1952 until 1977.

Regardless of the parties in power, in the 11 cabinets listed we find a woman acting either as minister or as junior minister. The Catholic party appointed the first woman minister in 1956. Marga Klompé was an unmarried woman with a doctor's degree in chemistry. She worked as a high-school teacher and became interested in politics during her work in the Resistance. She became involved with the Catholic party in 1946 and one of her first activities was to found a Catholic women's organisation. She entered parliament in 1948. Klompé was a Minister of Social Work in five different cabinets. Between 1963 and 1965, when in the coalition negotiations the Ministry of Social Work was lost to the VVD, Johanna Schouwenaar-Franssen was nominated as her successor at this ministry. Klompé returned to office in 1966 and stayed on until 1971. The third woman minister came from the Labour Party, Irene Vorrink, and she headed the Ministry of Health and Environment from 1973 to 1977. Like Klompé and Schouwenaar-Franssen, Vorrink also had a university degree. The two last-mentioned were married and had children, but at the time they became cabinet ministers the children no longer lived at home. Schouwenaar-Franssen, again like Klompé, was very active in women's organisations and in the party. She had chaired the Women's Organisation for University Women (*Vereniging van Vrouwen met een Academische Opleiding*) and was local councillor in the city of Rotterdam as well as member of the Senate since 1956. Vorrink studied law and worked in the civil service before

---

[6] J.C. Schokking, 1958, p. 42.

Table 5.3: Women in government, 1952-1977.

Cabinet (PM)	Year	Parties	No. women ministers	No. women junior ministers
Drees II	1952-1956	PvdA/KVP/ARP/CHU	0	1
Drees III	1956-1958	PvdA /ARP/KVP/CHU	1	1
Beel II	1958-1959	KVP/ARP/CHU	1	0
De Quay	1959-1963	KVP/ARP/CHU/VVD	1	0
Marijnen	1963-1965	KVP/ARP/CHU/VVD	1	0
Cals	1965-1966	KVP/PvdA/ARP	0	0
Zijlstra	1966-1967	KVP/ARP	1	0
De Jong	1967-1971	KVP/ARP/CHU/VVD	1	0
Biesheuvel I	1971-1972	KVP/ARP/CHU/VVD/DS'70	0	1
Biesheuvel II	1972-1973	KVP/ARP/CHU/VVD	0	0
Den Uyl	1973-1977	PvdA/KVP/ARP/PPR/D66	1	0

becoming a cabinet minister. She gained representative experience in the Senate, of which she had been a member since 1969.

During the same period two women served as junior ministers. In 1953 the first woman junior minister was appointed, dr. Anna de Waal, also from the Catholic party and, from 1971 to 1972, Sophia van Veenendaal van Meggelen, from DS'70, acted as the token woman. De Waal was a Junior Minister of Education and van Veenendaal van Meggelen a Junior Minister of Social Work.

Chapter 5

Table 5.4: Percentage of women MPs in each parliamentary party, 1948-1972.

	1948	1952	1956*	1959	1963	1967	1971	1972
KVP	6	7	5	8	8	7	6	7
CHU	11	11	8	8	8	17	10	0
ARP	0	0	0	0	8	7	8	7
PvdA	4	10	12	10	11	8	10	14
VVD	12	11	23	21	25	12	13	14
CPN	0	17	14	0	0	0	0	0
D66						14	9	17
DS'70							12	17
Total %	5	8	9	9	10	8	8	9
Total no. women MPs	5	8	13	14	15	12	12	14

* In 1956 the number of MPs in the Second Chamber was increased from 100 to 150 and in the Senate from 50 to 75.

In this second period, the representation of women did not rise above ten per cent, but as table 5.4 shows, more parties felt obliged to nominate at least one woman. The confessional parties were still rather reluctant to select women, even when the number of seats in parliament was increased. This really infuriated the Catholic women and they demanded more candidates. The VVD and PvdA had more women in their midst, but here too the actual number did not increase much with the expansion. The left-wing liberal party D66, entered parliament in 1967 with seven MPs including one woman. DS'70, a split from the PvdA, entered parliament in 1971 with one female delegate.

As in the period of the pioneers, the majority of the elected women came from an upper-class family, more so than their male colleagues. Having a politically active mother was still an important factor explaining the ambition to become an MP at a time when women and politics did not go together in many people's minds. Compared to the first period, however, only one third of women MPs had a

Table 5.5: Background characteristics of male and female MPs, 1946-1977.

	1946-1967				1967-1977			
	Men		Women		Men		Women	
	%	N (100%)	%	N (100%)	%	N (100%)	%	N (100%)
Social class: high (profession father)	51	317	70	27	51	228	82	28
Mother member of a political party*	21	122	31	13	32	104	42	19
Mean age when entering in years*	45	242	45	24	42	170	41	20
University educated	52	320	45	29	59	277	54	35
Married	96	27	47	15	92	105	63	30
With children	100	17	56	9	93	55	41	17

* These figures come from another source, the Dutch Parliamentary Survey, held in 1967 and in 1979.

Source: Parliamentary Documentation Centre.

politically active mother as opposed to two thirds in the first period. Men and women did not differ in terms of the mean age when they entered parliament. What changed over time was the importance of a university education as a selection criterion. Still, however, about half of the women MPs had a university degree and being married and having children was mainly a privilege for the male MPs. There was certainly a shift in attitude in the sense that mothers and wives were now allowed into politics, but party leaderships still preferred their female MPs to be unmarried and childless.

Women were present within the government and representative bodies based on a very restricted gender identity.[7] The women cabinet ministers all filled portfolios relating to the caring role of women in society. Women MPs also took on similar portfolios. In 1956, for example, four of the 13 women MPs participated in the committee for Social Work and Culture and three of them in the parliamentary committee for Justice. The other committees in which women took part were those for Education and Social Affairs. Being a token implies high visibility. The women MPs in this period tended to be stereotyped. They were evaluated not on their individual characteristics, but rather as *representatives of a group* – as women. This led to a heightening of the gender identity. An intriguing example is the fact that *all* female MPs, including those from the Protestant and Catholic parties, voted in 1955 in favour of a motion proposed by a Labour woman MP stating that 'except when abuse is apparent, it is not in the State's remit to prohibit the work of married women'. With this motion, the attempts of the government to limit the paid work of married women were finally stopped. The motion passed with the narrow margin of 46 to 44, thanks to the support of the women from the confessional parties.[8]

1975-1989: DEFENDERS OF WOMEN'S INTERESTS

The mid-1970s mark a turning-point in the political representation of women in the Netherlands. The Dutch political system had been confronted in the 1960s with developments such as depillarisation and secularisation, as well as with a growing demand for more political influence and a less paternalistic, more open

---

[7] H. van de Velde, 1994, p. 374.

[8] J. Plantenga, 'Double Lives: Labour Market Participation, Citizenship and Gender', in J. Bussemaker and R. Voet (eds.), 1998, p. 56.

attitude on the part of the political elite. In the late 1960s, women's organisations were also emerging, pursuing equal rights for men and women. The combination of these demands for more participation and for equal rights turned out to be a strong catalyst in the fight for equal political representation. After the elections in 1977, the percentage of women MPs increased from 9 to 14 per cent and four women junior ministers and one female minister were appointed to the cabinet formed in that year. From that time onwards, the debate focussed primarily on the question of how, not whether, to increase the participation of women in politics.

The demand for greater representation of women was heard in all parties. Although it was a centre-right cabinet that was formed in 1977 (CDA and VVD) in addition to the token female Minister of Social Work, four women junior ministers were appointed. The two CDA women were in charge of Justice and Women's Emancipation and the VVD women were appointed to the Ministries of Traffic and Health. An additional woman junior minister was appointed to the center-left cabinet of 1981, four came from the Labour Party and one from D66. The post of Minister of Social Work was still in the hands of the CDA. Together the junior ministers held the portfolios of Women's Emancipation, Social Affairs, Housing, Internal Affairs, and Health and Environment. The cabinet formed in 1982 contained two women VVD ministers, one for Development and one for Traffic. The three women junior ministers covered Women's Emancipation, Justice and Education. The CDA-PvdA coalition cabinet of 1989 appointed two women PvdA ministers in charge of the Ministry of Welfare, Health and Culture and of Internal Affairs and a CDA woman Minister for Traffic. Apart from these, three women junior ministers were appointed connected to the Ministries of Social Affairs, Economic Affairs and Internal Affairs.

Not only were more women appointed to the cabinets, but also in this period the strict gender criteria formerly applied when distributing the portfolios dissipated. The women government members were allocated to a range of different policy fields, including economy, internal affairs and traffic. Marital status also lost its relevance as a selection criterion – the majority of the appointed women were married and had grown-up children.

At the end of the 1970s, the economic, social and political position of women in the Netherlands was firmly on the public and political agenda. Both inside and outside the political parties, people were demanding equality between the sexes, including equality of political representation. Some parties established quotas (see chapter 6), and all larger parties set up party committees to facilitate the recruitment of women candidates.

Chapter 5

Table 5.6: Women in government, 1977-1990.

Cabinet (PM)	Year	Parties	No. women ministers	No. women junior ministers
v. Agt I	1977-1981	CDA/VVD	1	4
v. Agt II	1981-1982	CDA/PvdA /D66	1	5
v. Agt III	1982-1982	CDA/D66	1	1
Lubbers I	1982-1986	CDA/VVD	2	3
Lubbers II	1986-1989	CDA/VVV	1	4
Lubbers III	1989-1994	CDA/PvdA	3	3

Table 5.7: Percentage of women MPs in each parliamentary party, 1977-1989.*

	1977	1981	1982	1986	1989
CDA	10	15	13	20	22
PvdA	15	23	17	19	31
VVD	18	12	19	22	18
D66	25	24	50	11	33
CPN	0	33	67		
PPR	33	33	50	50	
PSP	0	33	33	100	
GL					50
EVP			100		
Total %	14	15	17	20	23
Total no. women MPs	21	22	25	30	34

* Percentages are based on the total number of deputies from the party in that year. The parties shown in the table are those with women in the parliamentary party.

The breakthrough in 1977 carried on into the 1980s. In the second half of the decade women's share of parliamentary seats went up to 20 per cent, and after the 1989 elections, to 22 per cent. The breakthrough of the Labour women came in 1989 when 15 out of 49 parliamentarians were women. Before that not even one fifth of the delegates were women. The elections of 1981 were very successful for the VVD. The party went from 26 to 36 seats. At the same time the proportion of women in the parliamentary party increased to 19 per cent. In 1989, when the VVD lost again, the proportion of women declined to 18 per cent. In 1982 three of the six D66 parliamentarians were women. This percentage dropped to 11 in 1986 and went back to 33 in 1989. In this period, the smaller parties on the left had always a relatively large share of women MPs. There was always at least one woman in the parliamentary party and sometimes this woman was even the parliamentary leader.

The same trends can be found in the party representation in the Senate. Here the overall percentage of women went from 5 in 1974 to 9 in 1977. In the 1980s the percentage continued to increase, reaching a level of 23 per cent in 1987.

Women MPs in the 1980s were still coming from good as well as from political families: 42 per cent of them had a mother who was also a member of a political party. Relatively fewer women than men had finished university, but compared to the overall percentage of adults with a university degree at that time, both men and

Table 5.8: Background characteristics of male and female MPs, 1977-1986.

	Men		Women	
	%	N (100%)	%	N (100%)
Social class: high (profession father)	46	127	90	31
Mother member of a political party	32	107	42	19
Mean age in years when entering	41	127	41	31
University education	64	224	53	49
Married	94	163	77	30
With children	92	123	61	41

Source: Parliamentary Documentation Centre.

women MPs were a highly educated group. Compared to their colleagues in the previous periods, these women MPs did not have to choose so often between motherhood and a political career. Although still less often than their male colleagues, a majority of the women MPs were married with children.

Gender identity seen in terms of a clear division between male and female MPs with regard to the issues they deal with inside parliament was again less strict in this period. Although the majority of women MPs were still more likely to sit on education, health and welfare committees, in this period women also occupied seats on committees on policing, defence, foreign affairs and finance.[9]

The women MPs in this period also represented women's interests. As in the previous periods, many women legislators had been active in women's organisations before entering parliament. Because of their work in these organisations, they were well known and thus were recruited by party leaders. Between 1975-1989, the public debate on women's rights and gender equality reached its peak in the Netherlands and issues such as the legalisation of abortion and the equalising of tax regulations were the subject of many political discussions. Some women MPs were prominent in demonstrations and other activities organised by feminist groups (see chapter 6). The majority, however, played the parliamentary game and voted according the party lines, even when, as feminists, they might well have voted differently. Women delegates from the Labour Party had particular difficulty with the strict application of party discipline.[10] But many female MPs identified themselves with the 'women's cause'. In 1978 a Parliamentary Standing Committee on Equality was formed, dealing with issues regarding the advancement of women in Dutch society. An even more clear-cut statement was the establishment in 1981 of the All-Party Women's Caucus (*Kamerbreed Vrouwen Overleg*, KVO). The main objective was to see whether women MPs of different political parties could be united on certain issues. They met every six weeks and participation was variable. About one third of the women legislators did not attend the meetings, because they did not believe that party lines could or should be crossed. As a PvdA woman MP stated: 'I am on the same wavelength as my party and not as CDA women or VVD women'.[11] The other two thirds did attend the meetings and appreciated the possibility of supporting each other in defending women's interests in

---

[9] M.H. Leyenaar, 1989, p. 171.

[10] A. Visser, 'Aanpassen of Dwarsliggen', in *Opzij*, vol. 13:10, 1985, p. 10.

[11] Rie de Boois, MP for the Labour Party, cited in A. Groen, *Vrouwen en het Binnenhof*, Den Haag, Staatsuitgeverij, 1985, p. 35.

their parliamentary parties. One of their activities was to publish a book of interviews with all women represented in the First and Second Chambers to 'discuss women's participation in politics and to mobilise other women to become interested in politics'.[12]

The emphasis in this period was less on gender differences than on the premise that gender should no longer be grounds for differentiation. Equality policies, as well as those aimed at increasing women's political participation, all started from the position that women are discriminated against and neglected, but not that they are different. The women MPs in this period can be viewed as defenders of women's interests. They extended the parliamentary agenda with issues of great concern to women and to increase their impact a parliamentary committee on women's affairs and all-women meetings were introduced.

1990S: PLAYERS

We can think of a group becoming significant when it reaches a critical mass of 30-35 per cent of the total arena to which it belongs.[13] The upward trend of women's representation continued in the 1990s and we find more women than ever in both government and parliament. Various developments had a positive impact on the empowerment of women. For example the economical and social advancement of women in Dutch society, especially the fact that women in the Netherlands caught up with men in higher education and that the majority of adult women were now involved in paid employment. A greater availability of child care made it easier for women to emerge from their private domains. More than ever it was now widely accepted that women might occupy political positions.

Another positive impact came from the formation of a so-called 'purple' cabinet, consisting of three parties, PvdA, D66 and VVD, in 1994 and in 1998.[14] The Christian Democrats, who were ideologically positioned between D66 and VVD, were kept out of government, something that had not happened since 1917. The cabinet that formed in 1994 and headed by a Labour prime minister, appointed four women out of 14 ministers and five women out of 12 junior ministers. Women were now in charge of the Ministries of Health, Traffic, Justice and Infrastructure.

---

[12] A. Groen, 1985, p. 7.

[13] R. Moss Kanter, *Men and Women of the Corporation*, New York, Basic Books, 1977.

[14] These cabinets were called purple because it mixed left (red) and right (blue).

Chapter 5

Table 5.9: Women in government, 1994, 1998.

Cabinet (PM)	Year	Parties	No. women ministers/total	No. women jun. ministers/total
Lubbers III	1989-1994	CDA/PvdA	3 / 15	3 / 11*
Kok I	1994-1998	PvdA/VVD/D66	4 / 14	5 / 12
Kok II	1998-2002	PvdA/VVD/D66	4 / 15	5 / 14

* The third woman junior minister was appointed in 1990, succeeding the junior minister at the Ministry of Economic Affairs who had to resign.

Table 5.10: Percentage of women MPs in each parliamentary party, 1994, 1998*

	1994 (%)	1998 (%)
CDA	27	32
PvdA	38	49
VVD	26	26
D66	50	43
GL	60	60
AOV	25	
CD	33	
SP	0	20
Total	32	37

* After the formation of the cabinet.
Source: *Vrouwenbelangen 1994, 1998*

After the elections of 1998, the coalition continued and again nine women were part of the government. This time two women ministers acted as the two deputy prime ministers meaning that they replaced the prime minister when he was unavailable.

In parliament the political parties still varied in their representation of women. The left-wing parties had more women parliamentarians than the VVD and CDA. The small orthodox Calvinist parties were still the most reluctant to select women candidates.

Now that many more women entered parliament, gender differences in demographic characteristics had almost disappeared. The average age of the women MPs in 1994 was 44.9, of the men it was 47.5. A majority of both groups had a university degree: 57 per cent of the women and 62 per cent of the men. Almost all women MPs were married or living together, just like the male MPs.

The greater number of women MPs is certainly a result of changes in the outlook of selectors. Pressure from the inside, especially from women's sections, as well as from the outside, such as the government and moreover the wish to modernise their image and to attract the votes of women voters, led to a more positive attitude towards political integration of women compared to 20-30 years ago. More than ever, party leaders were actively seeking women candidates.

A survey among candidates standing for parliamentary election conducted in 1994 tells us about attitudes towards the integration of women in politics.[15] When this survey was conducted 32 per cent of the MPs were women. What did they think about this number: should there be more, a few more, about the same or fewer women in parliament?

With the exception of the candidates of the small orthodox religious parties, the majority of candidates believed that there should be more women in parliament. Women candidates of Green Left and the PvdA were very explicit, while male candidates were a bit more reserved: about one third of the male candidates from D66, CDA and the VVD were satisfied with the 32 per cent representation of women.

Candidates were also asked to give their view on the relevance of several explanations for the under-representation of women in parliament. Not many believed that women do not belong in politics. Only very few male candidates thought that

---

[15] Candidates standing for the parliamentary elections of 1994 were interviewed. See for a report on this survey, M. Leyenaar and B.Niemöller, 'Legislative Recruitment in the Netherlands in the Grip of Institutional Reform', in P. Norris (ed.), 1997, pp. 120-137.

Table 5.11: Opinion about parliamentary representation of women, 1994 (%).

		GL	PvdA	D66	CDA	VVD	Small right	All
Many more	W	88	83	67	70	57	0	69
	M	81	13	31	6	24	6	26
A few more	W	12	17	33	30	43	0	26
	M	19	73	31	63	35	22	40
About the same	W	0	0	0	0	0	100	5
	M	0	13	39	31	35	33	25
Fewer	W	0	0	0	0	0	0	0
	M	0	0	0	0	0	39	8

Source: M. Leyenaar and B. Niemöller, 1997, p. 132.

women are not suited to the job or do not fit into parliament. The same is true for the statement that 'women tend to lose votes'. With regard to individual barriers such as the lack of education and professional experience about 20 per cent, both men and women, pointed to these as likely explanations. Interestingly enough, more women than men were of the opinion that women do not have enough confidence and therefore do not put themselves forward as candidates for political office. About 70 per cent of women candidates and 60 per cent of men viewed the strict division of labour between men and women as an important reason why women do not become candidates for parliament. The gender gap is larger with regard to possible institutional barriers: 40 per cent of women candidates agreed with the statement 'women are not given the opportunities by parties' as against 26 per cent of the male candidates. Consequently, male candidates were also less in favour of policies directed at changing institutions to increase the number of women in parliament. They were more in favour of training programmes than of quotas or of changing the hours of parliamentary sittings. Women, in contrast, approved strongly of quotas: 73 per cent against 25 per cent of the male candidates; and of more adaptable working hours: 42 per cent against 33 per cent. A majority of male and female candidates wanted to see more and better child-care facilities: 85 per cent of the women; 60 per cent of the men.[16]

At the end of this period the peak of the political debate on women's rights and gender equality was over and many of the inequalities to which it was addressed had been dealt with. As a result, gender orientation was also changing. A majority of women MPs still viewed the gender division of labour as an important source of inequality and they kept on working in parliament to change these gender roles. One important success of several women MPs was the parliamentary approval of *gender mainstreaming* as a governmental approach to overcome the remaining barriers to gender equality: equality policy had to be integrated into all regular policy. The effects of this 'Plan of Action on Gender Mainstreaming' were that from 1999, all ministries had to determine and implement at least three concrete projects aiming at gender equality, as well as specify in their budgets the amount of money spend on gender equality[17] (see also chapter 7). This policy plan took effect until the new cabinet took over in 2002.

At the same time, however, political identity had again become more important than gender identity. For example, the Parliamentary Standing Committee on Equality was abolished in 1994 as well as the All-Party Women's Caucus. The Caucus ceased to exist when in the 1990s attendance was steadily declining. We also witnessed a growing number of young and highly educated women MPs, who themselves experienced no gender discrimination in education and in finding a job, and who did not see any problems for women as a group. They did not view themselves as women representing women's interests, but as individual MPs representing their party. This attitude is also visible within parties. For example the women's section of the Labour Party decided to disband the organisation in 1995 and, since then, the party executive has taken responsibility for the formulation and implementation of affirmative action strategies (see chapter 7).

Thus at the start of the new millennium, with regard to their numerical presence, women have a firm grip on decision-making in both government and parliament. The Netherlands ranks fifth in the world list of countries with the high-

---

[16] *Ibid.*, p. 135.

[17] Ministerie van Sociale Zaken en Werkgelegenheid, *Plan of Action on Gender Mainstreaming*, Voorburg, 2002.

est parliamentary representation of women. But at the same time the interest in women's issues has waned and gender equality has a lower priority among the MPs.

In chapter 7 we shall look at the representation figures in the 21st century. But first we turn to a description of the participation of women in the other representative bodies – municipal councils, provincial councils, the European Parliament and in local and provincial governments.

LOCAL AND REGIONAL LEVEL

There are different theories regarding the level of decision-making and the electoral success of women. One theory is that the more important the political position, the less likely it is to find women candidates. This is because competition for top jobs is fierce and chances are highly determined by one's position in the relevant networks. Criteria such as a lengthy membership of the party, having filled a wide range of other representative and executive positions and continuous availability then become very important. Following this line of reasoning, we would expect to find fewer women in politics at the national than at the provincial and local levels. And, relatively, there should be more women in parliament than in government, given the scarcity of seats and importance of the latter body.

Another theory concerning the level of government refers to subject matter. For instance the issues that local councillors deal with are more recognisable and down-to-earth than some of the issues discussed in parliament. Many policy matters on the agenda at local level are especially important for women, such as child care, housing, traffic, schools and the subsidising of women's groups. In addition, contacts between local councillors and citizens are more direct and happen more frequently, compared to the contact of MPs with voters. Lastly, in the majority of municipalities, the job of a councillor is not full-time and hence it may be easier to combine this with the rearing of children and/or employment. This all leads to the expectation that we should find a higher representation of women at the local and regional levels than at the national level.

There are twelve provinces in the Netherlands. Each provincial council consist of 47-83 members and is headed by a provincial government in the form of a state governor appointed by the cabinet together with deputies appointed by the parties represented in the council.[18] The size of the government varies between three and nine deputies. Hardly any women have been appointed as state governor – only four since 1814. A woman governor twice headed the province of Drenthe: from 1974-1982 and from 1992-1994. In both cases it was a PvdA representative. The province of South Holland had a VVD woman as its executive from 1994-1999 and in 2003 the CDA appointed a woman governor in North Brabant. An important reason why the parties put so few women forward for the position of state governor is the fact that competition is very fierce given the status of the job. Former ministers are often granted these jobs, for example, as compensation for the loss of their seat in government. We also find relatively fewer women in the position of deputy than of provincial councillor. Here it is the (regional) party that decides who is to become deputy. Often these positions go to the people heading the list of candidates, who are often men. Sixteen women were elected to the provincial councils in 1919, a total of 3 per cent and this percentage had hardly increased in 1946 – to just 4 per cent (21 women). As at the national level, the 1970s were a turning-point for the provincial councils. In 1974, 12 per cent women were elected, in 1978 this was 16 per cent and in 1999 it was 31 per cent.

In 1919, at the first local elections after the introduction of women's suffrage, 88 women were elected to the municipal councils – less than one per cent. Until 1946, women's participation in the councils was no more than two per cent and until 1978 less than ten per cent. After this the percentage slowly increased to 22 per cent in 1990 and since then this figure has hardly increased.

With regard to the background of councillors there is data available from 1955 and 1981.[19] It appears that, compared to 1955, twice as many women councillors in 1981 were under 40 years of age: 35 per cent as opposed to 16 per cent. The same is true for the percentage of women that were unmarried or had been married: 31 per cent of women councillors in 1955, as against 14 per cent in 1981. Many more women in 1981 had a university education or were engaged in paid

---

[18] Until 2003, deputies were members of the provincial council when elected and stayed on as members during their job as deputy. The law was changed in 2003 allowing people from outside the provincial councils to apply for the position as deputy. The party the deputy is representing still appoints the deputy. After the elections of 2003 the vast majority of deputies still came from the council. They had to resign however when becoming a deputy.

[19] J. C. Schokking, 1955; M.H. Leyenaar et al., *De Helft als Meerderheid. Verslag van een Onderzoek naar Vrouwen in Politieke Functies*, Den Haag, VNG, 1983.

Chapter 5

Table 5.12: Percentage of women in political offices at the regional and local level, 1918-2003.[20]

Year	% Women provincial councillors	% Women provincial deputies	% Women local councillors	% Women local aldermen	% Women mayors
1919/1918*	3		1		
1931	3		1		
1946	4	3	2	1	
1954/1953	5	3	2	1	
1962	6	5	4	1	
1966	7	3	5		
1970	7	2	7	3	
1974	12	3	10	5	
1978	16	7	13	9	
1982	21	11	16	9	3
1987/1986	26	22	19	13	4
1991/1990	30	24	22	17	8
1995/1994	31	19	22	18	13
1999/1998	31	26	22	19	17
2003/2002	28	19	24	17	20

Source: M. Leyenaar, 2000; Ministerie voor Binnenlandse Zaken, *Voortgangsrapportages Vrouwen in Politiek en Openbaar Bestuur,* 1992-2003.

---

[20] For the completeness the figures of 2002 and of 2003 are added to the table. These developments, however, are discussed in chapter 7.

employment: 43 per cent and 33 per cent respectively in 1981 and 12 and 17 per cent in 1955.[21]

In 1919, there were around 1100 municipalities in the Netherlands. By 2003 this number had reduced to 480 as a result of a policy of combining smaller communities into larger ones. Local government consists of a mayor and aldermen. Until 2002, the aldermen were elected from the council and stayed on as council members during their position as alderman. Since then it is also possible for parties to appoint outsiders as their representatives in local government and aldermen are no longer members of the council. Mayors are appointed by the cabinet, however it is expected that at the end of the first decade of the 21st century, mayors will be directly elected. The executive of the municipality is responsible for the administration and for preparing and implementing central and provincial government decisions that affect the municipality in question.

So far, not many women have filled the position of mayor. It was only in 1931 that the precondition that the mayor had to be male was removed from the municipal law. At that time the Minister of Internal Affairs was still of the opinion: 'The physical as well as the spiritual conditions of women make them unsuitable for the office of mayor, for example will she be able to catch thieves, to pole vault, to clamber over barbed wire, to lower oneself in water pipes and to go on hands and knees trough woodland?'[22]

The first woman mayor was appointed in 1946. Since then the number has increased to 20 per cent in 2002 in the context of a formal policy of the Ministry of Internal Affairs to increase the number of women mayors (see next chapter). Although it is not a formal rule, the mayor comes often from the party that has a majority in the council. Another informal rule is that each party get a representative share of mayoral offices. Given the dominance of the confessional parties in the smaller communities, the CDA and its predecessors always had a large share of the 'mayor pie'. More recently, with the merger of smaller municipalities, the CDA had to give up many mayoral posts. Table 5.13 shows the number of mayors from each party as well as the percentage of women mayors.

---

[21] Number of respondents interviewed in 1955 were 259 women. In 1981 the percentages are based on 568 women councillors.

[22] Jonkheer Ruys de Beerenbrouck, cited in M.L. van de Sande, 'Mevrouw de Burgemeester...', in W. Derksen (ed.), *De Burgemeester, van Magistraat tot Modern Bestuurder*, Deventer, 1984, pp. 165, 166.

Chapter 5

Table 5.13: Women mayors.

Party	1986		1991		2002	
	Total	% women	Total	% women	Total	% women
CDA	406	2	339	3	174	11
PvdA	154	8	152	13	140	24
VVD	122	7	112	12	97	27
D66	12	8	14	36	30	30
GL	4*	25	3	0	6	50
Small orthodox parties	14	0	14	0	11	0
Other	3	0	0	0	2	0
Total**	714	4	634	8	460	20

* In 1986 there were three male PPR mayors and one female CPN mayor.
** Not including vacancies.
Source: Ministerie van Binnenlandse Zaken, *Voortgangsrapportage Vrouwen in Politiek en Openbaar Bestuur*, 2002, p. 20.

Table 5.14: Percentage women mayors according to size of the community, 2002.

Size	Total number municipalities	% Women mayors
< 8,000 citizens	41	29
8,001-14,000 citizens	115	22
14,001-24,000 citizens	128	23
24,001-40,000 citizens	97	13
40,001-100,000 citizens	55	13
>100,000 citizens	24	17

Source: Ministerie van Binnenlandse Zaken, 2002, p. 21.

In 2002, women held 91 of all mayoral offices: 34 of them were PvdA, 26 came from the VVD and 19 from the CDA, 9 from D66 and 3 from Green Left. The status of the position of mayor is very much dependent on the size of the municipality. Table 5.14 shows the distribution of men and women mayors over the different communities.

More women mayors are chairing local governments in small municipalities. In 2002, there were four cases of a woman being in charge of a city of more than 100,000 inhabitants. An intriguing question is whether there will be more or fewer women mayors when the selection procedure is changed and mayors are no longer appointed but directly elected by the citizens. Research has shown that, in general, women's rates of participation are higher when political positions are filled by appointment, rather then when the system calls for direct election of a candidate. The explanation offered is the fact that those doing the appointing have to account for their nominations, and find it useful to 'balance' appointments among relevant social groups.[23] Appointing public officials also makes it possible to influence the nomination process. In this case the Ministry of Internal Affairs, which does the appointing, tried to impose a policy of affirmative action on the people involved in the process. When mayors are directly elected, this will not longer be possible.

The assumption that the participation of women is easier to gain in local councils than in national assemblies, because eligibility criteria are less stringent and these are not full-time jobs, seems not to be true for the Netherlands. There are several explanations for this lack of progress at local level. First, we have seen that the Christian Democratic Party has the majority in most local communities and this party has been less favourable than others towards selecting women. A second explanation is that the majority of Dutch communities are rural, where the effects of the new women's movement were less pronounced than in the larger cities. There has always been a clear correlation with the size of the local community and the percentage of women councillors.[24]

A third explanation is the increasing fragmentation of the party system at local level. More political parties participate in the elections and a larger number of

---

[23] R. Darcy, S. Welch and J. Clark, *Women, Elections and Representation*, New York, Longman, 1987, p. 111; J. Mossuz-Laveau and M. Sineau, *Women in the Political World in Europe*, Strasbourg, Council of Europe, 1984, p. 50.

[24] Ministerie van Binnenlandse Zaken, *Voortgangsrapportage Vrouwen in Politiek en Openbaar Bestuur*, Den Haag, Ministerie van Binnenlandse Zaken, 2002.

parties is represented in the council, including the local lists. In one community, for example, it is possible to find nine different parties occupying the 17 available seats. Fragmentation of the party system is disadvantageous for women. When many parties with only a few candidates participate in the council, often only the first two people on the list are elected. Since women candidates are more often found at the lower places on the list, they will not tend to be elected.

A fourth reason is the merging of local communities into larger ones. For efficiency reasons communities are combined. For example in 1960 there were 1200 communities in the Netherlands, in 2002 there were less than 500. A merger also means the joining of the local party organisations active in the different communities. What then happens is that the local party leaders, who are often men, take the first places on the candidate lists.

The fifth explanation relates to the selection procedures of most parties. It is the local branch of a party that is responsible for candidate selection and in most parties the national executive has very little to say influencing the process. In general national party leaders are more concerned about female-male balance than are the local or regional branches.

The sixth reason explaining the lack of progress in the percentage of women councillors in elections taking place in the 1990s, is the increasing importance of the so-called local lists. Since the local election of 1990, there has been a greater interest in local political decision-making in the Netherlands. Now that people are less ideologically oriented, the pragmatic approach of local politics, dealing with day-to-day matters such as the arrangement of neighbourhoods and the fight against criminality and drug abuse, seems more attractive for many people to get involved in.[25] One of the consequences is the increasing attraction of local, independent, lists. These parties participate only in an election to one municipality and have no ties to a nationally organised party. There have always been local lists in the Netherlands, mostly in the southern provinces of Limburg and North Brabant, where Catholicism was the predominant religion. Because almost everybody was Catholic and voted for the Catholic party in the parliamentary elections, there was room at the local level for parties organised on other than a religious basis. Parties emerged because they represented a certain geographical part of the municipality or a certain local issue. We also saw parties established around a well-known local figure,

---

[25] P. Castenmiller, *De Levende Werkzaamheid. Politieke Betrokkenheid van Burgers bij het Lokaal Bestuur*, VNG Uitgeverij, 2002.

the local pub owner for example.[26] These days, however, we find local parties in the other provinces as well. In the local elections of 1990, local lists received 13 per cent of the total valid vote, in 1998 this increased to almost 23 per cent and in the elections of 2002 they managed 26 per cent of the vote. A side effect of the growing importance of local lists is the negative impact on the selection of women. Local lists tend to nominate fewer women to the councils than the nationally based parties participating in the local elections. In the local lists there is no tradition of affirmative action for women, nor are there any instructions from national party leaders to balance the list according to gender and ethnicity. Local lists can decide themselves how to arrange the selection process and consequently appoint fewer women to eligible places on the list.

A final reason for the lack of increase in the overall percentage of women councillors is the fact that women, once elected, tend not to return to office for a second time. A survey held in 2002 among local councillors shows that relatively more women leave the council during their first period of four years or decide not to stand for re-election. The main reason for this early 'retirement' is that combining the council, a job and the caring for children is too time consuming.[27] This is of course also an important reason for many women *not* to stand as a candidate for local office.

EUROPEAN LEVEL

The first 'parliamentary' meeting at European level took place in 1952 involving 78 members from six different countries. Over time many more countries have joined the European Union and consequently the European Parliament (EP) has increased in size. After the election of 1999 the EP housed 626 members from 15 different countries. Table 5.15 shows the representation of women delegates from the Netherlands.

Until 1979, national MPs were nominated to the EP. One woman MP was nominated in the Dutch delegation. Since 1979, MEPs have been directly elected by the citizens of each country. In the Netherlands this happens by a system of proportional representation with lists of candidates set by the parties. Women's representation has increased from 20 per cent in 1979 to 36 per cent in 1999.

---

[26] W. Derksen, *Lokaal Bestuur*, Amsterdam, Elsevier, 2001, pp. 30-32.

[27] P. Castenmiller *et al.*, 2002, pp. 28-30.

Table 5.15: Representation of women in the Netherlands delegation to the European Parliament, 1952-1999

Year	Netherlands delegation	No. of women	% Women
1952	10	1	10
1962	14	1	7
1973	13	1	8
1979	25	5	20
1984	25	7	28
1989	25	7	28
1994	31	10	32
1999	31	11	36

CONCLUSION

Up until the 1970s, women in the Netherlands played a marginal role in decision-making bodies; their representation was less than 10 per cent. A breakthrough occurred in the mid-1970s as more and more women became professional politicians.

Contrary to expectations, the under-representation of women is higher at local and regional level than at national level. Not many women can be found in the position of mayor, state governor, local alderman and provincial deputy.

With regard to party representation of women we can conclude that:

- For most political offices, the percentage of women representatives for the CDA and VVD are somewhat lower than for the parties on the left hand side of the ideological continuum, D66, PvdA and Green Left;
- The small orthodox parties are faithful to their belief that the proper place for a woman is in the home and not in politics;
- D66, Green Left and the SP, both relatively new parties compared to the others, have the highest representation of women.

Furthermore, we have seen that in the period 1918-1946, there was no conscious activity to select women as MPs. Only 'acceptable' women were chosen by the party leadership, which meant unmarried, upper-class and highly educated women. In the following period, 1946-1975, parties accepted that they should select at least one woman for the parliamentary party or cabinet. Those women were expected to defend and articulate the interests of mothers and home-makers. From the mid-1970s on, the under-representation of women in political decision-making became an issue on the agenda of parties, women's organisations and the government. When half of the population is consistently under-represented, the legitimacy of existing political structures might very well be called into question. Women's organisations insisted that women are more aware of their own needs and interests and are therefore better able to press for them. In this period, women MPs broadened the political agenda with issues such as child care, sexual abuse against women and the legalisation of abortion. In the fourth period, the 1990s, many have argued that any gender imbalance in political decision-making is an inefficient use of human resources. They state that women comprise half the world's pool of potential talent and ability, and their participation in politics would maximise the human and material resources of the state, for the common good. Women are now actively sought out during the selection of candidates at least for the offices of cabinet minister and member of parliament. Consequently the proportion of women MPs has increased to more than one third. But despite the larger numbers, specific interest for women's issues is waning somewhat. The women MPs of the 1990s are less inclined to define themselves as representatives of female citizens.

CHAPTER 6

EXPLAINING THE CHANGE IN ATTITUDE

'The soft approach has worked well.'[1] These were the words of the Deputy Secretary-General of the Ministry of Internal Affairs in 1995, when presenting the policies of the Dutch government designed to increase the percentage of women in politics and public office. What she meant by soft was that the policies of the government were based on the *persuasion* of relevant players such as political parties, external advisory bodies and other selectors – and not on *coercion*, for example through legal measures. The political representation of women in parliament and government was indeed something to boast about. Only in some Scandinavian countries were the relative proportions of women MPs and cabinet ministers higher, while in many other European countries there had been hardly any progress at all. The parliament of Belgium had, given this lack of progress, just accepted a law requiring political parties to select at least one-third female candidates and place these on their lists for parliamentary and local elections (see chapter 8). In other words, in the 1990s, the problem of ensuring that women were at the centre of political decision-making was clearly on the political agenda in most European countries as well that of the European Parliament. For example, in 1992, the European Commission created an *Expert Network Women in Decision-Making* whose main task was to disseminate information and to develop common European policies.

How can we explain this willingness in the Netherlands to share political power with women? There are three relevant sets of players with a decisive role in the empowerment of women: *women's organisations, political parties* and the *government*. This chapter deals with the strategies and policies of each of these sets of

---

[1] Benita Plesch, Deputy Secretary-General of the Ministry of Internal Affairs at a conference 'Strategies for a gender balance in political decision-making', organised by the European Expert Network Women in Decision-Making, Dublin, 23-24 March 1995.

players as well as the philosophy behind these. First, however, we need to sketch some of the background to the overall position of Dutch women.

SOCIAL AND ECONOMIC POSITION OF WOMEN

Employment and Education

Until the 1980s, the majority of Dutch women were not involved in paid employment. This is one of the reasons for the low political participation rate of women at that time. Employment gives women not only material independence, but also certain professional skills and greater self-confidence. In the Netherlands, unlike other countries of the European Union, women have never been a large part of the labour force. From 1900 to 1960, women formed around one-fifth of the working population, a number that varied only slightly during this period. Significant changes did occur, however, in the type of women who participated in wage labour. At the beginning of the 20th century, women comprised 23 per cent of the labour force. Most were working-class women and the wives of shop-owners and farmers. Many married women withdrew from the labour market in the 1950s for several reasons: a steady rise in their standard of living, a high marriage rate and the dicta of the Roman Catholic and Protestant churches that married women belong at home. The proportion of women in the working population declined from 24 per cent in 1947, to 22 per cent in 1960.[2] After 1960, the percentage of women in paid employment increased again, mainly caused by married women who carried on with their paid work until they expected their first child. Between 1960 and 1981, the proportion of employed married women rose from 7 to 33 per cent.[3]

There are several reasons for the relatively low rate of participation of women compared to other countries of the European Union before the 1980s. There is the late industrialisation of the Netherlands compared with Britain, France and Belgium. At that time Dutch capital had cheap male labour at its disposal and no great need for women and children in the labour force. The fact that the Netherlands was involved neither in the war of 1870 in Europe, nor in World War I meant that no shortage of men occurred. Later on, the relatively high wages and social security

---

[2] CBS, *Statistisch Zakboek*, The Hague, Staatsuitgeverij, 1979.

[3] C. Oudijk, *De Sociale Atlas van de Vrouw*, The Hague, Staatsuitgeverij, 1984, p. 192.

Chapter 6

benefits in the Netherlands, together with a high marriage rate, encouraged women to act as home-makers and carers, with the husband's role as breadwinner. This, combined with the role of the Dutch churches that propagated the ideology of family and motherhood, resulted in low participation levels at the labour market.[4]

Given this ideology of motherhood it was not very surprising that, in the 1930s, when unemployment figures were raising daily, several attempts were made by the government to ban married women from jobs in the civil service. One of the first times that women organised themselves as a group was to secure universal suffrage at the first decade of the 20th century. The second time was to protest against the restriction of women's right to paid labour. The first attempt to do that was in 1904 when a law was proposed stating that women civil servants were to be fired when they married. This proposal was defeated. Other attempts, however, were more successful, including the law proposed by a Catholic Minister of Social Affairs and accepted by parliament in 1937, which forbade married women (or women who 'lived in sin') to be employed. In 1935 a Committee to Defend the Right of Women to Paid Labour was founded, in which several women's organisations participated. The Committee was able to draw attention to this injustice with advertisements in newspapers and distribution of pamphlets. They also organised large protest meetings in Amsterdam and in other towns. As a result of all this pressure, the next Minister of Social Affairs – a socialist – discarded the contentious law.[5] However, after World War II, the government again tried to restrict married women's work outside the home. For example the Catholic Minister of Interior asked other ministers to reduce their employment of married female staff to a minimum. And in 1952 a report was published entitled *The Question of the Married Female Civil Servant* which suggested that female civil servants who marry should be dismissed, but that this regulation should not apply to women over 30 years of age, to women in leadership positions or to women who had been in service for 10 years or longer.[6] The attempts to restrict women's right to paid em-

---

[4] See B.T.J. Hooghiemstra and M. Niphuis Nell, *Sociale Atlas van de Vrouw, Deel 2, Arbeid, Inkomen en faciliteiten om werken en de zorg voor kinderen te combineren,* Rijswijk, SCP, 1993, p. 27; J. Plantenga, *Een afwijkend patroon. Honderd jaar vrouwenarbeid in Nederland en (West) Duitsland,* Amsterdam, Sua, 1993.

[5] W.H. Posthumus van der Goot *et al., Van Moeder op Dochter, de Maatschappelijke Positie van de Vrouw in Nederland, vanaf de Franse Tijd,* Sun reprint, 1977, pp. 267-281.

[6] Cited in J. Plantenga, 'Double Lives: Labour Market Participation, Citizenship and Gender', in J. Bussemaker and R. Voet (eds.), 1998, p. 56.

ployment finally ended in 1955, when parliament passed a motion submitted by a female Labour MP stating that government should remit from intervening.

The post-war welfare state was founded on the assumption of the nuclear family, with the husband as breadwinner and the wife as full-time mother. Bussemaker (1998) points out how the Dutch Government discouraged married women from entering or remaining in the labour market. For example, the tax system imposed negative incentives on a second income within the family and did not facilitate child care by making this tax-deductible. 'The identification of men with family maintenance meant that the male breadwinner earned a family wage and received child benefit, and that his wife and children were, by definition, included in his insurance provisions without the need for additional contributions'.[7] The general consensus was that to have married women participating at the labour market would be 'detrimental to healthy family relations'.

> A full time housewife was not only a major safeguard against miscarriages and infant mortality, she was also seen as a weapon against alcohol abuse and could play a positive role in the fight against anti-social behaviour in the broader sense.[8]

This view of the proper role of women came under fierce attack at the end of the 1960s and in the 1970s. Religion became less important in the lives of many citizens and, more importantly, the wave of feminism that swept over Holland questioned the 'naturalness' of this strict division of labour. The public debate on women's and men's roles in society, combined with the expansion of the service and public sectors of the economy, both of which employed a large number of women, are to be held responsible for the rise in the employment of women. In 1981 84 per cent of employed women had jobs in the service and public sector compared to 55 per cent of the employed men. In 1963, 70 per cent of women and 41 per cent of the men had jobs in these two sectors.[9] Contributing to this development was the availability of contraceptives as well as labour-saving devices such as central heating, showers and washing machines. Further, women's

---

[7] J. Bussemaker, 'Gender and the Sepration of Spheres in Twentieth Century Dutch Society: Pillarisation, Welfare State Formation and Individualisation', in J. Bussemaker and R. Voet (eds.), 1998, p. 30.

[8] J. Plantenga, 1998, p. 53.

[9] CBS, *Statistisch Zakboek*, The Hague, Staatsuitgeverij, 1979 and 1982.

Chapter 6

organisations demanded more and better child-care facilities and more women decided after they had a baby either to stay in paid employment part-time, or to re-enter the labour market after a few years of taking care of the child(ren). The government too became more inclined to increase the labour supply given the growing concern over the ratio of dependents to taxpayers.[10]

At the end of the 20th century, 51 per cent of women between 15 and 64 years old were engaged in paid employment, compared to 76 per cent of men. This is an increase of 12 per cent since 1990. Slowly the traditional gender division of labour is losing its impact.

However, a majority of women work part-time. Many mothers did not and do not feel comfortable with leaving children in somebody else's care for eight hours a day. And, because it was financially feasible, women with small children compromised and accepted part-time work. Although many more child-care facilities were created in the 1990s, as well as all kind of parental leaves schemes, this did not change the fact that 63 per cent of all women with paid employment had a *part-time* job in 2001. Compared to the other countries this is a very high figure; the average in the 15 EU countries is 16 per cent.[11]

The rise in the number of women involved in paid labour did not lead to the disappearance of gendered job segregation. In the 1970s, one third of all employed women worked in four occupations: sales persons, secretaries or receptionists, administrative positions, and in 'caring' jobs such as nursing and teaching. In comparison, one-third of all employed males worked in 14 different occupations. In 2000, 27 per cent of employed women had a job in the health-care sector against 5 per cent of men, and 20 per cent of men worked in industry against 8 per cent of employed women.[12]

There is still a significant difference in rates of payment: in 2000, women received on average only 78 per cent of the gross hourly payment for men.[13] Although more women than before can be found among managers – 16 per cent in 2001 –

---

[10] S. Gustafsson, 'Childcare and Type of Welfare States', in D. Sainsbury, *Gendering Welfare States*, London, Sage, 1994, p. 55.

[11] W. Portegijs, A. Boelens and S. Keuzenkamp, *Emancipatiemonitor 2002*, Den Haag, SCP/CBS, 2002, pp. 71-123.

[12] S. Keuzenkamp and K. Oudhof, *Emancipatiemonitor 2000*, Den Haag, SCP/CBS, 2000, p. 68.

[13] W. Portegijs *et al.*, 2002, p. 161.

there is still a gross under-representation of women in top jobs. For example, women fill less than 8 per cent of the top administrative jobs in the ministries.[14]

Overall, the position of Dutch women in the labour market is one in which family responsibilities are still crucial. This goes for the private as well as for the public sector.

With regard to general educational levels, we find the share of girls about the same as that of boys. About the same percentage of boys and girls continue their education, and more girls than boys finish their higher education and get a degree. For all women over 15 years of age, fewer women (19 per cent) than men (23 per cent) had a university or college (HBO) degree in 2001. But if we distinguish between age groups, then gender differences disappear or turn around: for the younger age groups relatively more women than men are higher educated. Segregation also exists in the education system: fewer women choose technical subjects or economics, and fewer men choose languages, medicine and teaching.[15]

One may conclude that in general the position of women in Dutch society has improved over the years: women in the Netherlands have caught up with men in higher education, and their participation in the labour force is still increasing. Economic factors, such as the shortage of employees in the 1990s and the expansion of the service sector in the years before, were largely responsible for these changes, but the fact that the cultural climate changed under the influence of equality policies had a big impact as well.

Equality Policies

The issue of gender equality has been on the agenda of the national government since the 1970s. There is a certain willingness in both state and society to promote and implement policy initiatives aimed at achieving an equal distribution of economic, social and political resources between men and women. A product of this culture of equality is the establishment of various governmental institutions that are responsible for dealing with different aspects of the advancement of women. In the Netherlands these institutions date from 1974. Against the background of the 'second emancipation wave' of the late 1960s, the government began to adopt policies designed to improve the position of women. Formulating an overall policy for women was a new departure. As Swiebel and Outshoorn describe it:

---

[14] *Ibid.*, pp. 182-191.

[15] *Ibid.*, p. 51.

The idea that it is part of the responsibility of government to have an overall policy on women, was new in 1974-1975; it was a deliberately staged innovation. As with other European nations, it can clearly be attributed to the revival of the women's movement at the end of the 1960s. At first the movement concentrated on rediscovering and redefining women's issues and on setting up its own mutual support facilities and campaigns. Soon it realised that government was indispensable for tackling many of the issues raised.[16]

The women's organisation Man Woman Society (*Man Vrouw Maatschappij*, MVM) organised a postcard campaign in 1974, capitalising on a change in government in 1973 to a centre-left coalition chaired by a Labour prime minister. Many women sent postcards to the prime minister with the message that it was time for an overall government policy on women. Following this, two governmental committees were set up. A National Committee 'Year of the Women' was inspired by the International Women's Year organised by the United Nations, along with an Emancipation Committee (*Emancipatie Kommissie*), that consisted of experts. This event marked the beginning of a specific government emancipation or equality policy for women. Previous policies on women had been embedded in general welfare provisions developed after the Second World War.

Amid some controversy, the Emancipation Committee managed to produce about one hundred recommendations. Although the government did not solicit most of its advice, some recommendations from the Committee were transformed into actual policy. A Junior Minister for Equality or, as it is called in the Netherlands, for Emancipation was appointed in 1977, attached to the Ministry of Culture, Recreation and Social Work and later to the Ministry of Social Affairs and Employment. A 'national machinery', a network of state institutions working on gender equality, was established. At its core was an administrative body to oversee government equality policy, the Department for the Coordination of Emancipation Policy (*Directie Coordinatie Emancipatiebeleid*, DCE). Part of the national machinery was the Emancipation Council, founded in 1981 as the successor to the Emancipation Committee. This was an independent advisory body, the main task of which was to advise the government on women's issues. Each ministry was required to seek the advice of the Council whenever their plans involved equal rights and/or opportunities for women. The Council could also issue advisory

---

[16] J. Swiebel and J. Outshoorn, 1991, p. 6.

reports on its own initiative and could draw the minister's attention to the possible effects of a ministry's policies on women.[17]

Another important result was the definition of equality policy as *inter-departmental*. The women's issue was not a phenomenon to be isolated in one department, but was to be seen as an aspect of policy in every conceivable field.[18] As a result, coordinating bodies were set up in each ministry.

During the first period, roughly from 1974 to 1981, the objective of governmental emancipation policy was to change attitudes, opinions and thinking on gender roles. A policy paper published in 1977, *Emancipation: Process of Change and Growth*, explicitly states that men and women should have a real choice to shape their own lives. Women should gain parity in terms of rights, education and participation, while men should become more involved in caring. At that time education was considered the appropriate policy weapon with which to attack beliefs about the roles of men and women and prevent future gender biases. Courses were organised for women with small children who wanted to improve their basic knowledge. These so-called 'Second Chance Comprehensive Schools' for mothers attracted a large number of eager students. Meanwhile, sons and daughters were educated using screened teaching material, in which '*papa*' did not merely '*fume une pipe*' but washed the dishes as well. As time progressed, more and more people came to realise that the inferior position of women in society was fundamentally rooted in social-economic structures. As a consequence, the Junior Ministry for Emancipation was moved from the Ministry of Culture, Recreation and Social Work to the Ministry of Social Affairs and Employment and with it the administrative unit, DCE. This Ministry is generally seen as a 'heavier', more important department than the Ministry of Culture, making this change appear to some to be a political statement. The junior minister in charge of this move was from the Labour Party and viewed as a feminist.[19] In 1982 a committee was installed consisting of women from the women's movement and civil servants from different ministries, whose task was to draw up an Emancipation Policy Programme for

---

[17] Emancipatieraad, *Emancipatieraad*, Den Haag, 1990, p. 5.

[18] J. Swiebel, 'De Vrouwenbeweging en de Beleidsorganisatie bij de Overheid', in *Katijf*, vol. 45, 1988, p. 15.

[19] J. Oldersma, 'More Women or More Feminist in Politics? Advocacy Coalitions and the Representation of Women in the Netherlands, 1967-1992', in *Acta Politica*, vol. 37, Autumn 2002, p. 288.

Chapter 6

1985-1990. This Programme was presented to, and accepted by, the Second Chamber in 1986 with many policy initiatives. It still forms the touchstone for all government emancipation policy. The starting point of the Policy Programme was the recognition of the structural imbalance of power between women and men, which is rooted in Dutch society. The result is that opportunities for women are fewer than for men. The main objective described in this Programme is 'a pluriform society in which everyone has the opportunity to lead an independent existence irrespective of their sex or marital status and in which women and men have equal rights, opportunities, freedom and responsibilities'.[20]

How can we evaluate the outcome of state-sponsored emancipation policy? First, women's policies have been quite successful when it concerns 'small' benefits to women. On the national as well as on the local level, a regular stream of subsidies has been available to set up women's groups, to finance activities of women's organisations, to set up women's health centres, rape crisis centres and shelters for battered women.[21] The DCE 'has given the women's movement a strong institutional backbone by funding a huge variety of women's initiatives and groups' according to Outshoorn (1998). She points out that the DCE has provided about € 35 million each year in setting up and maintaining a 'women's public policy support structure', including provincial and local women's bureaus.[22] Secondly, equality legislation has been introduced, such as the Equal Pay Act that was passed in 1975 and the Law on Equal Treatment of Men and Women in the Labour Market that passed through parliament in 1980. Since then, all kinds of social security regulations and fiscal laws have been made less family-oriented and more individualised. A Dual Wage Earners Act was passed in 1984 and in 1985 married women were included in old-age pensions.[23] Dutch laws and regulations have also been changed as the result of several directives of the European Community: women have their own right to unemployment benefits, pensions and

---

[20] Emancipation Policy Program, 1985, quoted in Saskia Keuzenkamp, 'You Cannot Make an Omelette Without Breaking Eggs. Emancipation Policy in the Netherlands', paper presented at the Fourth International Interdisciplinary Congress on Women, New York, 1990, p. 2.

[21] J. Swiebel and J. Outshoorn, 1991, p. 17.

[22] J. Outshoorn, 'Furthering the "Cause": Femocrat Startegies in National Government', in J. Bussemaker and R. Voet (eds.), 1998, p. 112

[23] J. Bussemaker, 1998, p. 33, see also D. Sainsbury, *Gender, Equality and Welfare States,* Cambridge, Cambridge University Press, 1996, p. 184.

Explaining the Change in Attitude

welfare and sickness benefits. In 1989 the Equal Opportunities Act prohibited any distinction between men and women in all areas concerning the labour market.

WOMEN'S ORGANISATIONS

Chapter four showed us that one of the first times that women organised as a group was to secure universal suffrage during the first decade of the 20th century. In 1894 the first organisation for female suffrage (VvVK) was founded, and many others followed. Since then there have been several issues, such as pacifism and the restriction of women's right to paid labour, that united many women. Most of these organisations, however, operated independently. Between 1920 and the 1960s there was no 'women's movement' in the Netherlands, in the sense of having a network of organisations aiming to organise women in order to advance their position in society.[24]

The emergence of two feminist groups in the late 1960s can be viewed as the start of the new women's movement. One is Man Woman Society and the other is called Wild Mina (*Dolle Mina*). It was mostly leftist-liberals in their 30s who participated in MVM, women as well as men. MVM focussed on equal rights and thereby directed its efforts towards convincing government and parliament to pass legislation guaranteeing equality. They discussed issues such as the 'double message' girls learned at school (they were educated but at the same time told to become housewives), the negative aspects of being a housewife (long working hours, dependency, little appreciation of these roles); the shortening of the work day so that both women and men could also take care of the children. MVM was very careful in pursuing its goals. They did not want to shock and estrange people, therefore their campaigns were always very 'proper'. As we have seen in the previous section, MVM often urged the government to act. It dissolved in 1988.

On the other hand Wild Mina, an offshoot of student and left-wing radical groups, had much stronger views about the oppression of women. For them doing housework was slavery, motherhood was oppression and abortion was to be legalised. Its members were partly anarchists and marxists. They used the media expertly by organising what were then shocking campaigns: women demonstrating for

---

[24] See J. Oldersma, 2002, p. 286.

legalisation of abortion showed their bare bellies with the text: 'boss of our own belly'. The conduct of these striking publicity campaigns in support of the legalisation of abortion, or the need for public toilets for women and children, proved very successful. The media provided good coverage and many women subsequently joined the group.

Oldersma (2002) describes how the issue of the political representation of women divided these early women's activists. The question was whether the movement should be dealing with numerical or with substantial representation. Should they fight to get more women in politics, regardless of their ideologies and political intentions regarding the role of women in society, or should the women's movement only support the idea of more *feminist* women in politics? During the 1971 parliamentary election campaign, MVM tried to get more women elected in parliament with a slogan 'Women vote for women'. Wild Mina, however, questioned this slogan: 'We wonder what we would gain if women should all of a sudden vote for "women" regardlessly. Are biological differences decisive after all? Are women (and men) not first and foremost human?'[25] Two other debates regarding women's political representation were important as well at that time. First there was the question whether *politics* was the right vehicle to articulate women's interests and fight for gender equality. The second schism was a matter of strategy: should one cooperate with men and with essentially male organisations such as political parties or should one fight through autonomous, women's organisations?

The debate on politics as the right place to advocate women's interests was initiated by Joke Smit, a member of the Labour Party in the council of the City of Amsterdam. She left the council after 18 months and made a famous farewell speech in which she rejected the culture of politics:

> The game of ridicule and being ridiculed has a name, it is called the political arena. In the political arena it is not a question of deciding on policies, rather it is a question of deriding the other, whenever you can. Even those who do not join in this game, consider it amusing or unavoidable. And this is sad. By doing so it is shown that politicians do not believe in their own statements, in

---

[25] I. Costera Meijer, *Het Persoonlijke wordt Politiek: Feministische Bewustwording in Nederland,* Amsterdam, Het Spinhuis, 1996, p. 144, cited in J. Oldersma, 2002, p. 292.

their own ideas. They talk about equal opportunities and protecting the weak, but they treat each other according to the law of the jungle.[26]

Other aspects of formal politics that were criticised by feminists in the 1970s were the limited scope of politics, the misuse of formalistic procedures and the strategic behaviour of politicians, instead of genuine care for the issues at stake.[27] Politics at that time was still restricted to the public sphere, to the world outside the home. Therefore it was extremely difficult for women politicians to raise issues such as child care or sexual abuse. And when they did they received patronising and offensive reactions. Procedures were used to remove issues of the agenda and to declare arguments out of order. 'Strategic behaviour is a term which is often a euphemism for a hypocritical way of acting. It means for example that when a decision has to be taken you are not voting according to your own ideas, but because you have to support your own or another party because of a "deal" that was made.'[28]

During its early years, from 1967 to 1974, the new women's movement focused on the pursuit of equal rights and on increasing public awareness of the fact that gender roles were not a consequence of 'natural inclinations'. The issue of the lack of political involvement by women was addressed in these years, but it was certainly not a focal point of the new women's movement. From 1974 onwards, activities to get more women in politics were gradually replaced by consciousness-raising groups, the first step towards developing a critique of patriarchy and power-relations between men and women.

In the mid-1970s there were many radical feminist groups that were primarily concerned with developing women's culture and campaigning against sexual violence and pornography. They started feminist publishing houses, feminist bookshops, women's centres and women's cafes. Many followers of Wild Mina were involved in these activities. In addition to these radical feminist groups, there was an autonomous socialist-feminist movement, which stood for both feminist and socialist change but sought to pursue its goals independent of male dominated political organisations, while not objecting to work with these for the right cause. They were prime movers in the struggle for the legalisation of abortion and other

---

[26] J. Smit 1988, 'Afscheid van de Gemeenteraad', in J. Smit, *Er is een land waar vrouwen willen wonen. Teksten 1967-1981*, Amsterdam, Sua, 1988.

[27] L. Janssen and M. Leyenaar, 'Growing Minority. Background and Behavior of Women in Local Politics', paper presented at the ECPR, Florence, 1980, p. 8.

[28] Ibid., p. 9.

Chapter 6

political issues. The differences between these two autonomous movements, radical feminism and socialist feminism, focused on (non-)cooperation with the left-wing political groups and men in general, and partly on lesbianism.[29]

The women's movement in the Netherlands has always been rather heterogeneous. As mentioned before, besides the feminist groups, there were also the traditional women's organisations, such as the Catholic Women's Club, the Dutch Organisation of Housewives, the Dutch Catholic Organisation of Farmers Wives, the Organisation of Academic Women and the Dutch Association of Women's Interests. Most of these long-standing women's organisations were associated with the Netherlands Women's Council, which acted as an umbrella organisation. A third category were the women's groups operating within other social movements, like women's factions in political parties and women's committees in trade unions, in churches and in universities. As in other Western European countries, many Dutch women also participated in *ad hoc* groups, like peace groups or groups directed against the use of nuclear power.

Combining forces was only possible in the 1970s and 1980s when there was a specific issue to pursue. Efforts were then made to overcome ideological divisions by setting up groups with a specific focus point. An important example in the history of the Dutch women's movement was the coalition formed to campaign in favour of the legalisation of abortion. Laws of 1886 and 1911 stated that women who had abortions, as well as the physicians who carried these out, were liable to be prosecuted. However, pregnant women could in practice have an abortion in special abortion clinics. When there were attempts to restrict this practice, the national committee We Women Demand (*Wij Vrouwen Eisen*, WVE) was formed in 1974, demanding that abortion should be removed from the criminal law and that it should be available through the National Health Service. Many different women's organisations joined WVE, autonomous and radical feminist groups as well as the women's factions of the leftist and liberal parties. The committee organised many different campaigns, for example large demonstrations in Amsterdam, sit-ins, and occupied an abortion clinic when the police threatened it with closure. They also formulated an alternative abortion law.[30]

---

[29] J. Swiebel and J. Outshoorn, 1991, p. 10.

[30] J. Outshoorn, *De Politieke Strijd Rondom de Abortuswetgeving in Nederland 1964-1984*, Den Haag, Vuga, 1986.

The Platform for Economic Independence (*Breed Platform voor Economische Onafhankelijkheid*) also reflected joint efforts to extend and intensify cooperation among political women's organisations, autonomous women's groups and women trade unionists. It was founded in 1982 when the women's faction of the Labour Party wrote to many women's organisations asking to join forces against the worsening of women's economic position during the ongoing economic recession. At the same time, the Dutch Women's Organisation (*Nederlandse Vrouwenbeweging*) – affiliated with the Communist Party – organised a meeting around this theme. The Platform for Economic Independence demanded just that – economic independence for women, a right to work and to welfare benefits, regardless of their marital or domestic status. The Platform lobbied politicians and organised study meetings and published reports on the issue. During the mid-1980s, more than 40 different women's organisations took part in the Platform, including the women's factions of most political parties and trade unions, as well as many so-called traditional women's organisations and interest groups. Participation was not formally organised and organisations could choose whether or not to participate in any given activity.[31]

Another example of an issue that brought women's groups together is the debate about the division of labour between men and women. The objective of the Association for Redistribution of Paid and Unpaid Labour (*Associatie voor de Herverdeling van Betaalde en Onbetaalde Arbeid*), founded in 1984, was a society in which there was no gender division of labour. Both men and women should be involved in paid employment and in caring tasks. One of the demands was a part-time working week of 25 hours for all. About 20 different women's organisations took part in the Association.

Both organisations, the Platform for Economic Independence and the Association for Redistribution of Paid and Unpaid Labour, challenged the traditional ideology of family wages, male breadwinners and housewives, and were important in convincing government and parliament to change relevant laws accordingly. One should be aware that, as mentioned in the previous paragraphs, all of these organisations were able to flourish, and indeed to exist, mainly because of financial support from the government.

---

[31] See also T. Ophuysen and I. Sjerps, 'Van vrouwen en de dingen die haar binden', *Katijf,* vol. 21, July 1984, pp. 19-23.

Chapter 6

During the 1980s, little doubt remained among women activists that politics, parliament and government were needed to get what one wanted. Active lobbies went on to convince decision-makers of the need for structural changes designed to allow men and women to enjoy equal opportunities. Of course there were still parts of the women's movement that rejected every involvement with politics, as became clear at a conference organised in 1982 on Feminism and Political Power. In her summery of the discussion Oldersma (2002) quotes one of the speakers as saying that radical feminists were still of the opinion that politics was irrelevant because 'in order to improve the world, one should start with oneself', while the revolutionary feminists shared this opinion because 'a revolution against patriarchs was needed'. However, many feminists present had already discovered the advantages of government subsidies and the discussion that went on was about how to use these funds, while avoiding 'encapsulation' and 'dirty hands'.[32] Acknowledgement by autonomous women's groups of the need to cooperate with politicians, supported the demand of the women's factions inside the parties for more women representatives in parliament. At the same time, as will be shown below, government institutions started to take to heart the under-representation of women in politics and public administration and commissioned surveys and other studies into the question of 'why so few'. Feminist bureaucrats kept the issue on the agenda and hired feminist academics to perform these studies.

But in general not many autonomous women's groups were much interested in the under-representation of women in formal decision-making. The traditional women's organisations viewed themselves as politically neutral and were not overly concerned with the question of a lack of political influence, while feminist groups were too busy being involved in defining a woman's world. There was one exception however – the Netherlands Association for Women's Interests, Women's Work and Equal Citizenship (*Nederlandse Vereniging voor Vrouwenbelangen, Vrouwenarbeid en Gelijk Staatsburgerschap*). Since its founding in 1894 as the Dutch Association for Women's Suffrage – it changed its name in 1930 – this organisation fought for equal political rights between men and women. In 1985, it started a campaign called 'Man/Woman: 50/50' aiming to mobilise voters to vote for women candidates and parties to nominate women to electoral bodies. Its objective was a

---

[32] J. Outshoorn, 'A Distaste of Dirty Hands: Gender and Politics in Second Wave Feminism', in T. Andreasen, A. Borchorst, D. Dahlerup, E. Lous, H. Rimmen Nielsen (eds.), *Moving On. New Perspectives on the Women's Movement*, Aarhus University Press, 1991, cited in Oldersma, 2002, pp. 297, 298.

balanced political representation by the year 2000. Since 1985, they have been a prime mover in calling attention to the under-representation of women in politics. Many different activities have been organised within the context of the campaign Man/Woman: 50/50. For each election, when the selection of candidates started they wrote letters to all political parties demanding the selection of women candidates. In the weeks immediately before the elections they set up publicity campaigns asking voters to vote for a woman candidate and, after every election, they published relevant figures and analyses. In 1992, they published ten suggestions how to get more women elected in local councils:

Ten suggestions for 35 per cent women in eligible places in 1994.

- Madam, you are wanted – political decision-making at the local level is important to women;
- Women, strengthen your candidacy by training or by engaging a mentor;
- Allies, motivate women and support them;
- Political parties, inform women about candidate selection and about the work of a councillor;
- Local party branches, decide upon target figures on women party representatives;
- Recruit women from other networks and organisations;
- Break through the 'looking for your own kind' principle;
- Select women local party leaders heading the list of candidates;
- Mark the names of the candidates with a M(an) or a W(oman);
- Vote for a woman.[33]

---

[33] A. Angerman and R. Meines, *Meer Vrouwen in de Politiek*, Stichting Burgerschapskunde, Nederlands Centrum voor Politieke Vorming, Leiden, 1993, p. 28.

Immediately after the disappointing outcome of the municipal elections of 1990, when the proportion of female councillors increased by only 3 per cent, the Netherlands Association for Women's Interests and some regional women's bureaus decided to found an Association for Women in Politics (*Vrouwen in de Politiek*, VIP) and to start a campaign: '1994: Elect Women in Politics' (*1994: Vrouwen Kiezen in de Politiek*) aimed at getting 35 per cent women into the local councils at the next election in 1994. A total of 29 organisations joined this Association, including the women's factions of five different parties, three organisations of black and migrant women, the regional women's bureaus and several training institutes. Many activities took place in the three years of its existence, from training sessions for women interested in becoming local councillors, to seminars explaining the objectives of the campaign. They also published two booklets: one about equality policy at local level and one with facts and figures about the political participation of women, together with interviews with women councillors. A theatre play was produced and posters were shown one month prior to the municipal elections with texts such as 'Will you vote for Adam or for Eve' or 'Will you vote for William or for Wilma'. Party leaders were invited and publicly questioned about their plans to increase the number of women on their lists of candidates. All of these activities helped to keep the issue on the political agenda, but the campaign did not lead to an increase in the local representation of women. In the 1994 municipal election many seats went to the local lists – parties without a national organisation and therefore without any policy obligation to select women (see chapter 5).

In general the women's movement has been an important mover in the process of empowerment of women. Although the main autonomous women's organisations were not primarily focussed on increasing the political participation of women, their demand for gender equality had a clear impact on government and parties in the sense that it made them more sensitive to the need for a balanced participation.

POLITICAL PARTIES

In the Netherlands, political parties have a monopoly on the recruitment for cabinet offices as well as the recruitment and selection of candidates for the representative bodies. Parties are the main gatekeepers of political positions. Since parties are free to organise the selection of candidates, they are ultimately responsible for the final number of women in the representative bodies.

Party Membership

Few people in the Netherlands are members of a political party. By the turn of the century, about 2.5 per cent of the electorate belonged to a party. This represents a sharp decline since the 1950s, when membership was still about 12 per cent of the population.[34] Moreover, it appears that not even 10 per cent of these party members can be considered as activists, by which we mean people who go to party meetings, discuss party matters, become a member of a local party board or participate in the selection of candidates. The conditions for becoming a member of a political party are outlined in party constitutions: people have to pay dues, be of a certain minimum age and possess Dutch citizenship or reside in the Netherlands. Some parties insist on specific conditions such as membership of a denomination (GPV), not being a member of another party (PvdA) or being of the male sex (SGP). Table 6.1 shows figures from 2000, based on estimates provided by the parties.

The proportion of female members varies in the larger parties between 24 per cent in the CDA and 36 per cent in the Labour Party. One explanation for the relatively low participation of female Christian Democrats is, according to a party report, that in most families only one person, that is the husband, subscribes.[35] The other parties vary in terms of the number of women involved in the party. Green Left estimates that about 44 per cent of its membership is female and the SP 36 per cent, while the percentages in the three smaller parties vary from 0 in the SGP to 27 per cent in the RPF.

Members can participate in the internal decision-making process of the parties. In most parties there is a central body, a national executive and regional and local branches. It appears from table 6.1 that, with the exception of the CDA and Green Left, the share of women in the executive is relatively lower than their share in membership. When we compare these figures with earlier data, it seems that the proportion of women in party executives has somewhat increased. In 1971, for example, 23 per cent of the Labour Party leadership were women with a figure of 14 per cent for the VVD.[36]

---

[34] G. Voerman, 'De ledentallen van politieke partijen, 1945-1995, in: *DNPP Jaarboek van Politieke Partijen 1995*, Groningen, DNPP, 1996, pp. 192-206.

[35] CDA, *Vrouwen en Mannen van de Partij. Een Onderzoek in het Kader van een Positief Actiebeleid voor Vrouwen in het CDA*, Den Haag, CDA uitgeverij, 1989, p. 130.

[36] M. Leyenaar, 1989, p. 134.

Chapter 6

Table 6.1: Party Membership of women, 2000.

Party	Total membership	% Women members	% Women board members
CDA	87,500	24	32
PvdA	61,614	36	27
VVD	52,000	31	27
D66	13,000	31	22
Green Left	14,000	44	47
SP	25,052	36	27
SGP	23,900	0	0
GPV	13,687	22	14
RPF	12,750	27	8

Source: M. Leyenaar, 'Vrouwen en Politiek in Nederland', in H. Daalder and H. Gosman (eds.), *Compendium voor Politiek en Samenleving,* Deventer, Kluwer, 2000, A1600-26.

What has been the role of parties in the empowerment of these women party members? Van de Velde (1994) has written an extensive study about the role of women in parties in the Netherlands. She showed how the parties' perceptions of women's political representation changed between 1919 and 1990 under the following influences:

- *Historical developments* such as the struggle for the right to vote and the new women's movement. Both of these occasions forced the parties to form an opinion on the political participation of women. Another example is the occupation by the Germans during World War II and the active role of women in the Resistance. As we have seen, especially in the religious parties, this caused some doubts as to firm ideas about the 'right' place of women;
- *External pressure* by, for example, autonomous women's organisations demanding a more active role of both parties and the government in increasing the political power of women. An increase in the political participation of

women became one of the objectives of governmental equality policy in the 1980s and was vigorously pursued (see below);

- *Internal pressure,* mainly by the women's factions of the parties, which kept the issue of the under-representation of women on the agenda of party leaders;
- *Changes in party strategies and in the party organisations.* Due to electoral considerations, there have been several occasions in the history of Dutch parties that an organisational change took place. The parties were then forced again to reconsider the role of women both inside and outside the party. Women's factions were restructured, and ideas were submitted designed to attract women voters. Increasing the number of women party members was part of the modernisation process. The CDA, for example, came to see the need for more women in its ranks, in order to get rid of its image as an old-fashioned group of middle-aged grey-haired men.[37]

The first two developments will be further discussed in the next section. Let us now go into more detail about the role of the women's factions in the 1980s and 1990s, the changes that took place in the selection processes, for example quota-setting, and the concrete actions parties took to increase the political representation of women.

Women's Factions

As already discussed in chapter 4, the representation of women in political office has always been a main issue of women's organisations within the parties. The emergence of the new women's movement also had an impact on women's factions. The women's section of the Labour Party – which since 1975 has been called the Red Women – clashed many times with the party leadership about feminist issues and the lack of participation of women both in party ranks and in representative bodies. For a while, all links between the Red Women and the Labour Party were broken off, but they were restored again in 1977. Under pressure from the Red Women, the party then debated quota-setting. Opposition to this was strong and, as a compromise, the 1977 party congress accepted *target figures* instead of quotas. Women were to occupy a minimum of 25 per cent of all the seats

---

[37] H. van de Velde, 1994, pp. 317-321.

Chapter 6

in representative and party bodies. However, there were no sanctions guaranteeing the implementation of this policy. In the end, the target figures appeared to function as a maximum, as opposed to a minimum, percentage. The 1987 party congress decided that the party should target a 50 per cent representation of women in all party offices, with an absolute minimum – in effect a quota – of 25 per cent. At that time, however, the representation of Labour women was already around 25 per cent. In 1992, this quota was increased to 35 per cent.[38]

When a single Christian party, CDA, was formed in 1980, the first draft of the new party rules included a rule that one fifth of the national executive should be women. But this suggestion did not stand up to the tough negotiations between the three parties.[39] In 1989, however, the Party Council adopted a resolution on the same issue, stating that the party needed to change its attitude towards the participation of women. It was decided that the party would recruit female members, pay attention to the political education of women and increase knowledge about affirmative action among regional and local party officials. It was also recommended that contracts be drawn up both between regions and local branches and between the national executive and regions in which targets for the percentage of women participants would be defined. These targets could vary between regions, corresponding, for example, the relative participation of women in a certain region.[40]

One party meant also a single women's faction, the CDA Women's Council (*CDA Vrouwenberaad*). The objectives of the CDA Women's Council were to stimulate the integration of women into the party, to increase the political consciousness of women and to contribute to the development of party policy.[41] The latter, in particular, has brought the women's organisation into conflict with other party bodies. Several times in the 1980s, the Women's Council voiced opinions on political issues that differed from the general point of view in the party. Generally, the Council assumed a much more radical stance on issues regarding women than the party itself. Around 1990, the CDA Women's Council included about 10 per cent of all women party members.[42]

---

[38] *Ibid.*, p. 235.
[39] A report on the development of party rules for the CDA in the archives of the CHU, 1978.
[40] Resolution accepted at the CDA Party Council, 16 December 1989.
[41] CDA annual party report, 1987, p. 57.
[42] H. van de Velde, 1994, p. 107.

One of the activities of the section Women in the VVD was to develop a database of qualified women, with the intention that this could be used by all parts of the Liberal Party when they were looking for a woman for a certain position. In practice, however, this database was rarely used. The position of Women in the VVD changed radically in 1984. Before then it was assumed that all female party members were affiliated with the women's section. From 1984 onwards, female members were required to sign up separately for the women's organisation. In 1990 the organisation had about 4000 members – approximately 12 per cent of the total number of female party members. This change in the membership rules was a reaction by the party leadership to the fact that the women's faction was increasingly expressing its own political views. Now Women in the VVD could no longer claim to speak for 'all liberal women'. The need for a separate women's organisation has always been questioned within the party, not only by male party members, but by many liberal women as well.[43] With reference to the participation of women in the party, liberal ideology in general seems to have been more of an obstacle than an encouragement. The notion that all party members already had equal opportunities to participate restrained the party from implementing special measures for the participation of women and obstructed the development of an overall view on the actual positions of men and women.

The same kind of attitude could be found in D66. They also held the opinion that affirmative action did not fit in with their progressive-liberal ideology. Consequently there was never a separate women's faction, but instead, since 1979, there has been an internal party committee responsible for emancipation of women *and* men (*Politiek Emancipatie Aktiverings Centrum*, PEAC). D66, however, had a greater 'moral' right to declare this, since they always had relatively more women than the other parties participating in their party boards and elective offices. The attraction of D66 to women can be partly explained by the time of emergence, 1966, and its appeal to young, well-educated and progressive people. D66 always favoured gender equality, but was against separatism and affirmative action.

The fact that the Communist Party (CPN) did not have a separate women's faction was because of the very strong ties with the Netherlands Women's Organisation (*Nederlandse Vrouwen Beweging*, NVB) an organisation of communist women. In the 1980s, the Communist Party went through a process of feminisation. In 1984, the party accepted a resolution that both marxism *and* feminism should be

---

[43] As is clear from letters from party members to the party magazine.

regarded as the party ideology. The Communist Party had set a 50 per cent quota for women back in 1982.⁴⁴

Gender equality and feminism also played an important role in the other left-wing parties. Almost from the foundation of the PPR in 1968, women were participating in the party executive. By 1971 gender was already a criterion for the composition of internal and representative bodies. However, implementation came only in the 1980s: in 1986, 46 per cent of the members of the national party executive were women. In the PPR, like the CPN, oppression of women was a subject of intense debate, in which the women's faction, founded in 1978, played an important role.⁴⁵

In the PSP party manifesto of 1971-1975 there was already a chapter dealing with gender equality, and women played a substantial role in the party organisation. By the mid-1970s women party members had created study groups. The women in the PSP did not want to form an official women's faction, but preferred to stay autonomous. Their influence however was quite substantial: at the party congress of 1980 it was decided that the objectives of the party should be a socialist *and* a feminist society. From that time on, the enemies were capitalism *and* patriarchism.⁴⁶ It is therefore no wonder that the Green Left, the successor of the CPN, PPR and PSP has always been very supportive of feminist issues and of the demand for a greater representation of women. Green Left has had two female parliamentary leaders and right from the start at least one-third of the MPs were women. There has been no formal women's section, but women party members and representatives form an informal network and meet periodically.

In the SP there never has been a separate women's section. The increase in seats for the party since it entered parliament in 1994 has been to the advantage of women: of the nine SP representatives in the Second Chamber in 2003, four are women.

The orthodox Calvinist parties, of which the SGP has been represented in parliament since 1922, were never much in favour of participation of women in politics. The SGP has not changed its views on this issue. For example, when a number of women wanted to become members of the SGP, the reaction of the party was to decide formally, at a party conference in 1993, that women could neither become members nor stand as candidates. In 1997 they changed their party statutes

---

⁴⁴ L. Koeneman *et al.*, 'Het Partijgebeuren: kroniek van de partijpolitieke gebeurtenissen van het jaar 1984', in *DNPP Jaarboek van Politieke Partijen 1984*, Groningen, DNPP, 1985, p. 28.

⁴⁵ H. van de Velde, 1994, pp. 271-290.

⁴⁶ *Ibid.*, pp. 241-268.

accordingly: Article 4 of the party statute states that only men over 18 years old and who endorse the SGP views can become a member of the party.[47] One woman filed an official complaint about discrimination against women with the International Court of Justice in The Hague. The Court, however, ruled in favour of the party: the freedom of the constitutional right to associate was more important for the Court than the constitutional ban on sex discrimination. This ruling was undoubtedly inspired by the unwillingness of the state to interfere in the political parties.[48]

The other two orthodox Calvinist parties, GPV and RPF, are more forthcoming towards women. They not only allow women members, but also stimulate women to become more involved in party matters by organising special seminars on gender equality. These two parties merged in 2000 into a new party called Christian Union and for the first time in the history of their parliamentary representation a woman was elected in the parliamentary party at the elections of May 2002. She was number seven on the list, but was elected by preferential votes and was entitled to the last (fourth) seat of the parliamentary party.

Selection Criteria

Since there are no laws or regulations prescribing how parties recruit their representatives, procedures differ among the parties. In all parties local, regional and national party bodies are involved and the whole process takes about a year. In the past, most parties' regional branches initiated the process of candidate selection by suggesting names of candidates. The national party board constructed an advisory list of candidates on the basis of these suggestions. Local party groups discussed this list again and an adapted list was finally decided upon by the national party congress consisting of delegates from all over the country.

This influential role of the local and regional branches was a hangover from the 1960s. As a result of the wave of democratisation in this decade, the organisational

---

[47] See www.clara-wichman.nl/proefprocessenfonds.

[48] M. Braun, 'Beginsel Vast: Staatkundig Gereformeerde Vrouwenstemmen', in *De Groene Amsterdammer*, vol. 117:46, 1993, p. 14; M. Braun, 'Staatkundig Gereformeerde Gewetensnood: Beginselvastheid door de Eeuwen Heen', in *Nemesis*, vol. 10:1, 1994, pp. 12-16; M. Braun, 'De Hoogmoed van het Mannelijk Lid: de SGP, de Nationale Constitutie en de Rechten van de Mens', in *Nemesis*, vol. 12:1, 1996, pp. 1-3; R. Grabijn-van Putten, *Ik Wil het Gewoon Vertellen: Over Vrouwenlidmaatschap van de SGP*, Boekencentrum, Zoetermeer, 1996.

structure of parties also democratised. The wishes of the rank and file had to be taken into account by including them in the selection process of MPs. Some parties, such as the Labour Party and D66, even introduced membership referendums: all members could make their preferences known by filling in postal ballots. The Labour Party abolished this procedure not long afterwards, but it has always been in use with D66.[49] In the late 1980s, parties started to feel uneasy with both their selection procedures and the outcome of these in terms of the composition of their parliamentary parties. Since then the parties have been changing the procedures under the influence of the debate on institutional reform (see chapter 9).

Parties were dissatisfied with the selection process for various reasons. It was felt that the parliamentary party consisted of too many white, highly educated males of whom the majority came from the public sector. Moreover many believed that more effort should be put into the recruitment of young candidates. It was felt that criteria such as professional experience, ties with interest groups and debating skills should be valued more highly than simply a long party career. Lastly it was argued that national party leaders too often had to 'beg' for a place on a 'regional list' for their own candidates.[50]

The pressure for greater leadership involvement not only came from inside the parties. Women's groups, both inside and outside the parties, were demanding a fairer representation in terms of gender. The national parties were also aware that the parliamentary parties were facing increasing public scrutiny given the growing dissatisfaction with politics and politicians. Accordingly, the four main parties altered their recruitment practices, providing their national party organisations with a more dominant role. With the election of 1994 coming up, the larger parties explicitly announced their aim of looking for more women and younger candidates. A long party experience and previous experience in representative bodies was replaced as a selection criterion by being young, having good communication skills, having ties with civic groups and preferably job experience in the private sector. The introduction of television in parliament also put much more emphasis on looks and performance as a debater. The fact that a lengthy party career is not

---

[49] In 2002 the Labour Party reintroduced the referendum among members enabling them to elect the party leader. The VVD too is considering a members referendum.

[50] R. Hillebrand, *The Antichambre van het Parlement*, Leiden, DSWO Press, 1992; R. Koole and M. Leyenaar, 'The Netherlands: The Predominance of Regionalism', in M. Gallagher and M. Marsh (eds.), *Candidate Selection in Comparative Perspective*, London, Sage, 1988, pp. 190-209.

seen as a necessary asset in order to become a serious candidate works also in favour of women, since in each party there are fewer women party members and women tend to be members for shorter periods than do men. Two examples of changed selection procedures can be found in the Labour Party and in D66. The Labour Party now finds its potential candidates for the parliamentary party through advertisements in the national newspapers, and about 50 per cent of all applicants are women. It seems that women are more inclined to put themselves forward when invited in such a transparent and open procedure. The reform D66 introduced in the 1994 election was that regardless of a candidate's place on the D66 list, if he or she got at least 25 per cent of the votes one needs for election (0.67 per cent of the total valid vote), this person will automatically become part of the parliamentary party. A regulation like this is favourable to the election of women candidates, because in general they get relatively more preferential votes than male candidates. Later, in 2002, this internal D66 rule was incorporated into electoral law, valid for all parties and all candidates (see next chapter).

So, changes in the selection procedures turned out to be advantageous to women. As we have seen in chapter 5, in the parliaments elected in 1994 and in 1998, about one third of the parliament were women, the average age was 46 years and 44 years in the respective parliaments, and almost half of the members were newcomers.

Affirmative Action Plans by Parties

The ideas of the new women's movement in particular found their way into the more left-wing political parties around the world. This was also true in the Netherlands where the Labour Party and the parties that would later form Green Left were first in adopting explicit policies to enlarge women's political representation.[51] But other parties followed their example. An important stimulus was financial support by the government. From the mid-1980s organisations could apply for a government grant to hire someone who would help them to advance the position of women within the organisation. With the exception of the SGP, all parties applied and hired someone for three years to set up affirmative action strategies. The GPV and RPF, who did not subscribe the government's policies on gender equality, used the money for training. The new positive action plans were based on many facts and figures about the participation of women in the party. Using these figures,

---

[51] H. van de Velde, 1994, pp. 175-196.

party executives tried to convince members of the necessity for affirmative action. Many other concrete recommendations were made. Since then, quite a few of these recommendations have been implemented. For example, the VVD and CDA created a 'Human Resource Database' of names, background characteristics and career intentions of women party members, so that selectors could not claim 'there are no women available'. Another example is the introduction of cadre training courses for women. In the three large parties, special training courses were organised for women members to enhance their chances of being selected for councils or the parliament. Most parties also provided funds for child-care support for members who wanted to participate in party activities. Furthermore, the Labour Party and Green Left introduced 'shadow council members'. Women who were still hesitant to put themselves forward as candidates for councils would assist the elected council members in order to gain experience and confidence. What did not work so well were the plans of CDA, VVD, Labour Party and Green Left to set up contracts between the national executive of the party and the local and regional party branches about the intended percentage of women participating. This was a kind of flexible quota system – agreed percentages were related to the percentage of women party members in particular local or regional branches. More generally, implementation by the local and regional branches appeared to be one of the major problems with the affirmative action plans of the parties. The party executives, stimulated by the financial aid of the government, formulated positive action plans, but the local and regional branches had to carry them out, especially with regard to candidate selection for municipal elections. Because of the relative autonomy of the party branches, there was no guarantee of implementation and therefore the policy did not fulfil expectations, especially with regard to women's representation at local level.

In 1991, the financial grant of the government to increase the participation of women in the parties ended. However, most parties continued their activities in this area and set up party committees for overseeing further implementation of their recommendations.

In general, Dutch parties have been very reluctant to introduce quotas for women. This hesitancy of the parties can also be seen in the general opinion of party members regarding quotas. In a survey of party members held in 1986, respondents were asked about the desirability of quota-setting in their party. One third of the men and more than half (54 per cent) of the women who responded were in favour of quota-setting. These gender differences appear in every party. In a survey held in 1994 among candidates for the parliamentary election in that year, it was also found that women candidates approved much more strongly of quota-setting: 73 per cent against 25 per cent of the male candidates.[52]

The left-wing parties have all flirted with quotas, but it has never been the main instrument used to guarantee the participation of women. Internal debates on quota-setting had more the effect of 'opening peoples' eyes. Selectors, especially at the local and regional levels, were reminded that they should think about the selection of women candidates and look for them actively.

To summarise, the general attitude towards the political integration of women has lately become quite positive. In the 1990s practically all parties in the Netherlands practiced some kind of affirmative action policy for women. Another important development has been a broadening of the range of characteristics that selectors look for in political leaders. Selection criteria such as a long party experience and previous experience in representative bodies have been replaced by being young, having good communication skills and ties with civic groups and preferably job experience in the private sector. The growing trend of having more women in the parliamentary parties is undoubtedly a result of this change in attitude. The fact that these days many more women have the same educational level as men, as well as similar professional experience, has also helped to redress some of the imbalance.

Men and women party members, whether candidates or MPs, nevertheless still differ in their explanations for the under-representation of women, as well as in their preferred solutions to this problem. Women more often pointed the finger at the parties, while a considerable number of men were still inclined to 'blame the victim'. Consequently women party members have always been more in favour of quota-setting as an instrument to reach a gender balance in political decision-making.

GOVERNMENT

Governments can indirectly affect the chances for women to become involved in politics by setting values, rules and procedures. In countries where there is legal protection against all types of sex discrimination, there are more women in politics than in countries where no equal opportunity laws exist.[53] Governments can be

---

[52] See M. Leyenaar and B. Niemoller, 'The Netherlands', in P. Norris (ed.), 1997, p. 135.

[53] United Nations Study, *Women in Politics and Decision-Making in the Late Twentieth Century*, Leiden/Boston, Martinus Nijhoff Publishers, 1992, p. 104.

Chapter 6

instrumental in changing peoples' attitudes, opinions and mentalities concerning the roles of women and men. Besides the provision of legal, social and political equality, other important indirect measures that have an impact on women's political participation are the improvement of access for women to education and labour markets as well as the provision of institutional arrangements for combining motherhood with paid employment. In the previous sections, we discussed the social and economic position of women in the Netherlands as well as the equality policies and the equality infrastructure. Now we turn to the concrete policies and activities the Dutch government has undertaken to directly promote the political participation of women.

One of the first times that the newly installed administrative infrastructure for equality mentioned the need for government interference in politics is in a report published by the Emancipation Committee in 1977:

> Except appointments in civil service functions, the government can nominate persons in delegations for international negotiations, in advisory bodies and in public office. Though especially the last two types of appointments are mostly made in accordance with private (non-governmental) organisations, this is nevertheless an important policy instrument.[54]

According to Oldersma (2002) the government's response was negative, because a policy to increase women's participation in politics and in public offices would not be compatible with 'democratic traditions'. The governments' point of view was that the constitutional right to freedom of organisation meant that there should be no interference with political parties, which must be free to organise the candidate selection process as they see fit. With regard to the nomination of public officers, the government's view was that *merit* should be the only criterion, not sex. It was only the nomination of women to internal committees and international delegations that met with some approval.[55] The Emancipation Committee tried again during the formation of a new cabinet in 1977. They asked the 'formateur' for a Minister for Equality Policy and for ministers who would be gender-sensitive. They wanted the new cabinet to carry many women ministers, now that enough

---

[54] Emancipatie Kommissie *Aanzet voor een Vijfjarenplan, Revisie Positie van de Vrouw, Rolverdeling Vrouw-Man*. Emacipatie kommissie, Den Haag, 17 March 1977. Handelingen Tweede Kamer, 76-77 14496 nos. 1 and 2.

[55] J. Oldersma, 2002, p. 11.

capable women were available. A high number of women cabinet ministers would be an example for many other women wanting to participate in public life.[56] Although at that time the government was reluctant to introduce concrete measures, this lobbying of the Emancipation Committee did have an impact on the numerical representation of women. In the 1977 cabinet, one woman minister and four women junior ministers were appointed, including the nomination of a Junior Minister for Equality Policy.

From the beginning, the empowerment of women has been part of governmental policy-making on women. In the first *Policy Plan on Equal Opportunities* (or Emancipation) of 1977 a separate paragraph refers to the position of women in politics. The government wants more women involved in politics, but it explicitly rejects interference with political parties: 'It would not be justified to set conditions in the subsidising of parties such as the condition to organise training courses for female party members'.[57] There is also no intention to establish a quota system, because 'this does not fit in our democratic-political system'.[58] The *Emancipation Policy Plan 1985-1990* has no very strong focus on the need to improve women's representation in politics. One concrete policy was the financial support of political parties enabling them to hire an affirmative action officer. Another intention mentioned in the *Policy Plan* was the nomination of more women in external advisory boards.[59] In the *Emancipation Policy Plan 1990-1995* an overview for each ministry is presented, dealing with policies and activities with regard to the advancement of women. Based on this overview, the *Policy Plan* concluded that there was a lack of progress in three fields, including the participation of women in political decision-making.

Government facilitated activities by political parties and women's organisations through a generous subsidy policy. It was also instrumental in increasing available knowledge on women's under-representation by organising conferences and by commissioning research projects. The fact that the government did not want to interfere directly in the organisational structure of parties did not mean it could not

---

[56] Emancipatie Kommissie, *Organisatie Emancipatiebeleid*, Nota aan de kabinetsformateur, Den Haag, 26 May 1977.

[57] *Emancipatie. Proces van Verandering en Groei,* Den Haag, 1977, p. 21.

[58] *Ibid.*, p. 21.

[59] Tweede Kamer der Staten-Generaal, *Actieprogramma Emancipatiebeleid 1987-1990*, Vergaderjaar 1987-1988, 20255, nos. 1-2, p. 9.

offer parties financial support to tackle the problem of the under-representation of women. As was already noted in the previous section, nearly all parties took up this grant and appointed someone in charge of drawing up an affirmative action programme. Another organisation that accepted the grant was the Association for Women's Interests, Women's Work and Equal Citizenship, which used the money to develop and implement its campaign Man/Woman: 50/50. The government also financed several large conferences on the subject of women and politics. The Ministry of Internal Affairs took a particular interest in the subject and in 1983 organised a conference on 'Women in Political Offices' to which the Prime Minister, the Minister of Internal Affairs and the Junior Minister of Equality Policy gave speeches on the need for more women in representative offices. The year before, the DCE, under the auspices of the (feminist) Junior Minister of Equality Policy, financed a conference under the title 'Feminism and Political Power'.

Another important government activity was the financing by ministries of research into the absence of women in politics. Already in 1983, the Ministry of Internal Affairs had commissioned a large research project explaining the limited political representation of women at local and regional level.[60] Around the same time, the Ministry of Cultural Affairs commissioned the writing of a so-called trend report on women and political power.[61] Several other large-scale commissions for research followed, including a study into the motives of female and male councillors for quitting after one term in office.[62] The outcome and results of these conferences and research projects helped to define concrete policies.

The breakthrough regarding concrete policies on women in politics and public administration happened in 1990, however, when two women ministers and one female junior minister, all from the Labour Party, turned to the Emancipation Council and formally requested an advisory report on the under-representation of women in politics and public offices. The advisory committee was asked to answer four questions:

- What obstacles are there for women who want to participate in politics?

- What can the government, political parties and other civil organisations do to remove these obstacles?

---

[60] M. Leyenaar *et al.*, 1983.

[61] M. Leyenaar and S. Saharso, *Vrouwen en politieke macht*. Den Haag, Ministerie van WVC, 1983.

[62] P. Castenmiller *et al.*, 2002.

- What kind of agreements are possible between the government and political parties in which both declare themselves in favour of increasing political participation of women?
- What concrete recommendations does the Council suggest in the sphere of research, legalisation, subsidies and information?[63]

The Emancipation Council hired an expert and in 1991 the report was published.[64] In the introduction of the advisory report, three reasons were advanced to legitimise a state policy on this issue:

- The outcome of political decision-making touches upon the lives of *all* citizens and it is therefore unjust that half of the population, women, is greatly and systematically under-represented;
- Without governmental interference, equal access to political offices will not be reached in the near future, because people in power will not give up their positions voluntarily;
- A balanced participation of women and men in political decision-making is part of the Convention on the Elimination of all forms of Discrimination Against Women (CEDAW) that the Dutch government was going to ratify.[65]

The report clearly rejected the view of women as deficient citizens: given the small number of offices, there were enough capable women available. The reason that women did not participate in politics on an equal basis with men was not the fault of women, but of the system. A strong focus was placed in the report on convincing the political parties to adapt their selection procedures in ways that promoted the access of women. On the basis of the text of the advisory report, the government presented a policy programme on 'Women in Politics and Public Administration' that was accepted by the parliament in 1992. A team of civil servants from the Ministry of Internal Affairs was appointed to take charge of the

---

[63] Emancipatieraad, *Vrouwen in Politiek en Openbaar Bestuur*, Den Haag, Emancipatieraad, 1992, p. 30.
[64] The author of this book was hired to write this advisory report.
[65] Emancipatieraad, 1992, p. 7.

implementation of these policies and, in 1996, the policy was evaluated extensively.[66] What were the relevant policies and were they implemented?

The policy programme started with *target figures* for a relative increase of women in representative bodies and an absolute increase of the number of women mayors. Three elections were due in 1994 (the parliamentary elections, the local elections and the election for the European Parliament) and two in 1995 (for the provincial council and for the Senate respectively). The government set a target of 30 per cent women representatives in each of the elected bodies at the end of 1995, 100 women mayors (in 1991 there were 51 women mayors out of a total of 637), one woman state governor (out of twelve), 15 per cent women members of existing external advisory bodies and 50 per cent women in new advisory bodies to be established after 1992. At the end of 1995, the target figures for the representative bodies were achieved, with the exception of the local councils. In 1995 there were 80 women mayors, an increase of 23 (40 per cent). In the external advisory bodies, the average was 16 per cent women, one per cent above the target of 15 per cent.

The second concrete instrument mentioned in the policy programme was the *monitoring* of women's political participation and the intention to inform the parliament yearly about the progress. The first publication of *Women in Politics and Public Office: a Progress Report* was published in 1993 and since then the Ministry of Internal Affairs has published it annually.[67] Every year this progress report is send to the parliament and discussed in the Parliamentary Committee on Internal Affairs. This yearly act of accountability certainly has helped to keep the issue on the parliamentary agenda.

A third policy was the agreement to use the *half-yearly talks* between the Minister of Internal Affairs and the leaders of the political parties for discussing the progress or lack of progress of the parties to increase women's political participation. These high-level meetings have presumably done much to raise awareness and commitment by the leaderships of the parties.

Further, it was announced in the policy plan that potential changes of the electoral system would be scrutinised for possible effects on the election of women. This was actually done in 1995 when the government was seriously considering changing the system from proportional representation with lists to a mixed sys-

---

[66] Ministerie van Binnenlandse Zaken, *Kabinetsstandpunt Vrouwen in Politiek en Openbaar Bestuur*, Kamerstuk 22 777, no. 1, 1992.

[67] Ministerie van Binnenlandse Zaken, *Vrouwen in Politiek en Openbaar Bestuur*, Voortgangsrapportages 1993-2003.

tem, as is found in Germany. Two women experts were asked to apply a Gender Impact Assessment (GIA) test of this possible change.[68] The outcome of applying the GIA to the proposal to change the electoral system was that the representation of women in parliament would stay the same or diminish under the proposed electoral system. This was one of the reasons why the government of the day put this proposal on ice.

Several policy intentions in the programme referred to the appointment of mayors. The Ministry of Internal Affairs was to prepare a study of possible *gender biases in the criteria* used in the selection process for mayors. State governors, who are responsible for the nomination of mayors, were to be requested to *nominate at least 50 per cent qualified women candidates*. Exceptions were only acceptable when it was clearly justified. Although the report on gender-favourable selection criteria was never written, the number of women mayors did increase slowly. One reason for the slowness is the ongoing process of the amalgamation of municipalities resulting in fewer available mayoral posts. In other words, competition for these positions has been getting fiercer, with many incumbents available for fewer posts, leaving little room for newcomers – women. In 2002, the target of 100 still had not been met: 91 of the then 460 mayors (20 per cent) were women.

Another important policy that was announced in the policy programme considered the *membership of external advisory boards*. The government nominates members of these boards, and usually the board itself brings forward a suitable candidate using its own network. In 1991 only 12 per cent of all members of the 90 different advisory boards were female. In the policy programme of 1992 it was

---

[68] A GIA has been applied to the policy proposal to change the current electoral system from a system of proportional representation with a single, national district to a system with five districts. The GIA report included the following steps. Step 1 was a short paragraph about the relevance of this proposal for the equal opportunities process. Step 2 was a description of the policy proposal. Step 3 involved a description of the current situation: the number of women represented in the parliament. Step 4 covered the trends: what could be expected about the representation of women if the electoral system did not change? In step 5 the policy proposal was analysed in more detail: what are the central concepts, what is the objective and how does these relate to the gender division of labour and access of men and women to political resources? Step 6 summarised the possible effects of introducing five districts instead of having one. A comparison with similar electoral systems in Europe was made as well as a hypothetical calculation of the representation of women in parliament, on the basis of the outcome of the election of 1994, assuming the new electoral system had already been in use. The last step consisted of a summary of the effects of the change on the numerical representation of women.

announced that for those external advisory bodies with less than 15 per cent women members, the nominating organisations were requested to nominate only women candidates. Only when it was established that no qualified women were available could a male candidate be nominated. Those advisory boards with between 15 and 50 per cent women members were advised to nominate more women. New committees however, should have 50 per cent women members from the start. When a new law on the advising structure was drafted in 1994, the 50 per cent 'rule' was part of it.

Since 1992, the relative percentage of women members in the advisory councils has increased gradually and in 1995 the target figure of 15 per cent was achieved. However, in 1997 when the whole advisory structure was reorganised and a completely new set of councils came in place, the legal requirement that new councils should contain 50 per cent women was not applied in every advisory council. In 2002 the average female representation was 25 per cent in the 28 advisory bodies. The highest women's representation (46 per cent) could be found in the advisory board related to the Ministry of Education, the lowest (19 per cent) in the advisory boards connected to the Ministry of Welfare and Sport.[69]

In total, the policy programme of 1992 contained 19 concrete activities for the government to carry out. The 1996 evaluation report on this policy programme not only showed progress in numerical representation, but also an increase in 'goodwill' with regard to the empowerment of women. Many other relevant players, such as political parties, civil organisations and voters had become convinced that more women should take part in political decision-making. In 1996, the Ministry of Internal Affairs, announcing further measures and new targets for the years 1996-2000, published a second policy programme.[70] Between 1996 and 2002, several activities were undertaken by the government to further the political advancement of women. The activities initiated or financed by government ministries, mainly the Ministry of Internal Affairs, included:

- In 1995, the agency Toplink was established (financed by three ministries) as a mediating organisation between individual women, advisory boards and boards of private and public organisations looking for suitable women

---

[69] Ministerie van Binnenlandse Zaken, *Vrouwen in politiek en openbaar bestuur,* Voortgangsrapportage 2002, p. 34.

[70] Ministerie van Binnenlandse Zaken, *Vrouwen in politiek en openbaar bestuur. Kabinetsstandpunt 1996,* Den Haag, 1996.

to nominate. Since its founding, many women have been placed in boards of companies and organisations. The government grant ended in 2002.

- A recruitment pool was set up for migrant and black women with an interest in entering local politics. These women were mobilised to participate and offered training.
- Experiments have been organised in several local councils to study the impact of the organisational culture on the functioning of individual council members.
- Research has been financed into the selection of women and migrant candidates to fight local elections, with a specific focus on non-traditional methods for recruiting potential candidates.[71]
- Several conferences have been organised on the issue, including public meetings with the leaders of political parties.
- Grants have been issued to women's and civic organisations for campaign activities around elections, the training of potential candidates, press activities etc.
- Research has been financed to study the reasons for leaving the local council after one period (four years) of serving, because there was reason to believe that more women than men were leaving the council.[72]
- Proposals were made to compel local governments to set up provisions for child-care facilities for council members.[73]
- A bill was submitted in 2001 concerning the replacement of women MPs who became pregnant. The common practice was that pregnant MPs either were not replaced at all or, mainly in small parliamentary groups, by the next person on the list of candidates. However, there was no legal guarantee that this replacement would withdraw after the pregnancy leave. This new

---

[71] M. Leyenaar, B. Niemoller and A. van der Kooy, *Kandidaten Gezocht. Politieke Partijen en het Streven naar Grotere Diversiteit onder Gemeenteraadsleden*, Amsterdam, IPP, 1999.

[72] P. Castenmiller *et al.*, 2002.

[73] See Ministerie van Binnenlandse Zaken, Voortgangsrapportages *Vrouwen in Politiek en Openbaar Bestuur*, 1993-2001.

bill should guarantee both the replacement *and* the return of the mother in parliament.

The Dutch government has been a prime mover in empowering women as co-agents in decision-making. Since the 1980s, governmental institutions have been intervening in the problem of the under-representation of women in politics and public administration. They have been providing funds for further research; they have subsidised political parties enabling them to define affirmative action plans; they have subsidised women' organisations in order to keep the issue on the agenda and to lobby with the parties to select more women; they have facilitated education and training for women candidates and with concrete measures and legal actions they have pressured selectors such as parties, state commissioners, advisory boards to change selection criteria in order to enhance the chances for women.

CONCLUSION

In this chapter the previously described process of the empowerment of women in the Netherlands, from pioneer to player, has been elaborated. Social, economical and political developments have been taken into account. Social forces included the decline in the importance of religion and the changing of cultural norms with regard to social roles of men and women. From the 1960s onwards, church attendance has been declining steadily and, for many religions the churches no longer determine people's way of living. At the same time, feminists, active in many different organisations, were raising doubts about female and male roles in society. They criticised women's submissive role and the lack of choices and opportunities many women have. The government has supported these changes both through equality policies and by providing child-care facilities. A network of state institutions concerned with matters of gender equality has facilitated these developments immensely.

There are also economic developments, such as periods with a shortage of employees, that helped women's empowerment. One of the big changes has been the influx of women into the labour market. The expansion of the service sector at the expense of industry helped women to get into the labour force. In the 21st century more than half of all adult women are engaged in paid employment. They also caught up completely with men in their education.

From having a confessional, patriarchal, breadwinner/home-maker mindset, the Netherlands has slowly evolved into an increasingly secular and individualised society in which emancipatory ideas have taken root and spread effectively. By the late 1970s, 13 per cent of parliamentarians were women. As a result of pressure from women's organisations combined with the adoption of positive action by parties and the government, the parliaments of the 21st century consist of more than one-third women.

The question that remains is whether this is a long-lasting development or a short-term phenomenon. The lack of progress at the local level points to the latter. In the next chapter we enter the 21st century and provide an overview of the current situation and predict the future empowerment of women.

CHAPTER 7

EMPOWERMENT OF WOMEN IN THE 21st CENTURY: LONG-LASTING DEVELOPMENT OR SHORT-TERM UPHEAVAL?

Watching party leaders campaigning for the parliamentary election of 15 May 2002, one was again inclined to conclude that only men participate in politics in the Netherlands. Not one woman took part in the many televised debates between party leaders. There was no colourful distraction, only dark grey, dark blue and black suits, light shirts and suitable, not too flashy, ties. The image of politics as a man's game was again clearly consolidated by these daily television reports.

In 2002 and 2003, four elections took place in the Netherlands, two parliamentary, one local and one election of members to the provincial councils. In this chapter we use the results of these four elections to answer the question of whether the upward trend in women's political participation was not a trend after all, but instead a short-term upheaval. Can we really speak about a change in attitudes of political parties and government in terms of a greater sense of gender equality and a greater willingness to share power?

First we analyse the four elections in more detail and then we turn again to the three players that were instrumental in the process of empowerment: women's organisations, political parties and the government. At the start of the 21st century, are there still women's groups demanding an equal share of the political pie? And what happened to the women's factions working inside the political parties? In 1995 an internal party committee in charge of affirmative action replaced the women's faction of the Labour Party (PvdA). Was this an effective move and did other parties follow this example? Further, given the general advancement of women in Dutch society, one wonders whether the government is still upholding the state institutions on equality. And what about the further implementation of the policies directed at increasing the participation of women in politics and public offices? The chapter concludes with an appraisal of the empowerment of women in the Netherlands in the near future.

THE 2002 AND 2003 ELECTIONS

Parliamentary Elections

At the beginning of the 21st century, politics in the Netherlands is in turmoil as it is in many European countries. Many citizens are turning away from the traditional parties and new parties are entering the political arena, addressing more explicitly than ever the issues of immigration and personal safety.

In the Netherlands, the 2002 parliamentary elections led to a change in government: a centre-right government replaced a centre-left government. After eight years of absence, the confessional party, CDA, was back in power again. In the run-up to the parliamentary elections of 2002 it became clear that relations between the three governing parties were tense and that the coalition was unlikely to last. The break-up of the coalition was hastened by the arrival of a new party, Liveable Netherlands (*Leefbaar Nederland*, LN), formed by independent local councillors and others as a protest against the governing parties. This new party challenged the lack of transparent decision-making, government indecisiveness, and the inability of the 'purple cabinet' to solve problems such as hospital waiting lists and growing crime rates. Furthermore, LN placed the issue of immigrants, and especially the question of their lack of integration in Dutch society, high on the political agenda. The popularity of LN really increased with the selection of a party leader. Pim Fortuyn, a former professor in sociology and columnist came forward to take up this role. His flamboyant public performances, along with his open homosexuality and direct manner in dealing with the media, made him a popular leader. However, his individualistic leadership style was also a drawback, as he was not willing to be bound by the strictures of party discipline. In February 2002, matters were brought to a head when the executive of LN dismissed Fortuyn as their leader. Fortuyn, by now convinced of his electoral attraction given his high poll ratings, founded his own party, List Pim Fortuyn (*Lijst Pim Fortuyn*, LPF) and submitted a list of candidates for the election of May 2002. Fortuyn was murdered 9 days before the parliamentary elections. The effects of all this on the election results are described by Andeweg and Irwin (2002):

> This first murder of a political figure in 330 years sent a shockwave through the country and led to an unprecedented public display of mourning. Amidst accusations that, by 'demonising' Fortuyn, the Left and the media had created a climate of opinion that made the assassination possible, the elections went ahead as scheduled on 15 May. Exit polls showed that the murder changed the preference of 12 per cent of voters. Some voters used the ballot box to send a

message of condolence, but others, apparently fearful that polarisation would destabilise the country, produced a last-minute swing towards the Christian Democrats.[1]

As predicted by the polls, the coalition parties were severely beaten in the elections. The PvdA went from 26 per cent to 15 per cent (23 seats) the VVD from 25 to 16 per cent (24 seats) and D66 from 9 to 5 per cent (6 seats). Voter support shifted to the opposition CDA and the new LPF. The CDA became the largest party with 29 per cent (43 seats). LPF received 17 per cent of the total vote and won 26 seats in parliament, the first time in history that a new party had gained such a high level of support.

The arrival of LPF on the stage shook the Dutch party system. Its policies appealed to a significant section of the public, harbouring a growing sense of powerlessness and a loss of confidence in the government. The violent death of its leader served to reinforce its message as a populist party, appealing to a dissatisfaction among voters that was expressed at the general election. Politics had become too professional and politicians too alienated from citizens. When interviewed by the media, neither government ministers nor party leaders seemed to give straight answers, nor were they able to admit to failures. The straightforward way of communicating used by Fortuyn, evident in the many televised debates during the campaign, was a welcome change from the somewhat arrogant attitude of the 'old' male political leaders.

No women were present during these debates, since the campaign revolved around those ranked number one on the lists of candidates from each party and in no party had a woman reached that position. However, when one takes a closer look at the different lists of candidates for these parliamentary elections, one finds the names of women candidates in second place. With the exception of the new party, List Pim Fortuyn, and the small religious parties all other political parties placed a woman candidate second. The outgoing governing parties, PvdA, the VVD and D66, nominated their women ministers, while the opposition parties selected their best-known women parliamentarians for these slots. This, of course, was a clear signal of the changed climate with regard to the integration of women in party politics. Party leaderships were making a statement to female members and voters by placing prominent women right behind the number one on their lists.

---

[1] R. Andeweg and G. Irwin, 2002, p. 99.

Table 7.1: Representation of women in the 2002 parliament, by party (grouped from left to right).

	SP	GL	PvdA	D66	CDA	VVD	LN	LPF	CU	SGP	Tot.
No. seats	9	10	23	7	43	24	2	26	4	2	150
% Women	44	60	48	43	39	25	0	11	25	0	35

Further down the lists, more women candidates were present, the centre-left parties leading with 40-45 per cent women candidates and the Christian Democratic and conservative parties following with 25-35 per cent. Table 7.1 shows the percentages women MPs after the election of 2002, grouped by party.

So, although the absence of women politicians on television during the campaign consolidated the image of politics as a masculine monopoly, the electoral system ensured that, when the chips were down, women entered parliament in relatively large numbers. A gender balance was almost achieved in the left-wing parties, while in the parliamentary party of the CDA more than one third were women. Of the established and larger parties, only the VVD stayed somewhat behind with 25 per cent. The Christian Union achieved a similar percentage as a result of preferential votes for the first woman candidate on the list, in the number seven slot. She collected enough preferential votes for direct election in the parliamentary party. The new parties, LPF and LN, however, bucked this trend, with only three and zero women respectively. Given the large number of seats won by LPF (26), the result was that the overall percentage of women in parliament went down from 38 per cent in 1998 to 35 per cent in 2002. The absence of women LPF candidates can be explained by the fact that the candidate list was drawn up in a hurry and that the selection of candidates was done by one man only (Fortuyn), who used his own (male) network, rather than by a well-oiled party organisation. Besides using his own network, Fortuyn also selected people who got in touch with him requesting to be put on the candidate list. This too worked to the disadvantage of women candidates, since women do not put themselves forward so easily as men do. Further it seems that women were less eager than men to believe in Fortuyn's parliamentary adventure. According to the newspapers, he did try to

Table 7.2: Representation of women in the 2003 parliament, grouped by party.

	SP	GL	PvdA	D66	CDA	VVD	LPF	CU	SGP	Tot.
No. seats	9	8	42	6	44	28	8	3	2	150
% Women	44	62	48	33	32	29	12	33	0	37

solicit some well-known women for his list, but did not succeed in convincing them to stand for election.

The coalition government formed after the 2002 elections consisted of the CDA, VVD and LPF. Of the 14 ministers, only one (i.e. 7 per cent), the Minister of Education, was a woman and four women were among the 14 junior ministers (28 per cent). The Christian Democratic prime minister clearly did not argue very strongly for more women ministers. After eight years in opposition, there were many male candidates waiting impatiently for a cabinet post, and the pressure from the women's faction was not strong enough to resist this. In the VVD, some prominent and well-known party women did criticise the absence of women VVD ministers in public, putting forward the names of many capable women, but without success. In the LPF, there were simply no women to complain. In contrast to the situation in the left-wing parties, the leadership of the VVD and LPF did not fear that they would lose women voters and party members should they overlook women when forming the cabinet.

The coalition government formed after the 2002 elections lasted only 87 days. Internal fights, especially among the politically inexperienced LPF ministers, caused the fall of the cabinet in October 2002. Another reason to dissolve the cabinet, at least for the VVD and CDA, was the low rating of the LPF party in the opinion polls, leading to the expectation that the LPF would lose a large share of its votes if new elections were to take place.

In the elections of January 2003 the LPF lost 18 of their 26 seats and the traditional parties again took the centre of the political stage. Although 20 parties participated in the elections, no new party succeeded in winning seats. Table 7.2 shows the distribution of seats for each party and the percentage women MPs.

Empowerment of Women in the 21st Century

Compared with the previous election, the CDA, LPF and D66 had relatively fewer women elected to the parliamentary party. But the overall percentage of women increased again, largely as a result of the near doubling of seats won by the PvdA, from 23 to 42, a party with a relative large share of women candidates, combined with the losses of the LPF (from 26 to 8), a party with a low share of women.

The analysis of the number of votes each individual candidate received in these elections shows the electoral attractiveness of women candidates to the voters. As explained in chapter 4, the electoral system allows for the casting of preferential votes. In the election of 2003, 80 per cent of the electorate voted for the party leader, the first person on the list of candidates. 20 per cent voted for another candidate and these we call preferential votes. A candidate who receives 25 per cent of the total number of votes necessary for a seat is directly elected, regardless of his or her place on the list of candidates. A list of all candidates who received preferential votes is provided in table 7.3. Table 7.3 does not include the names of the persons who head the lists.

Many more female than male candidates received preferential votes, especially considering the fact some of them were placed low on the lists of candidates. Two candidates were elected whose place on the list would not have made them eligible: for the second time Mrs. Huizinga from the Christian Union, who was placed as number four on the list while the party only collected three seats, and Mr. Nawijn, a former LPF minister.

Even if preferential voting has little impact on the final composition of the parliament, because those who receive these votes already are placed on eligible slots, it does strengthen the candidate's position within the parliamentary party. The number of preferential votes is a kind of power-base for representatives, for example in the internal negotiations on the division of the portfolio among the MPs of the same party.

With regard to the composition of the 2003 government, the lobby by women's organisations to appoint more women into the cabinet had a clear impact. Emulating the list of names of VVD women put forward by prominent VVD politicians, several autonomous women's organisations submitted lists of potential women candidate ministers; these lists were published in a widely read monthly feminist magazine and reported in the newspapers.

When the coalition was finally formed after 4 months of negotiations, there were five women ministers out of 16 (31 per cent) and five women junior ministers

Chapter 7

Table 7.3: Women and male candidates (not the first persons on the lists) who were directly elected by preferential votes in the parliamentary election, 2003.

Women candidates	No. of votes* women	No. of votes men	Male candidates
J. van Nieuwenhoven, PvdA	217,715		
E. Terpstra, VVD	184,828		
M. van der Hoeven, CDA	128,433		
A. Kant, SP	83,651		
		68,526	C. Eurlings, CDA
N. Albayrak, PvdA	66,644		
M. Schultz, VVD	59,437		
L. van der Laan, D66	58,588		
		45,538	J. Remkes, VVD
		38,934	H. Kamp, VVD
A. Hirsi Ali, VVD	30,785		
		25,854	B. Dittrich, D66
M. Vos, Green Left	24,988		
		22,732	F. de Grave, VVD
		21,209	H. Nawijn, LPF
T. Huizinga, CU	19,560		
		18,268	J. Atsma, CDA
A. Schreijer-Perik, CDA	16,862		

* Votes needed for a seat: 64,363. Once a party has enough votes for a seat, then the number of votes needed for direct election in the parliamentary party regardless of the place on the list is 16,091.

out of 10 (50 per cent). This time both the CDA and the VVD tried hard to find suitable women candidate ministers.

Local and Provincial Elections

Women have yet not succeeded in gaining more political power at local and regional level. Table 7.4 reports results of the local elections of 2002. Comparing tables 7.2 and 7.4 it is clear that each party delegates a smaller share of women to local councils than to parliament. The use of shorter lists with fewer candidates being elected, combined with the fact that women candidates find themselves at lower slots on these lists, causes the relatively low participation of women. In chapter 5, several reasons were provided for the lower level of representation by women in the local councils, among which was the rise of local independent parties, who nominate fewer women candidates than local branches of the national parties. In the local elections of 2002 these so-called local lists received 26 per cent of the popular vote and only one fifth of their delegates were women.

The popularity of local lists can be explained by the same phenomenon that caused the huge electoral success of List Pim Fortuyn. Many people turned their backs on the traditional political parties and were disenchanted with the traditional way of communication practiced by politicians. Local people are founding their own parties, focussing on local issues and many local citizens prefer these parties to the well-known national parties. And, as mentioned before, local lists tend to nominate fewer women to the councils than the local branches of national parties.

The overall percentage of women councillors hardly increased in 2002. Since most of the aldermen still come from the council, a low percentage of women councilors results in a even lower percentage of women aldermen since they are often recruited from the top of the lists. Only 16 per cent of the aldermen are women, a decrease of two per cent compared to 1998.

The 2003 elections for the provincial councils generated lower percentages of women representatives. Compared to the previous elections in 1999 the percentage of women provincial councillors actually decreased, from 31 to 28.

In contrast to the local elections, this decrease cannot be laid at the feet of a specific group of parties, such as the local independent parties. List Pim Fortuyn selected only three women to the provincial councils (18 per cent), but given their size the impact of this relatively low percentage is quite small. As in the 2003 parliamentary elections, List Pim Fortuyn shed most of its former glory and won only 2 per cent of the total vote. The reluctance of the small confessional parties with a share of six per cent of the total vote to nominate women to eligible places had a far greater impact on the representation of women at the provincial level.

Chapter 7

Table 7.4: Representation of women in the 2002 elected local councils, grouped by party. In 2002 there were 9080 councillors and 1687 seats for aldermen.

	LL*	SP	GL	PvdA	D66	CDA	VVD	CU/SGP	Other⁋	Tot.
% vote	26	2	4	15	3	24	16	5	0.4	100
% women councillors	20	34	40	28	25	24	24	7	12	23
% women aldermen	13	20	25	16	34	17	18	3	0	16

* Local (independent) lists. These are parties that participate in the election of only one community.

⁋ Other parties are often combinations of lists of existing parties.

Table 7.5: Representation of women in the 2003 elected provincial councils, grouped by party. In 2003 there were 763 seats.

	SP	GL	PvdA	D66	CDA	VVD	LPF	CU/SGP	Other	Tot.
% vote	5	7	26	4	29	18	2	6	2	100
% women councillors	26	41	34	35	27	25	18	6	31	28

A total of 68 deputies, again often coming from the councils, further govern the 12 provinces. Only 13 of them (19 per cent) are women.

The four elections do not show a consistent picture. The presence of women in the decentralised elected bodies is still very low and hardly any progress has been made on this. We even find a decrease of women politicians in both governing bodies and provincial councils. The question is whether this means that the parties' attitudes towards the integration of women have become more negative. To put this to the test we have to look more closely to the *parliamentary* representation of women, since the influence on the selection by the party leadership is much more prominent. Given the results of the 2003 parliamentary election, I conclude that the decline in the relative number of women MPs in 2002 was not a sudden relapse by party leaders into the old days of thinking that 'women do not belong in politics'. What became very clear in this 2002 parliamentary election, and even more so during the government formation, is that the bottom line is all about sharing political *power*. Sharing power is more difficult than sharing education, taxes, or wages. Without an explicit message by the party leadership and supportive selection practices, equal participation of women in both representative politics and governments is unlikely. Party leaderships use their own (old boys') networks as recruitment pools, while men in general are also more inclined to put themselves forward for powerful positions. In the absence of specific support, women lose the power struggle for an eligible place on the candidate list or for a cabinet post, not least because they are not so eager to fulfil these positions. At the local and provincial level this support is clearly lacking.

THE PRIME MOVERS IN THE 21ST CENTURY

Chapter 6 described the ideas and activities of the women's movement, political parties and government that resulted in the empowerment of women. In this chapter we turn back to these prime movers and find how they are operating at the beginning of the 21st century, setting out to answer the question of whether the political advancement of women in the Netherlands is a long-lasting development or only a short-term development.

Women's Movement

Gender equality and the improvement of the social, economic and political status of women are, in 2003, still grounds for organisation. A list of relevant websites of

Chapter 7

Dutch women's organisations collected by the International Information Centre and Archives for the Women's Movement (IIAV) indicates 291 links. And on a website that lists women's organisations all over the world, 112 groups can be found in the Netherlands in 2001.[2] Many of these organisations are small and have one specific objective or support a certain group of women. Examples are Women Studies Centres, Lesbian organisations, Groups Against Violence, National Network of Women in Sports and Muslim Women. They receive government grants for a short period of time and for specific objectives.

There are a few organisations that receive *structural funds* from the government. These survived the restructuring of the financing of women's organisations in 1996. At that time several groups were forced to merge and to become more professional. From *ad hoc* groups with loose organisational structures, the organisations that remain have become more professional, with paid employees and offices equipped with modern communications technology. Lobbying is these days a well-paid profession while networking, direct mailing and high-level meetings have replaced the demonstrations and *ad hoc* mobilisation of female citizens. The main state-funded organisations are E-Quality, Opportunity in Business (OiB), the IIAV, the Women's Alliance, the Foundation against Trafficking in Women, Transact and the Clara Wichmann Institute. However, the appearance of a centre-right government in 2002 combined with large cuts in the budget, resulted in the ending of grants for three of these organisations – OiB, the Women's Alliance and the Clara Wichmann Institute. All three organisations are now trying to continue their activities with *ad hoc* grants from the government and other institutions or by consultancy work.

Opportunity in Business advises private companies about the advancement of women employees. It was launched in 1996 at a high-level meeting with political and business leaders. The then woman Minister of Economic Affairs had personally invited several CEOs from large companies to support this initiative. Their companies became paid members of OiB and in return received advice on how to increase the participation of women employees. OiB has 33 paying members and the intention is to operate independently of government funding in the near future. Between 1997 and 2002 OiB received € 50,000/year. The Women's Alliance was created in 1993 as a merger of the Platform for Economic Independence and the Association for the Redistribution of Paid and Unpaid Work (see chapter 6). This umbrella organisation houses a large number of member organisations,

---

[2] See www.euronet.nl/fullmoon/womlist.

including the women's secretariat of the Federation of Netherlands Trade Unions and rural women's organisations. Until 2002 they received an annual grant of € 250,000. The Clara Wichmann Institute is specialised in women and law and the Ministry of Justice funded them with € 450,000/year. From 1995 until 2002, Toplink was also funded yearly with € 200,000. They set up a large database with names of highly qualified women and mediated in filling vacancies in executive and advisory boards.[3]

Referring to the other, still funded, organisations, E-Quality is an expertise centre on gender and diversity, established in 1998 after a merger of four different centres of expertise. E-Quality receives around € 2 million annually. The IIAV houses the archives and library of the women's movement and provides databases with information on experts and organisations. Their grant is € 1.2 million per year. The Foundation against Trafficking in Women attends to the interests of women working as prostitutes and who suffer coercion, violence and exploitation. It receives an annual € 250,000 from the Ministry of Health. Transact is also funded by this ministry to combat sexual violence. They receive € 1.4 million per year. Further there are many organisations who apply for *ad hoc* grants to be used on gender equality events. In 2003 the Department for the Coordination of Emancipation Policy (DCE) spent around € 15 million in supporting specific activities and women's organisations.

Apart from this national support structure, there are the Provincial Emancipation Bureaus, financed by the provincial governments and local bureaus in Amsterdam, Rotterdam and The Hague. They provide services ranging from information on provincial grants to a database with names of able women to serve in boards of organisations and companies. Here too there is a tendency to professionalise and an intention to become independent from government grants in the future by merging with other organisations.

The women's movement in the 21st century continues to exist in the sense that many groups and organisations still tend to promote women's issues and specific groups of deprived women. To conduct their activities they receive *ad hoc* grants from local, provincial or national governments or from specific funds set up to support certain objectives. They operate mostly locally and are not very well known to the general public. We have seen that there is also a professional, government-

---

[3] Ministry of Social Affairs and Employment, Department for the Coordination of Emancipation Policy, *The Netherlands Five Years after Beijing*, 2001, pp. 49-52.

Chapter 7

subsidised women's movement in place, although fewer and fewer organisations can count on these subsidies. This part of the women's movement, however, tends to focus more on the economic position of women in society, rather than on their lack of political power. Unlike in other countries, where large organisations lobby consistently for a greater participation of women in politics, such as the Women's Political Association in Ireland, the Women for Parity in France and the Political Association of Women in Greece, there is no such organisation in the Netherlands. Only the relatively small Man/Woman: 50/50, part of the Netherlands Organisation for Women's Interest, is still active during each election. They publish the results on their website and try to put pressure on the political parties to nominate more women candidates to eligible places on their lists. Apart from them, lobbying for more women MPs or more women cabinet members happens on an *ad hoc* basis, as during the 2003 government formation, when three women's organisations published a list with names of potential women ministers.[4]

Political Parties

In the 21st century, the debate on political representation inside political parties has clearly shifted from involving more women to the inclusion of women *and* ethnic minorities. As was explained in the previous chapters, in the 1990s, political parties, with the exception of the small religious parties, became convinced of the public wish to increase women's political participation and, consequently, they defined active strategies for the nomination of women candidates. The ongoing decline in membership of the larger parties and the continuing negative public opinion of party politics made parties even more convinced of the need to enlarge their support base and now they have also started to more actively recruit candidates with an ethnic background. Predictions are that non-Western immigrants will be 14 per cent of the total population in the Netherlands in 2015.[5] Given the high percentages of ethnic voting (people from a certain ethnic background prefer to vote for one of their own), political parties acknowledge the need for candidates from ethnic backgrounds. In 2002, 11 MPs (7 per cent) were of an ethnic background and eight of them were women. In the local councils 2.4 per cent of all representatives were from an ethnic background.

---

[4] *Trouw*, 7 November 2002.

[5] W. Portegijs *et al.*, 2002, p. 24.

The more or less full acceptance by party leaderships of the need for gender representation in politics, together with the criticism by younger women and men of positive discrimination, has had its impact on the existence of women's factions within the parties. The PvdA was the first party to abandon its women's organisation in 1995 by replacing it with a party committee for emancipation of women and ethnic minorities and thus making this issue the responsibility of the whole organisation. They started a specific training programme (ROSA) directed at the scouting, recruiting and training of women and ethnic minority candidates. In 2000 this was replaced again by the PvdA Women's Network (*PvdA Vrouwen Netwerk*, PVN). A multi-ethnic women's network has existed within the PvdA since 1996. A network seems to be a much looser organisational structure with no statutes, rules or regulations, headed by a more or less flexible group of women party members. It also allows non-members to participate. The objectives of both PvdA networks are to increase women's participation in both the party boards and in the representative bodies and to press for women's issues and women's perspectives in all policies.

The women's faction of the VVD followed in the footsteps of the PvdA. In 2002 the Organisation of Women in the VVD ceased to exist and a new Liberal Women's Network (*Liberaal Vrouwen Netwerk, LVN*) was established. In principle all 17,000 women members of the VVD belong to the network. The idea is to involve not only party members but also women from outside the party, and to create one large network of liberal women. The main objective is equal opportunities for men and women, as well as to increase the number of women in leadership positions in order to disseminate liberal thought. The LVN is more embedded in the VVD than the PVN in the PvdA. One member of the national leadership is responsible and acts as the chairperson of the Steering Committee of the LVN. The Steering Committee is advised by a national LVN committee with representatives of the provincial party boards. The reason to establish the Liberal Women's Network and dissolve the women's faction was to be 'more modern, more adequate, more efficient' and to shift the responsibility from women members to the party leadership as a whole, integrating the fight for equal opportunities in both the party organisation and party policies. Apart from the Steering Committee and the national LVN committee, thematic groups have been established, each consisting of three to six members. Each thematic group researches and discusses a certain topic and advises the two committees on the appropriate course of action.

Green Left started its Feminist Network (Femnet) in 1997. Femnet is not a critical lobby group, but 'an open network where Green Left members and supporters interested in gender issues can meet to discuss these issues'.[6] Femnet can also be viewed as a database of feminist experts to which party leadership or selection committees can turn in search of a woman candidate. In 2003, around 250 men and women were part of Femnet. There is a small coordinating group in charge of communication with its members and with the party organisation. Once a year there is a meeting of all Femnet members. Since 1997 they have organised training courses for women Green Left local councillors, workshops on employment and care, while Femnet has also commented on several government policies on women.

D66 set up a national committee in 1996 called 'Women/Men Rights Committee' (*V/M Rechten Commissie*) of 45 D66 members dealing with equal treatment and equal rights of women and men. The Committee focuses primarily on the party organisation. They advise the national executive, the parliamentary party and other internal party branches on these matters. The objectives are to promote equal treatment of women and men, to promote a balanced participation of women and men in politics and to promote the debate on these objectives within the party organisation. The Committee meets seven times a year and subgroups, formed around certain issues, prepare policy documents.

So far the women's faction of the CDA has not changed its organisational structure. They are still organised according to the party structure with representatives at national, regional and local level and a seat is reserved for them on the national executive. In 2003, the membership was around 4000. Although a greater representation of women is the focal point of the women's faction, so far they have not been very forceful or capable of convincing party leadership to nominate an equal share of women. The fact that the CDA Prime Minister Balkenende appointed only one woman minister to his government in 2002 has been interpreted, among other things, as a clear indication of lack of influence by the women's faction.

Despite the fact that the Socialist Party never had a separate structure for discussing gender issues (see chapter 6), it is an attractive party for women. In 2003, 40 per cent of all SP members were women and it is one of the few parties with a growing membership. The fact that the SP has several prominent women in the parliamentary party probably had an impact. In the 2003 parliament, four women and five men represented the SP.

The women's sections of the political parties have clearly changed in character. As the digital leaflet of Femnet states explicitly, women's sections are no longer supposed to fight party leadership. Gender issues, as well as the demand for a

---

[6] Green Left, digital leaflet on Femnet.

greater participation of women both in and outside the party, should be fully integrated in party policies and organisations. The concept of a separate women's organisation where women party members plot against the party does not fit the political style of the 21st century. Participation of women and women's issues are to be the responsibility of the *whole* party, not solely of women. Explicit affirmative action policies, such as quotas, also do not belong to this new approach. This does not mean that gender is not an important criterion in the selection procedures, but the parties' wish is that the nomination of women happens 'automatically', without the need for extra measures.

The sharp contrasts may have disappeared, but women party members still exercise external pressure, for example on the government. What is still in place is the Political Women's Conference (*Politiek Vrouwen Overleg,* PVO), consisting of women delegates from the national executives from PvdA, CDA, VVD, D66 and Green Left interested in gender matters. There are no funds and the chair rotates among the parties. The level of activity depends on the dedication of the chairing party, but in general activities involve discussing women's interests with women ministers, setting up meetings with women's organisations around elections, coordinating the input on gender matters to the party platforms, organising expert meetings and lobbying government *formateurs.* An example is the writing of a joint letter to the Minister of Internal Affairs demanding action against the religious party the SGP for not allowing women to become members of the party (see also chapter 6).

Government

The third 'prime mover' in the process of empowerment of women is the state. Chapter 6 showed the active role of various cabinets, especially from the Ministry of Internal Affairs, in influencing parties' attitudes towards the necessary integration of women in politics. As is the case with the political parties, the point of view of the government towards women's empowerment, and consequently its policies, has evolved. In 2000, still under the auspices of a centre-left coalition cabinet and a Social Democrat prime minister, a short and medium-term *Multi-Year Plan on Emancipation Policy* was presented.[7] This policy plan also forms the basis for the

---

[7] Ministry of Social Affairs and Employment, Department for the Coordination of Emancipation Policy, *Multi-Year Plan on Emancipation Policy. Short and Medium Term,* 2000.

policies and concrete activities of the two centre-right governments that came into power in 2002 and 2003.[8]

As stated in the introduction of the *Multi-Year Plan on Emancipation Policy*, the starting point is different from that of the 1980s and 1990s.

> What once were controversial issues have gradually become a matter of course. During the past 15 years, women have joined the labour market in large numbers, while men are spending more time on children and housekeeping. Women are progressing to more senior positions, albeit very slowly. Domestic and sexual violence has become recognised as a problem. Emancipation policy focuses on improving the quality of society. A society, free of discrimination and violence, in which gender is a logical part of policy, and in which conditions are created for the freedom of choice and flexibility of individual citizens as a result of changing requirements regarding living patterns and life cycle.[9]

In this quote, both the policy focus and the policy approach become visible. Important issues in the 21st century are the combination of work and care for men and women, human rights, including the promotion of equal rights, combating violence against women and a more equal distribution of power. Apart from these issues, the policy programme discusses the role of information technology in the emancipation process.

The chosen approach is a 'two-track policy'. On the one hand there is a need for policy 'that promotes change, places new issues on the political agenda, proposes new instruments and creates strategies with social partners on the basis of an overall policy'. On the other hand there is a policy 'that anchors emancipation objectives in all areas of regular policy'.[10] The latter is referred to as the strategy of gender mainstreaming and it is clear that this approach has permeated the strategies of both government and political parties in relation to women's empowerment. We return to the concept of gender mainstreaming at the end of this chapter.

Combining Work and Care

Government policy is now to improve labour participation in general and that of women in particular. As the policy programme *Multi-year Plan on Emancipation*

---

[8] Ministry of Social Affairs and Employment, *Beleidsbrieven 2002* and *2003*.

[9] *Ibid.*, p. 5

[10] *Ibid.*, pp. 11, 12.

Policy (2000) points out: 'Higher labour market participation not only increases women's economic independence, but also the support base for social security provisions'.[11] The aim of the government is to make provisions that allow for a combination of work and care, shared by members of a household. In 2001, 53 per cent of all women between 15 and 64 had a job outside the home for more than 12 hours a week, compared to 39 per cent in 1990. However, compared to the 77 per cent of all men in this age category, the labour market participation of women is still low. As pointed out in chapter 6, another gender difference is the number of hours that men and women are employed. Table 7.6 shows the relevant percentages, grouped by educational level.

Many more men than women work full-time. The level of education for women is decisive in whether they continue with a paid job after having babies: only seven per cent of university-educated women work less than 20 hours a week, while the percentage is 26 for women who only finished primary school. Of the latter group only 26 per cent have a paid job of more than 12 hours a week, while the proportion for women with a university degree is 88 per cent (not in the table).[12]

Government policy directed to improve women's participation in the labour market has always been somewhat contradictory.[13] On the one hand there are the policies to encourage women to (re)enter the labour market or to work more hours, while on the other hand government stresses the need for care by the family and community, because the cost of professional care is so high. This message, combined with the wish of many individual women to bring up their children at home, has led to there being many part-time women employees. Another consequence is the postponement by women of the age at which they start to have children. The average age of doing this is now 29 and there is a growing number of women who decide not to have children at all.[14]

In general in the 21st century, a model of one-and-a-half breadwinners has replaced the model of a male breadwinner living with a housewife who takes care of the children. Men work full-time and most women continue their paid employment after having children, but do this part-time.

---

[11] *Ibid.*, p. 17.

[12] W. Portegijs *et al.*, 2002, p. 74.

[13] T. Knijn, 'Participation through Care? The Case of the Dutch Housewife', in J. Bussemaker and R. Voet (eds.), 1998, p. 74.

[14] W. Portegijs *et al.*, 2002, pp. 23, 24.

Table 7.6: Percentage of employed men and women, number of hours they work and educational level, 2001.

| | Women | | | Men | | |
	12-19 hours	20-34 hours	>34 hours	12-19 hours	20-34 hours	>34 hours
Total (age 15-64)	18	45	37	2	10	88
Basic education	26	43	31	3	11	86
University education	7	42	51	1	13	86

Sociaal en Cultureel Planbureau and Centraal Bureau voor de Statistiek, *Emancipatiemonitor*, 2002, p. 74.

Another interesting development is the replacement of 'motherhood ideology' with 'parenthood ideology'. Now that more women opt to continue working after the first child is born, they also want their young husbands to get involved in some of the caring tasks. And more and more (young) men are now demanding to be able to work part-time so that they can share in the giving of care. A committee advising the government about future developments on paid and unpaid employment recommended opting for the 'combination scenario'. Knijn (1998) describes the content of the combination scenario:

> Its ideal is a working week of 29-32 hours for both parents of young children. It aims to reach this redistribution of paid and unpaid work by changes in the fiscal and social insurance system, by extending public care provisions and by giving employees a right to part-time and flexible working weeks'.[15]

---

[15] T. Knijn, 'Participation through Care? The Case of the Dutch Housewife', in J. Bussemaker and R. Voet (eds.), 1998, p. 76.

The government followed up on this recommendation and since then several policies have been implemented. The Working Hours Act has been passed which provides that employers are required to take account of employees' personal circumstances in policy on working and rest periods, as has the Working Times Act. The latter allows workers to coordinate work and care on a structural basis, by providing the right to reduce working hours. Employers cannot refuse their employees the right to work part-time.[16] The Work and Care Act arranges for a more flexible system of leave and introduces the right to short-term paid care leave of a maximum of ten days a year.[17] What also made a difference was the Shop Hours Act of 1996, which allows shop-owners to define their own closing hours, with the restriction of a fixed number of hours a week. Food shops, for example, may now be open at night and on Sundays.

In order to make employers more receptive to the wish of employees to combine work and care, the 1998 government established a so-called Daily Routine Committee (*Commissie Dagindeling*) with a former male director of a large department store supervising it. The project invited companies and organisations to submit plans for combining wage labour and care. The committee scrutinised all these plans and many of them received funding in order to be implemented. For a period of four years, 1999-2003, € 55 million has been spent on experiments. 'The purpose of these experiments is to achieve a better match between working hours and the opening time of schools, child-care facilities, shops and other facilities ... The results of these experiments will be applied to future policy.'[18]

Another interesting policy document is the study Course of Life (*Verkenning Levensloop*), published in 2002. The central idea is that, instead of one main activity in a certain period of life, such as learning, working, taking care of the children or enjoying a pension, people should opt for combinations of these activities. One keeps on learning (life-long learning), women do not quit their jobs to take care for the children, but instead opt for a few hours less, and the same is true for the husbands. These 'lost' hours are made up for in a later stage of life, when the children have grown up or when one decides to stay on after reaching pensionable age.

In short, emancipation of men and women in the 21st century is very much focussed on the equal sharing of paid and unpaid labour between husband and

---

[16] Ministry of Social Affairs and Employment, 2000, p. 30.

[17] *Ibid.*, p. 38.

[18] Ministry of Social Affairs and Employment, 2001, p. 56.

wife, between men and women. The government is trying hard to change attitudes of Dutch men and women towards the division of labour, by introducing all kinds of facilities, as well as convincing employers of the necessity of the 'combination scenario'.

Empowerment

What about the governments' focus on the empowerment of women? Breaking through the 'glass ceiling' of management and political positions is still an item on the emancipation agenda. The government is worried about the fact that, regardless of the general advancement of women in education and professional experience, only a few women reach top positions. Many women are stuck at the middle levels. In the *Multi-Year Plan on Emancipation Policy* published in 2000, targets are set for 2010. But, as the report states clearly, such targets are not set in stone. They show the ambitions of the cabinet, but they have to be realised by others, such as political parties, social organisations, companies and non-profit organisations, local and regional authorities. The idea is that the targets make it possible to monitor developments over time and to see whether efforts have been successful or whether additional measures are needed.[19] In two different tables we show some figures on women's share of top management and decision-making positions at the beginning of the 21st century. The first table concerns high-level management positions, the boards responsible for the daily operation of the enterprises, including the CEO, and the boards of commissioners, which advise the company or organisation on the long-term policies. Being a commissioner is not a full-time job, depending on the size of the company or organisation, it takes a few hours a week/month. The second table concerns the public sector.

In general we find more women in the boards of commissioners than in the daily boards. Only very few women are involved in running the business on a day-to-day basis. In the welfare sector, however, especially in those areas where relatively more women operate such as youth care and child care, many more women take part in the running of the organisations.

Not many women are present at the highest administrative levels of the ministries, despite a ten-year policy of affirmative action. Given the scarcity of these jobs, competition for them is of course very fierce. Of the 24 members of the Council of State, two are women. The Council of State is formally presided by the Queen (the third woman), but in practice the vice-chair is in charge. Of the five

---

[19] Ministry of Social Affairs and Employment, 2000, p. 62.

Table 7.7: Women's share in decision-making positions, 2001.

	% Women on boards	% Women commissioners
Private companies (500 largest)	1.8	5.5
Chambers of Commerce (22)	11	8
Pension funds (15)	11	13
Employers organisations (5)	4	4
Trade unions (4)	42	26
National health care institutions (9)	23	20
Hospitals (16)	5	24
Youth care (7)	33	30
Child-care organisations (8)	48	37
Universities (12)	5	6

Source: W. Portegijs *et al.*, 2002, pp. 179-188.

members of the Netherlands Court of Audit, one (the chairperson) is a woman. The 25 per cent female members present in the external advisory boards is the consequence of the law on the composition of advisory boards, including a directive on gender. At the highest levels of the police, only four per cent are women and six per cent of the chairs of the Independent Administrative Bodies are women. However, women did successfully break into the world of justice: 41 per cent of all judges are women and there are 38 per cent female public prosecutors.

In the *Multi-Year Plan on Emancipation Policy* targets range from 20 per cent for the senior posts in the private sector to 50 per cent in government and parliament. The intention was to reach these targets by continuing to put pressure on parties, among others, by providing money to set up specific projects such as recruiting programmes for ethnic minorities women and young talent wishing

Table 7.8: Share of women in high-level public positions, 2001.

Position	% Women
Secretary General Ministry	8
Deputy secretary general ministry	0
Director general Ministry	9
Deputy director general ministry	7
Council of State	16
Netherlands Court of Audit	20
Members external advisory bodies	25
Chairpersons independent administrative bodies (ZBOs)	6
Judiciary	41
Public prosecutors	38
Chief of police	4

Source: W. Portegijs *et al.*, 2002, p. 190.

to participate.[20] The two governments headed by Prime Minister Balkenende (2002 and 2003) have adopted all these policy intentions including the target figures mentioned above. A greater participation of women in politics and public administration is one of the three central issues of Cabinet Balkenende II that started to govern in 2003. The other two are a greater participation of women in the labour market and to overcome the use of violence against women.

Gender Mainstreaming and Empowerment

The approach used by political parties and Dutch cabinets in the 21st century to overcoming the remaining barriers to gender equality is *gender mainstreaming*:

---

[20] *Ibid.*, p. 66.

integrating equality policy into all regular policy. In the political parties, gender issues and women's participation are now explicitly the responsibility of the whole party organisation and not solely of the women's sections. The government, too, embraces gender mainstreaming as a promising strategy. For example, from 1999 until 2002, according to the *Plan of Action on Gender Mainstreaming*, all ministries had to determine and implement at least three concrete acts of emancipation and report these to the parliament.[21]

This approach originates from the Council of Europe, which defines it as 'the (re)organisation, improvement, development and evaluation of policy processes, so that a gender equality perspective is incorporated in all policies at all levels and at all stages, by the players normally involved in policy-making'.[22] Mainstream policies and programmes have to be adjusted in a way that gives equal consideration to the values and needs of both sexes. Many policies are in theory gender-neutral, while in practice they are gender-blind. Mainstreaming means making women and women's real-world circumstances visible to policy and decision-makers. Gender mainstreaming is viewed by the Dutch government as a new phase in equality policy. It follows 'the phase in which the emphasis was on introducing formal equal rights and ensuring that women also had access to all important living spheres'.[23] Four developments make the implementation of gender mainstreaming attractive:

- a culture of equality,
- women's general advancement,
- an increasing insight that society benefits from gender diversity, and
- gender expertise.

Compared to 20 years ago there is now a culture of equality in place. We have seen in the previous chapters that the Dutch state is certainly willing to promote and implement policy initiatives aimed at achieving an equal distribution of economic,

---

[21] Ministry of Social Affairs and Employment, Department for the Coordination of Emancipation Policy, *Netherlands Interdepartmental Plan of Action and Final Report on Gender Mainstreaming*, 2002, p. 5.

[22] Council of Europe, *Gender Mainstreaming: Conceptual Framework, Methodology and Presentation of Good Practices*, Council of Europe, Strasbourg, May 1998, p. 15.

[23] Ministry of Social Affairs and Employment, 2002, p. 5.

social and political resources between men and women. A product of this culture of equality has been the establishment of various governmental institutions that are responsible for dealing with different aspects of the advancement of women. As a consequence, without under-estimating the difficult circumstances of many women – divorced women, single mothers, elderly women, who live in poverty without any prospects for change – the position of women in Dutch society has improved.

A third development is the acknowledgement of the need for so-called 'diversity': results are improved when management teams or decision-making bodies are of a mixed composition in terms of gender and ethnicity.

The fourth factor is gender expertise. In the past 20 years or so, a great deal of knowledge has been accumulated about gender roles. Most academic research, often conducted in universities within departments of women's studies, started out by studying the unfair treatment of women, with the view that women's studies should contribute directly to women's liberation. These days the focus of research is the gender concept: what are similarities and differences between men and women and what is the meaning of gender for the functioning of our society? We also find statistics are much more readily available on the position of men and women in society. It is easier to apply gender mainstreaming when facts and figures on men and women are available.

Given all these trends and developments, another approach to implementing equal opportunities policy was clearly needed, one that would conquer the shortcomings of equal opportunities policy. Gender mainstreaming is now viewed as such an approach.

One of these shortcomings of equal opportunities policy is that it has always been mainly a *women's* affair. The political will to achieve greater equality between women and men by including the gender perspective in general policies, is not a matter of routine. It is still very difficult to get *men* interested in gender matters. Both governmental institutions and women's organisations did not succeed fully in disseminating their ideas to those who do not belong to their own group. The lecture hall with 99 per cent women in the audience attending a meeting on work-life balance, child-care facilities or violence against women is a familiar sight.

Finally, the fact that feminism has far fewer supporters than it once did is also a reason to introduce gender mainstreaming. Most people are in favour of equality, but see this as something to be reached gradually and not by too much preferential treatment.

However, the application of gender mainstreaming carries a real danger. To attain equality and to reach a balance of power, special women's departments or departments of equal opportunities have presented many 'women-specific' policies. Women themselves have fought for their rights at all levels of society, inside and outside institutions and within their own organisations. The danger is that mainstreaming will be used to displace or eliminate these specific women's programmes or organisations, before there are any guarantees of an integration of women's needs and interests in general policies. We have witnessed the disappearance of women's sections in parties and the cabinet that was installed in May 2003 discarded the Secretary of State for Equal Opportunities and gave the portfolio to the Minister of Social Affairs instead. This Minister announced in October 2003 his wish to do away with the portfolio of Equal Opportunities or Emancipation. In future cabinets there should be no room anymore for a Junior Minister or Minister of Equal Opportunities. The main argument is that equality between men and women should now be the sole concern of the separate ministries, without the need for specific coordination and for political responsibility. [24] To underline this intention, a Monitor Committee has been installed in 2004 whose task is to evaluate the performances of the separate ministries with regard to equal opportunities.

CONCLUSION

By the beginning of the 21st century, women had definitely become a force to be reckoned with in Dutch politics. Albeit at a very slow pace, 'pioneers' and the 'tokens' had been replaced by 'defenders of women's interests' and 'players'. Since 1977, the number of women involved in political decision-making has been increasing, reaching 37 per cent women MPs after the parliamentary elections of 2003. The sudden decrease of women's parliamentary representation after the 2002 parliamentary election to 35 per cent does not call this conclusion into question, since it can be attributed to one new, populist, party that gained 17 per cent of the seats and sent only three women (11 per cent) to parliament. The parties on the left nominated around 50 per cent women candidates to eligible places on their lists, while CDA and VVD nominated around one-third women candidates. And for the first time in history a woman standing for a small orthodox religious party was elected, not because she was placed high on the candidate list, but because of preferential votes. However, the outcome of the local elections of 2002 and regional elections in 2003 in terms of the representation of women shows us the

---

[24] See the speech by Minister A. de Geus of Social Affairs, www.emancipatieweb.nl.

Chapter 7

importance of the 'goodwill' of party leaderships. Without an explicit plan and associated selection procedures, a balanced participation of women in the representative bodies is clearly difficult to achieve. Without these extra measures women still tend to lose fights over the allocation of power or even decide not to fight at all.

Today's women MPs differ from those elected in the previous century. They are much more diverse in background, while being married or having young children is no longer an obstacle to selection by the parties. In contrast to the situation in the previous century, there are no clear-cut women's issues to lobby for jointly, such as the ban on employment for married women or legalisation of abortion or the expansion of public child-care facilities. Women MPs can no longer be labelled as feminists, mothers or housewives according to the interests they stand for in parliament. In the 1980s and 1990s, when women came to be a substantial group they changed the content of the political agenda. Issues as child care, sexual violence, combining paid and unpaid work are fully fledged political issues these days. In the 21st century, gender differences in parliamentary behaviour are slowly disappearing. Male MPs are also dealing with so-called women's issues. Compared to the situation 10 or 20 years ago, the women who now enter politics, especially at the national level, make a conscious decision to do so. They are welcomed and sought-after, often by using new instruments of recruitment and new criteria for selection. We learned that the PvdA, for example, finds its potential candidates for the parliamentary party through advertisements in national newspapers. In the two parliamentary elections in 2002 and 2003 about 50 per cent of all applicants to these advertisements were women. Women are more inclined to put themselves forward when invited in such a transparent and open procedure. The fact that a lengthy party career is not seen as a necessary asset in order to become a serious candidate works in favour of women.

From the description of the empowerment of women in the Netherlands it becomes clear that three factors have been instrumental: women's organisations, political parties and the government. They used many different strategies in order to increase the number of women in representative bodies. The strategies ranged from raising awareness among citizens to 'wild' demonstrations, from quota-setting or new selection criteria within parties to financial pressure on party leaderships from the Minister of Internal Affairs.

The roles of these three types of player have changed. The women's movement has taken on a new appearance: from being a participatory movement defining women's strengths, it has become an institutionalised and professional network of organisations working on gender equality. The government now structurally finances only a few organisations. The national machinery is still in place, but the number of institutions has declined. There is no longer an external advisory committee on gender issues and the Junior Ministry for Emancipation has been abolished. The core administrative unit, DCE, still exists, but its coordinating task is under attack by the Minister of Social Affairs who has Equality in his portfolio, using the argument that gender mainstreaming is now the policy approach.

With regard to the focus of equality policies, a substantial part of the funds available for gender equality are spent on projects to combine paid and unpaid labour by women *and* men. Increasing the share of women in politics and public administration still has the attention of the DCE, but at a lower level of intensity. Monitoring progress by annual publication of the relevant figures is an important instrument to keep the issue of women's empowerment on the parliamentary agenda. Specific activities of the Ministry of Internal Affairs are the passing of a law on pregnancy leave for MPs and the financing of a training course for migrant women who aim to enter politics.[25]

Considering the role of the political parties, we have seen that the traditional centre and left-wing parties are willing to share power with women. In the 1990s, they adopted all kinds of policies to increase the participation of women. Now they are extending this policy of inclusiveness to groups of immigrants, taking into account the steady growth in the population and the strong ethnic voting patterns.

Two important questions remain open with regard to the future empowerment of women. The first is whether there will be enough women who are willing to play the political game. So far it is only at the local level that women are more reluctant than men to enter and continue with council work. The main reason is the burden of too much work: the combination of a job, politics and family with the number of evenings and weekends one has to spend in council or party activities. There has been no lack of women candidates for office at the national level. At this level, however, we see a reluctance of women to go for the highest-level political jobs: party leader, state governor, minister and prime minister. Given the scarcity and thus popularity of these jobs, women have to put up a fight to get these positions.

The second open question is whether the continuous decline in the membership of political parties can be reversed if the political parties broaden their support base. A related issue is the general turmoil within the party system. We have seen that the arrival of new, conservative parties on the political scene lowers the chances

---

[25] Ministerie van Binnenlandse Zaken en Koninkrijksrelaties, 2002, p. 4.

Chapter 7

for a future gender balance in both representative bodies and government. If this remain the case, then institutional guarantees, such as laws on the gender composition of lists of candidates may also become necessary in the Netherlands. In the next chapters we continue the debate on institutional arrangements for increasing women's participation in politics (chapter 8) and on the so-called 'crisis of politics' (chapter 9).

PART III:
DEBATES AND DEVELOPMENTS IN EUROPE

CHAPTER 8

PARTY QUOTAS, PARITY AND 'PANDA' LAWS

The third and last part of this book explores recent European debates and developments on the empowerment of women. This chapter explores arguments on whether a gender balance in representative bodies should be enforced by legislation, and on the contrary view that quota legislation is outdated in the 21st century and that a gender balance is better attained by convincing the main selectors in political parties. At a time when party politics is not very popular, a more representative parliament could be the answer, especially when this would result in greater interest and involvement of citizens. Thus the following chapter discusses how best to make use of the current crisis of party politics in Europe to enlarge women's political participation.

In the southern European countries – Italy, Greece, Spain, Portugal – as well as in Belgium and France, there is a strong women's lobby in favour of quota legislation. Here the concept of 'parity democracy', a 50-50 political representation of both sexes, is seen as the key objective in the struggle to get more women into political positions. In the northern countries however, the legislative approach is firmly rejected on the grounds that it takes sexual differences as fundamental. Here, we find quotas that are set voluntarily by parties themselves. These have been most effective, as we saw in the overview of the parliamentary representation of women presented in chapter 2.

The Belgian federal parliament accepted a quota law for elections in 1994, followed in 1999 by the French parliament, which passed a parity law. The legal requirement that 50 per cent of the representative bodies should consist of women put the principle of parity into practice. Portugal in 1997, Greece in 2000 and Italy in 2003 have changed their constitutions so that electoral laws can be amended to introduce gender quotas. The implication of all this, and the question of whether other European countries will follow, is the issue addressed in this chapter. First we discuss in general terms the use of quotas as a strategy for the empowerment of women. We make a distinction between voluntary quotas set by parties and quotas imposed by law. In order to understand the pros and cons of quota legislation, the

Chapter 8

concrete examples of France, Belgium, Greece, Italy and Portugal are described. The chapter closes with a consideration of whether quota legislation can be expected in other European countries, for example in the ten accession countries.

VOLUNTARY QUOTAS INTRODUCED BY PARTIES

The most effective way to enlarge women's representation in parliament is to use gender quotas as part of the procedure to select candidates. The use of quotas has always been viewed as an important explanation why relatively many women can be found in the parliaments of the Scandinavian countries, because here parties were already setting quotas in the 1970s. Applying gender quotas means that women must constitute a certain number or percentage of the members of a body. Quotas are transitional or temporary measures, the aim of which is to overcome current imbalances that exist between men and women. Quota-setting relocates the problem of under-representation from the individual woman to those who select the candidates for representative office.

Despite its effectiveness, quota-setting is one of the most controversial of the policy instruments designed to create a gender balance in political decision-making. In general, support for quotas comes from those 'on the outside wanting in', that is women within parties. With quotas they want to guarantee the election of a number of women simultaneously, thus avoiding the presence of a token woman. Opponents of quotas claim they are discriminatory, promote token women, and undermine the ethos of equality. Women are lent a hand because of their symbolic value, not because of their talents, qualifications and experience.

We have seen in the previous chapters that in most parties, women's factions lobbied for the introduction of quotas and were often met with resistance from the party leadership. After all, selecting more women meant fewer male candidates in eligible places on party lists. Several strategies have been used to overcome this fierce resistance. The so called two-stage strategy is well-known: women in the parties first pushed for quotas within party structures and, having achieved 30-40 per cent women on the party boards, it became possible to have the party leadership adopt quotas for elective bodies. This happened in the Norwegian Labour Party in the 1970s.[1] A second strategy is to introduce quotas and at the same time

---

[1] D. Dahlerup, 'From a Small to a Large Minority: Women in Scandinavian Politics', in *Scandinavian Political Studies*, 1988, vol. 11:4, pp. 275-298.

expand the number of seats on the party board. This means that already selected male party officials do not have to give up their seats. This strategy was applied in the Social Democratic Party of Denmark, which doubled the size of internal party boards while introducing two vice-chairpersons, making it possible to implement a quota of 40 per cent.[2] A third strategy is to introduce quotas for elective offices gradually so that male incumbents can get used to the idea that after one, two or three elections they have to make room for female candidates. Dahlerup (1998) describes the experience of a local branch of the Swedish Social Democratic Party that, prior to the 1970 election, wanted women to be nominated on eligible places on the list of candidates. However, the men had long years of political experience, which was also much needed. The party decided that the first ten names on the list would continue to comprise experienced men, but men and women candidates would alternate in all other positions on the list. At the election in 1973 that followed this change, local party leaderships decided to alternate the names of men and women after number five on the list; before the 1976 election, the whole list was organised in this manner.[3]

Even after a party accepts the principle of quota-setting, there remain problems to solve. First there is the issue of sanctions. Many quota regulations do not include a sanction when quotas are not met. The only 'sanction' parties sometimes apply is the publication of the names of local or regional party bodies that have not met the quotas. Another matter is the choice of a quota (20, 25, 35, 40 or 50 per cent), which can be a matter of pragmatism or of principle. Many European political parties pragmatically chose a percentage that was equal to the percentage of their female membership. The main question in deciding on a quota of course concerns the meaning of representation: do delegates represent party members, voters, the electorate or all citizens? Without going into the philosophical discussion of the concept of political representation, it is hard to defend the view that delegates represent only party members. In the majority of European countries, party membership is very low. In the Netherlands for example only 2 per cent of the electorate carries a membership card. The problem with using the percentage of women voters for a party as a quota is that the number of votes coming from men and women can fluctuate from election to election: in some elections more women vote for a

---

[2] D. Dahlerup, 1998, p. 102.

[3] *Ibid.*, p. 104.

Chapter 8

party, in other more men are attracted to that party. The concept of parity takes the number of women citizens as a guiding principle, in which case women should fill 50 per cent of all political positions. When a party sets a quota too low, there is a danger that selectors will use the figure as a maximum instead of a minimum. As we have seen, this happened in 1985 with the Dutch Labour Party when it adopted a quota of 25 per cent. This percentage was often used as a ceiling: when 25 per cent women on the list of candidates or on the party boards was reached, this was used as an argument for not selecting any more women.[4]

The Scandinavian countries were the first to use quotas to create a gender balance in representative offices. As was mentioned in chapter 2, by 1974, the Liberal Party in Sweden had told its selectors to nominate at least 40 per cent women, and changed this in 1984 to the 'zipper' system: every second place on the list had to be taken by a woman candidate. Other Swedish parties followed their example, which accounts for the fact that we now find more than 40 per cent representation of women at all political levels. In Denmark, quotas emerged in the Socialist People's Party in 1977 and in the Social Democrat Party in 1983. During the 1980s, the number of women in the parliamentary party increased substantially. In Finland, however, no quotas are in use. Women party members demanded participation in all bodies at a level corresponding to their membership. Most parties accepted this as a kind of internal rule but did not impose it.[5] The Norwegian Labour Party introduced a quota for women of 40 per cent in 1983, which increased the proportion of women in the parliament from 33 per cent in 1981 to 42 per cent in 1985.[6]

In 2003, we find quotas in most other countries as well, especially in the Social Democratic, Socialist and Green Parties. For example, the German Socialist Party (SPD) changed its party regulations in 1988 to require that at least 40 per cent women be selected for the internal party bodies and 25 per cent for the candidate lists for parliamentary elections. In 1998 the latter quota increased to 40 per cent. The Democratic Socialist Party (PDS) and the Green Party in Germany apply a quota of 50 per cent together with the zipper system.[7] Of the newly formed parties in Italy in the 1990s many apply quotas for women: the Green Federation uses a 50

---

[4] H. van de Velde, 1994, p. 235.

[5] S. Bergman, 'Finland', in B. Hoecker (ed.), 1998, p. 101.

[6] F. Rubart, 'Der Fall der Norwegen', in B. Hoecker (ed.), 1998, p. 356.

[7] See www.db-decision.de.

per cent quota, the Communist Reformation Party a 40 per cent quota, as do the Democrats of the Left, while the Italian Democratic Socialists apply a 33.3 per cent quota and the Italian Popular Party one of 20 per cent.[8]

In table 8.1 we find some evidence for the contagion theory presented by Matland and Studlar (1996). They argue that traditional parties feel obliged to select more women if another, usually small leftist party, starts to support the representation of women, for example with quota-setting. In the beginning this will be true for parties that are ideological neighbours of the party with gender quotas, but over time more parties will follow.[9]

Setting quotas for candidate selection does not mean automatically that the same percentage of women representatives will be elected. In a list-PR system, as we have seen in chapter 3, this depends heavily on the places of women candidates on the list. There are many examples of parties reaching the quota of female candidates set by the national party leadership on the total list, but failing to get the same percentage of women into the parliamentary party or the local councils. This is because women candidates have found themselves often placed in the lower slots on party lists. The zipper system was introduced to avoid this. Depending on the size of the quota, every other second place, or every third place on the list has to be filled by a woman.

Voluntary quotas are easy for parties to implement in countries with list-PR electoral systems. It is up to the party whether to balance their list of candidates according to gender, professional status or age. The more seats a party can count on, the easier it is to take into account all these criteria when deciding upon the composition of the list. Quotas work differently in an SMP electoral system, however. Since each constituency has a single seat, it is simply not possible to introduce quotas at constituency level.

How, then, can something equivalent to a quota system be introduced under SMP electoral rules? The Labour Party in Britain confronted this problem, when it

---

[8] See www.quotaproject.org.

[9] R. Matland and D. Studlar, 'The Contagion of Women Candidates in Single-Member District and Proportional Representation Electoral Systems: Canada and Norway', in *The Journal of Politics*, vol. 58:3, 1996, pp. 707-733.

Table 8.1: Parties using quotas for the composition of the parliamentary party, 2003.

Country	Parties	Country	Parties
Austria	Green Party 50% SPÖ 40% ÖVP 33%	Italy	Green Party 50% PRC 40% PPI 20% DS 40% SDI 33%
Belgium	SP 25% PS 20% Ecolo 50% for the top 2 places	Luxembourg	Green Party 50%
Denmark	No longer any quotas	Netherlands	PvdA 40%
Finland	None	Portugal	PS 25%
France	PS 50%	Spain	PSOE 40%
Germany	SPD 40% Green Party 50% PDS 50% CDU 33%	Sweden	SAP 50% VP 50% MPG 50%
Greece	Pasok 20%	UK	None
Ireland	DL 40% Green Party 33% Labour Party 20%		

Source: www.quotaproject.org

See appendix for full name of the political parties used in this table.

adopted quotas following Labour's defeat by the Conservatives in 1992. By then it had become clear that there was a gender gap in voter support for the party.[10] It was suggested that, if women had voted Labour in the same proportions as men, the party would have won the 1992 election. This finding, reflecting as it did the connection between the party's modernisation strategy and the demands of women, stimulated the Labour leadership to introduce positive discrimination in the form of quotas. By 1992, a quota of 40 per cent women on all party decision-making units was in operation but the participation of women in parliament was still low, reaching only 14 per cent of elected Labour representatives in 1992. Nonetheless, the return of 37 women for the Labour Party in 1992 almost doubled their representation in the previous parliament. In this result lay the basis for the advancement of women in the next election. In 1993 the party's annual conference agreed that women should be candidates in half of the constituencies where MPs were retiring and in half of the most winnable seats. The device used to affect this was the 'all-woman shortlist', where constituency parties retained their jealously guarded right to select their own local candidate, but could select from woman candidates only. The Labour Party organised regional meetings to decide which constituencies were to have all-woman shortlists. When the quota was not reached, the national party was allowed to impose this on unwilling constituencies.

This strategy was successful, due in large part to the support of the party leadership. In addition, the issue had been extensively debated within various groups and ancillary party organisations, including the powerful trade union sector, the 'new left' Labour Coordinating Committee, the Labour Women's Action Committee and other internal feminist advocacy groups. However, the policy of favouring women candidates through all-woman shortlists hit resistance among the party's constituency organisations, especially among disappointed male aspirants. In January 1996, two male aspirants challenged the legality of the all-woman shortlist at an Industrial Tribunal. They argued that, as this selection procedure concerns access to employment, the all-woman shortlist was a discriminatory mechanism against men. The Tribunal upheld their case, agreeing that all-woman shortlists contravened the Sex Discrimination Act. This ruling had a negative effect on the subsequent selection of women candidates, but did not lead to a 'deselection' of the 35 women who had already won a place on the ballot. All of the women candidates chosen in this

---

[10] Parts of this text on quotas and quota legislation has been published before in M. Leyenaar, B. Niemöller, M. Laver and Y. Galligan, 1999, pp. 28-31.

Chapter 8

way prior to the ruling of the court were elected to parliament, illustrating the effectiveness of the all-woman shortlist in conjunction with the strategy of placing women in winnable seats.[11] In order to avoid similar court cases in the future, the Labour Government submitted a bill in parliament in October 2001 to exclude matters relating to the selection of candidates by political parties from the scope of the Sex Discrimination Act. 'The key objective for this Bill is to enable a political party, should it wish to do so, to adopt measures which regulate the selection of candidates for certain elections in order to reduce inequality in the numbers of men and women elected, as candidates of the party'.[12] The bill was accepted by the House of Commons.

The Labour Party in Scotland and Wales, where new parliaments were installed in 1999, used another way to enforce quotas: twinning. Two local parties each in a different constituency, select their candidates jointly with a requirement that one man and one woman be selected. Party members have two votes, one for a woman and one for a man. The man and woman with the most votes is selected. Due to this system of twinning as well as the fact that in both regions a mixed (AMS) system is used, the representation of women in the Scottish parliament in 1999 was 37 per cent; in the Welsh parliament after the election of 2003 it was 50 per cent.[13]

An alternative to the policy of twinning is 'parallelism' or 'dual mandate'. Parties select two candidates, a woman and a man. Each constituency returns two legislators, one of whom would be elected from a female list of candidates and one from a male list. The voters have two votes and would vote for both lists.[14] This of course requires a change in the national electoral law away from SMP, since two-seat constituencies have to be introduced, rather than just a change in party selection procedures.

The example of the Labour Party shows that setting quotas by parties operating in an SMP system is possible, but the consequences, women replacing men as candidates, are much more visible than when a certain percentage of a list is re-

---

[11] J. Lovenduski, 'Gross Britanien', in B. Hoecker (ed.), 1998, pp. 167-188.

[12] Explanatory notes Sex Discrimination (Election Candidates) Bill. The bill was introduced in the House of Commons on 17 October 2001 and was accepted.

[13] F. Mackay, F. Myers and A. Brown, 'Towards a New Politics? Women and the Constitutional Change in Scotland', 2003, pp. 84-98; and in the same volume P. Chaney, 'Increased Rights And Representation: Women and the Post-Devolution Equality Agenda in Wales', pp. 173-184.

[14] See www.quotaproject.org.

served for women. The resistance of male potential candidates is likely therefore to be even more forceful.

We have seen that, although controversial, in the 1980s and 1990s quite a few parties, usually Social Democratic, Socialist or Green parties, adopted gender quotas often under pressure of the women's section working within the parties. The overall pattern is that quotas have a positive effect on the selection of women candidates. Those parties that have set quotas do tend to have more women as their representatives than parties without quotas. Quotas have an eye-opening effect on the selectors, who will put more effort into their search for potential women candidates. They also encourage women aspirants to put themselves forward as candidates.

Because quotas in political parties are self-imposed and temporary measures, their very success can be a reason for their eventual abandonment. Danish left-wing parties cancelled the quota system in the mid-1990s because it was seen to have outlived its usefulness, so that quotas no longer belonged to the current *zeitgeist*. As we mentioned before, a similar trend can be seen in those countries where the overall position of women has improved. More and more women in their 20s and 30s who themselves had every opportunity to educate themselves and find an interesting job, oppose quota-setting because they do not want to be viewed as a 'protected species in danger of extinction'.[15] Often they also oppose the existence of separate organisations for women. The lack of support from (younger) women is one of the reasons why some parties have not only abolished quotas, but also discarded the women's section of the party.

However, we also see a quite different trend in those countries where the representation of women in political decision-making has hardly increased over the years. The reluctance by political parties in these countries to adopt gender quotas or to take other measures likely to contribute to an improved gender balance has resulted in increasing demands for constitutional and legislative measures guaranteeing a gender balance in political decision-making.

---

[15] In Italy a constitutional reform bill demanding possibilities for quotas was nicknamed the 'Panda' Law (see the section on Italy).

Chapter 8

QUOTA LEGISLATION

When political parties do not impose quotas and there is hardly any progress in women's political representation, governments may take up the challenge and adopt quota legislation for political offices. In some cases the constitution is amended either with explicit gender quotas for certain political functions or in such a way that makes it possible to pass national legislation such as electoral laws demanding substantial representation of women in politics. As we have seen in the British case, constitutional provisions on equality and sex discrimination form an obstacle in adopting gender quota laws. Laws favouring one sex over the other run the risk of being declared unconstitutional. This is what happened in the 1980s in France and Belgium and, ten years later, in Italy. One obvious way of dealing with this problem is to change the constitution in such a way that quota laws are acceptable to constitutional courts.

According to the Global Database of Quotas for Women in 2003, 38 countries have constitutional quotas or electoral quota laws. In five of these countries, such regulations are valid only at sub-national level. Table 8.2 lists the countries concerned and the type of quota law in force in each.

In many of these countries quota legislation was introduced in the 1990s, often after strong pressure from women's organisations. One of the reasons why male political leaders went along with quota legislation is, according to several authors, the wish to display a modern and democratic image.[16]

Imposing quotas by law is more controversial than having voluntary quotas set by the parties themselves, and a lot of negotiation over the final text is necessary before parliament is willing to pass the law. Typical arguments for and against gender quota laws can be teased out in a discussion of the French case.

---

[16] M. Hunt and M. Jones, 'Engendering the Right to Participate in Decision-Making: Electoral Quotas and Women's Leadership in Latin America', in N. Craske and M. Molyneux (eds.), *Gender and the Politics of Rights and Democracy in Latin America*, England, Palgrave, 2002, pp. 32-56; B. Marques- Pereira, *La Representation Politique des Femmes en Amerique Latine,* Brussels, L'Harmattan, 2001.

Table 8.2: Countries worldwide with quota legislation, 2003.

Country	Type of quota law	Country	Type of quota law
Argentina	CQ/EL	Korea	EL
Armenia	EL	Macedonia	EL
Belgium	EL	Mexico	EL
Bolivia	EL	Morocco	EL
Bosnia and Herzegovina	EL	Nepal	CQ/EL
Brazil	EL	Pakistan	EL
Costa Rica	EL	Panama	EL
Djibouti	EL	Paraguay	EL
Dominican Rep.	EL	Peru	EL
Equador	EL	Philippines	CQ/EL
Eritrea	CQ	Sudan	EL
France	CQ/EL	Taiwan	CQ
Guyana	CQ	Tanzania	CQ/EL
Honduras	EL	Serbia and Montenegro	EL
Indonesia	EL	Uganda	CQ/EL
Jordan	EL	Venezuela	EL
Kenya	CQ		
Quota legislation only for the sub-national level			
Bangladesh	CQ	Namibia	EL
Greece	CQ	South Africa	EL
India	CQ		

Source: www.quotaproject.org
CQ: constitutional quotas
EL: electoral quota laws

Chapter 8

FRANCE

In 1945, the first election that French women were allowed to stand, 33 women were elected to parliament; 50 years later, in 1994, the figure was about the same. It is thus no wonder that French women demanded a law guaranteeing equal access to political functions for both men and women. The demand was for *parity*: all elected bodies should be composed of an equal number of men and women. The concept of parity sprung from that of '*democratie paritaire*', introduced by the Council of Europe in 1989. This is a model of democracy in which 'women are fully integrated on an equal footing with men at all levels and in all areas of workings of a democratic society'.[17] The slogan was that there could be no true democracy without the full representation of each sex. Around 1992, several associations and groups were formed in France with the objective of bringing about a change in the constitution that would enforce parity in the representative bodies.[18] From then until the passing of the law in 1999, a fierce debate took place between intellectuals and politicians, embracing and opposing the proposal for constitutional change.

The main arguments used in this debate range from the very pragmatic to the very normative and are summarised by Allwood and Wadia in their book *Women in Politics in France, 1958-2000* (2000).[19]

Arguments in Favour of Legally Imposed Quotas

One of the most convincing arguments in favour of legally imposed quotas is the lack of progress made over more than 50 years of women's representation in politics. After women were allowed to stand for election, everybody expected that their presence would increase gradually, for example through participation in local councils in which women would gain experience and expertise. This simply did not happen: representation of women in politics remained very low, especially at national level. Since balanced representation was clearly not going to occur 'naturally', specific measures seemed necessary.

A second argument refers to women's role in society and to the gap between politicians and voters. As in other European countries, representative politics in

---

[17] K. Van Ebbenhorst-Tengbergen, 'Presentation of International Programme of Action to Promote the Participation of Women in Decision-Making', CDEG, Dublin, 1996.

[18] G. Allwood and K. Wadia, 2000, p. 193.

[19] *Ibid.*, chapters 8 and 9.

Table 8.3: Presence of women in the French parliament (per cent).

	1958	1962	1968	1974	1980	1986	1993
Assemblee nationale	2	2	2	2	5	6	6
Senate	2	2	2	3	2	3	4

Source: G. Allwood and K. Wadia, 2000, p. 28.

France has a bad reputation with citizens. There is a growing gap between citizens and the political elite, demonstrated by decreasing turnout rates and a public dissatisfaction with the political class (see also chapter 9). Bringing more women into the political elite would, according to some adherents of parity, be a way to bridge this gap, because women's closeness to daily life problems would appeal to voters.

The biggest polemic, however, concerned women's exclusion from democracy and the meaning of citizenship for women. Those in favour of parity claimed that it would improve the status of women as citizens and their opportunity to participate fully in politics. They argued that women were not citizens in the same way as men: the declaration of universal rights did not mean that these rights were universal to everyone. According to parity advocates, women's exclusion at the time of the French Revolution was justified by the creation of two separate spheres: a public sphere associated with men and a private sphere in which women were active.

> Women who were associated with nature, reproduction and the family, constituted a separate category with a specific role in democratic life. They were responsible for maintaining moral standards and this was done in the private sphere. Men who where associated with reason were responsible for making laws, and this took place in the public sphere.[20]

---

[20] *Ibid.*, p. 216.

Since then, the universalistic nature of French politics in a way included only male citizens. Parity advocates speak out for a universalism which recognises sexual differences *openly* and does not deny them: 'the collectivity, whose interests are encapsulated in representative democracy, is comprised of two genders, who should equally contribute to decision-making'.[21] For them 'naming sexual difference [is] the only way to eliminate its pertinence and to remove the discrimination produced by a false universalism which denies the possibility of inequalities by declaring that rights are equal and universal'.[22] The duality of humanity is stressed: 'together, women and men combine to define and perpetuate the species. Together, they should combine in equal numbers to organise communal life. Not in the name of the difference of one sex in relation to the other, but in the name of their dual participation in the human race'.[23]

Further, parity is advocated on the grounds that it would produce a more representative democracy. This, of course, relates to the views one holds on representation. First, the representative acts in what he or she perceives to be the best interests of the electorate, regardless of the social or cultural category voters belong to: the elected body as a whole represents the people as a whole. A second view is that the representative body should reflect the diversity of the electorate and MPs are elected by 'their own' constituents and are accountable to them. Adherents of parity belong to the group with the second view. Another argument is that parity guarantees a more balanced political agenda, including more topics of special concern to women. They refer to the 'Scandinavian experience' where women MPs placed women's issues on the parliamentary agenda. Finally, those in favour state that, once parity is accomplished in the elected bodies, this will influence other spheres of power as well, such as economics and civil society. Sharing of power between men and women will then become more acceptable in business and in large social organisations.[24]

---

[21] G. Halimi (1994), cited in G. Allwood and K. Wadia, 2000, p. 219.
[22] E. Sledziewski (1993), cited in G. Allwood and K. Wadia, 2000, p. 219.
[23] F. Gaspard and C. Servan-Schreiber (1993), cited in G. Allwood and K. Wadia, 2000, p. 219.
[24] G. Allwood and K. Wadia, 2000, chapter 9.

Arguments against Legally Imposed Quotas

Opposition to a parity law was of course fierce, since it was much more fundamental and far-reaching than asking political parties to set quotas. The opponents brought two main arguments forward. The first referred to the debate on citizenship and the universalistic character of French political institutions. Since parity distinguishes between categories of citizens, it is contrary to universalism, according to which all citizens are equal and sex, age, ethnicity, physical ability are, or should be, irrelevant to an individual's public life. From interviews with politicians and members of the legal profession Sineau (1995) concludes that the dominant view of the politicians on universality is that people are one and an undivided category: 'Equality is assured by the political irrelevance of differences and to attach political significance to membership of a certain community is dangerous to the cohesion of the nation.'[25] The concept of parity was criticised because it sees sexual difference as fundamental and seeks its legitimacy in the fact that humankind consists of two sexes, women and men, and the belief that this ought to be represented in strict terms of parity at all levels of representation.[26] Opponents of parity accused the adherents of suggesting that there are only two, a masculine and feminine, perspectives on the world, whereas there are multiple feminine and multiple masculine points of view and men can possess feminine virtues and vice versa. They also pointed to the fact that women, including women MPs, are not a homogeneous group with a single interest. They referred to the fact that interviews held in 1997 with parliamentarians showed that a majority of the French women MPs were against a parity law.

Related to this argument is the second main criticism of the concept of parity. If sex is a criterion for representation, why not other group characteristics as well? Politicians in particular voiced a fear of demands for representation from other under-represented groups, once a law on parity had passed the Assembly. The counter-argument was that women do not constitute a social category, because they are present in all social categories and that sexual difference is fundamentally

---

[25] M. Sineau, 'Parite et Principe d'Egalite: le Debat Francais', in Ephesia (ed.), *La Place des Femmes*, Paris, 1995, pp. 518-523, cited in G. Allwood and K. Wadia, p. 217.

[26] J. Outshoorn, 'Parity Democracy: A Critical Look at a "New" Strategy', paper presented at the ECPR Joint Sessions of Workshops, Leiden, 1993.

Chapter 8

different from all other categorisations because 'it is immutable and it is the only one recognised by French law and noted on the birth certificate'.[27]

A third more or less principled argument is that a parity law would interfere with the autonomous position of political parties. According to the fundamental right of freedom of organisation, political parties should be 'free' to organise the recruitment and selection of candidates as they want.[28]

From Theoretical Concept into Law of the Land[29]

Although women's representation in the French *Assemblée Nationale* increased from 1.9 to 5.4 per cent at the end of the 1970s and the percentage of women local councillors from 2.4 to 8.3 per cent, the continuing low level of women's representation was reason for the then female Minister of Women's Affairs and Family to suggest the use of gender quotas in local elections. In 1980 a bill was sent to parliament demanding that each sex should at least secure 20 per cent of all places on the lists for the municipal elections. Only three MPs voted against the bill but it still failed, because it did not reach the Senate before the end of the parliamentary session. A second attempt was made by a woman MP by way of an amendment to a government bill on municipal election reform. The amended bill was overwhelmingly accepted by the *Assemblée Nationale* (476 in favour and 4 against), but this time it fell because it was declared unconstitutional by the French Constitutional Court. In its ruling, the Court referred to Article 3 of the Constitution stating that national sovereignty belonged to the people and must be exercised by them directly or through their representatives. It may not be exercised by a section of the people (women). Further it referred to Article 6 of the Declaration of the Rights of Man and the Citizen which states that all citizens are equally eligible for all public functions, posts and appointments, according to their ability and with no distinction other than their qualities and their talents. According to the ruling it was unconstitutional to divide voters or candidates into categories. The publicity surrounding the introduction of the bill and the ruling by the Constitutional Court generated broad public support for increasing the presence of women in parliament. Women

---

[27] F. Gaspard, 'La Parite: Pourquoi Pas?', in *Pouvoirs*, vol. 82, 1997, pp. 115-125, cited in G. Allwood and K. Wadia, 2000, p. 210.

[28] Based on G. Allwood and K. Wadia, 2000, chapter 9.

[29] Based on G. Allwood and K. Wadia, 2000, chapter 8.

outside the parties founded associations for parity and increased their pressure on the parties to support a constitutional change and to implement parity in their own organisations. Political parties sensed this and became more supportive of gender quotas. The Green Party for example embraced the principle of parity for their candidate list for the European election of 1989. In the 1994 European elections, more parties submitted a list balanced according to gender, including the Communist Party (PCF), the Socialist Party (PS) and of course the Green Party.

From that time on several attempts were made in the national parliament to pass bills on parity or gender quotas, but most of these attempts came from small parties and were defeated. Representation of women in politics then became an issue in the presidential campaign of 1995. Almost all presidential candidates declared themselves in favour of a substantial increase in women's representation and of measures designed to achieve this. One suggestion by Jacques Chirac – presidential candidate and later president – was to link public financing of political parties to the number of women elected in the parliamentary parties. After the presidential election the demand for parity stayed on the agenda and, with a parliamentary election due in 1997, the Socialist Party decided in September 1996 to reserve 165 of 555 constituencies for women candidates. Due to the application of this affirmative action rule, the overall representation of women in the *Assemblée Nationale* increased from 6 to 11 per cent. Other parties followed suit in the regional elections of 1998, nominating many more women to eligible places on their lists: overall, 37 per cent of candidates on the lists were women, and the percentage of women elected rose from 13 per cent in 1992 to 26 per cent in 1998. Table 8.4 shows us that gender as a selection criterion was not used only by the leftist parties.

Table 8.4: Percentage of women candidates and elected female regional councillors, 1998.

	Green Party	Communist	Socialist	RPR	UDF	FN
Places on the lists	35	43	39	34	32	*
Elected	34	26	35	27	23	17

* Figure not mentioned by Allwood and Wadia.
Source: G. Allwood and K. Wadia, 2000, p. 197.

Chapter 8

The cantonal elections held in the same year, however, showed a completely different pattern, with only 8 per cent of those elected being women. As discussed extensively in previous chapters, the electoral system is probably the main cause for the large difference in results between elections at different levels, with the regional elections using a list-PR system and the cantonal elections using an SMP system.

At that time, however, all parties agreed in principal on the need for a larger representation of women and most parties were in favour of a law on parity. Given the many different arguments used in favour of parity, it was possible for each party to pick an argument of their liking to endorse the concept. Another reason for the willingness of parties was the popularity of the concept of parity with the general public. It was a simple and catchy demand: women constitute half of the population and should occupy half of the seats in the representative bodies. Polls taken in 1994 and in 1996 show an overwhelming support (62 and 71 per cent) in favour of the introduction of parity into the Constitution.

The parliamentary election of 1997 resulted in a socialist prime minister working together with a republican president. Lionel Jospin, true in this regard to his campaign pledges, announced a constitutional amendment on parity during his general policy statement to the National Assembly. Both men, Jospin and Chirac, sensing the electoral support for parity and the demand for action, came forward in 1998 with a bill for constitutional reform. After being scrutinised by the other cabinet ministers, the bill presented to the parliament proposed to insert the following text into Article 3 of the Constitution: 'The law determines the conditions in which the equal access of men and women to political office is organised'.[30] The *Assemblée Nationale* passed the bill with little opposition, but the Senate (a reform of the constitution needs to be passed by both institutions, with approval of three-fifths of a special Congress of both Houses meeting at Versailles) rejected the bill in January 1999. The majority of the Senate, while declaring their support for the goal of increasing the number of women in representative bodies, argued that parity would endanger universalism; that it would lead to demands for representation of other 'minority' groups and, since parity was easier to implement in a list-PR system, the bill was a means of introducing the system of proportional representation for national elections through the back door. Chirac personally negotiated with the opposing senators and ultimately succeeded. In March 1999, Article 3 of the Constitution was amended with the following text: 'the law favours the equal

---

[30] G. Allwood and K. Wadia, 2000, p. 198.

access of men and women to elected mandates and appointed posts'.[31] Another bill, modifying Article 4 of the Constitution which concerns the role of the parties in the electoral process, was also accepted by both Houses: 'parties favour the equal access of women and men to electoral mandates and appointed posts'.[32] The Congress of both Houses was held at the end of June 1999 and these texts were passed by 741 votes to 42. These constitutional reforms made room for the introduction of quota laws. In December 1999 the government tabled a bill requiring political parties to include 50 per cent women on lists in elections under PR, and for the parliamentary elections (using SMP) between 48 and 52 per cent of all *candidates* presented in the constituencies had to be women. For the European and senatorial elections the proposed law stipulated that the male and female candidates had to be placed alternately on the list. For the municipal and regional elections three out of every block of six candidates had to be women.

The stipulation about where on the list women candidates had to be placed was one of the main issues in the debate that followed in January 2000, in which a number of amendments were proposed. One, for example, proposed that, in order to be admissible for those elections where list-PR is used, party lists must observe 'alternating parity'; in other words, this would have required that parity was to be brought about by requiring each list to be divided, from top to bottom, into blocks of six candidates of whom three must be women. But the Senate rejected all these amendments and a joint committee consisting of members of both Houses, was convened to explore possible compromises. Since this committee too failed to arrive at any agreement, in the end the original text put forward by the government was submitted again and then passed both Houses as well as the Constitutional Court. The resulting law also carries a financial penalty for non-compliance. Parties that do not respect a balance between the number of men and women among their candidates will receive less funding from the state. For the elections using proportional representation the sanction is more effective: electoral authorities reject lists presented by the parties that do not comply with the quota requirements.[33]

---

[31] The original text of Article 4 is: '*La Loi favorise l'egal acces des femmes et des homes aux mandates electoraux en functions electives.*'

[32] The original text of the modification of Article 4 on the role of parties is: '*Ils contribuent a la mise en oeuvre du principe enonce au dernier alinea de l'article 3 dans les conditions determines par la loi.*'

[33] See www.quotaproject.org.

In 2001, the first elections took place under the new regime of quota legislation, which applies to municipalities with 3500 inhabitants or more. In the previous elections of 1995, 21 per cent of those elected as local councillors, deputies and mayors had been women. In 2001 the corresponding figure increased to 47 per cent.

The result was less dramatic in the 2002 parliamentary elections because the parties did not in practice adhere to parity. In total, 38 per cent of all candidates were women and the UMP in particular, a right-wing coalition of parties supporting President Chirac lagged behind the others with only 20 per cent women candidates. The Socialist Party did somewhat better with 36 per cent, as did the National Front with 49 per cent. But many of the women candidates did not win the seat in their constituency and only 12 per cent women were elected in the *Assemblée Nationale*. In the end the parties accepted the financial sanctions of the quota laws, rather than nominating women candidates in constituencies where the party in question could expect to win the seat.

BELGIUM

Belgium preceded France in the area of quota legislation by adopting a law in 1994 imposing a minimum percentage of candidates of each sex. In the same way as in France, the first attempt to introduce quota legislation happened in 1980, when a woman senator from the Flemish Christian People's Party (CVP) put forward a bill to the Upper House demanding that no more than three quarters of the candidates on the electoral list presented at *local* elections should be of the same sex. Contrary to the situation in France, both Belgian society and Belgian jurisprudence were accustomed to the application of quotas on behalf of specific categories of citizens, since the Belgian political system is defined in large part by a language and a regional cleavage. The existence of plural social identities based on language (Flemish, French, German) and region (Flanders, Wallonia and Brussels) and the need for representation of these identities in the political institutions was by that time already widely recognised and implemented.

As in France, the main reason to present a bill imposing gender quotas on electoral lists was the very low representation of women in politics.

Thus the objective of the bill was to accelerate the slow increase in the level of women's representation. The explanatory statement accompanying the bill further referred to the various party statutes that already embedded gender quotas, stating a need for uniform regulations. Apart from these more pragmatic grounds, advocates of the bill underlined in the parliamentary debate that principles of equality and non-discrimination were not being used in a gender-neutral way. A denial of the fact that there are two sexes, men and women, and that they do not function in society in the same way, results in discrimination against women. Vogel-Polsky (1994) phrases it as follows:

> All citizens are treated as equals at a formal level. Such a perception of equality is based on the presumption that citizens face similar backgrounds. In daily life, men and women often face very different living conditions, which are not so much shaped by a conscious choice than by societal structures. A formal notion of equality does not take into account such a reality.[34]

The bill was received enthusiastically in the parliamentary committee and was supported by Senators belonging to the Francophone Christian Democrats, the Flemish Social Democrats, Liberals and Regionalists.[35] But before the bill could be discussed and voted upon in the plenary session, the Council of State rejected it on the grounds that it was unconstitutional, referring to the principles of equality and non-discrimination.

As is shown in table 8.5 there was hardly any increase in women's representation in Belgian politics between 1980 and 1990. The first attempt to pass gender legislation had not stimulated the political parties to appoint many more women to safe seats. Thus, as in France, a second attempt to introduce a bill in the Lower House followed in 1991, this time demanding a gender quota of 20 per cent for the national representative bodies. This time the bill was not voted upon, because new elections were due.

The women's section of the (Flemish) Christian People's Party (CVP), Woman and Society (*Vrouw en Maatschappij*) has been very instrumental in paving the way to quota legislation. Right from their foundation in 1974, they lobbied intensively for a greater participation of women in the party and for an increase in women's representation in the political bodies. They had already convinced the

---

[34] E. Vogel Polsky, 'Les Actions Positives, les Quotas au Crible du Droit de l'Egalite', in K. Arioli (ed.), *Quoten und Gleichstellung von Frau und Mann*, Basel, Heibing & Lichtenhahn, 1996, cited in P. Meier, 'On the Theoretical Acknowledgement of Diversity in Representation', in *Res Publica*, 2001, vol. 4, p. 558.

[35] P. Meier, 'Gender as Part of Political Identity. Gender Quota in Parliament, Government and Advisory Committees in Belgium', paper presented at the APSA, Washington DC, 2000.

Table 8.5: *Women's presence in the Belgian Parliament (percentages).*

	1946	1950	1958	1968	1974	1978	1987	1991
Lower House	1	3	4	4	7	8	8	9
Senate	6	4	3	0	7	10	8	11

Source: L. van Molle and E. Gubin, 1998, p. 367.

party in the 1970s to adopt a 20 per cent quota for internal nominations and, in the beginning of the 1990s, party leaders gave in to their demand for one-third female candidates on CVP electoral lists. During the selection of candidates for the local elections of 1991, party leaders *asked* local party branches to nominate at least 33.3 per cent women candidates. When Woman and Society lost the internal party battle for an official quota of one third on all candidate lists of the CVP, the only option left was quota legislation to be reached through parliamentary assent. At that time the CVP was also in government and Miet Smet, founder and former chair of Woman and Society, was Junior Minister of Women's Affairs. She succeeded, together with the (male) Socialist Minister of Internal Affairs, Louis Tobback in drawing up a new quota law. Meier (2000) describes the legislative process.[36] The first draft submitted to the Council of Ministers stipulated that electoral lists contain a maximum of two thirds of candidates of the same sex. A difference with the previous bills was that this time the *place* on the list was also mentioned: the quota applied to the safe (expected to be eligible) and contestable seats. Another new element was the application of sanctions to parties who did not respect the law. Three sanctions were suggested:

- parties would lose the privilege to use a single list number across the various electoral districts;[37]

---

[36] P. Meier, 2000.

[37] It is very important for a party to be able to use the same identification number throughout the country.

- their allotted time on television for campaigning would be restricted; and
- their right to distribute campaigning material using lower mail rates would also be restricted.

Again the Council of State reviewed the draft bill and this time it did not declare it unconstitutional. The Council of State ruled that the draft bill respected the constitutional goal of equality between the sexes, since the quotas could be applied to both male and female candidates. However, the Council did reject the application of sanctions, arguing that they were out of proportion.

It was then decided to set up a small working group consisting of the party leaders of those four parties participating in government in order to negotiate a text that was acceptable to all parties. The result was a weak compromise: the law should be temporary; it should not be applicable to national elections; it should not make reference to the place on the list and it should only contain one sanction, i.e. the ruling that slots on the lists that were legally reserved for the under-represented sex cannot be taken up by candidates of the other sex and will stay blank.[38] In the end the Council of Ministers accepted this compromise with the exception of the qualification referring to the type of elections: according to the Council of Ministers the bill should be applied to *all* elections and the quota should be increased gradually starting with a 25 per cent quota applicable to the local and provincial election of 1994 to a 33.3 per cent quota to be in use at the elections in 1999.

As was expected by many women who had worked hard to get a quota law passed through parliament, the fact that there were no restrictions for the parties on *where* to place women candidates meant that, although parties did reach the quota for female candidates, they failed to get the same percentage of women in the parliamentary party, since women candidates found themselves placed in the lower slots of the party lists. That was why members of the Green Party submitted another bill demanding that women and men should alternately occupy the first and second place of the list. They argued that it is more effective to have a few women on strategically important slots than to have many women on ineligible places. This bill, however, failed to pass through parliament.

---

[38] Say that a party submits a list of 10 candidates of which two are women. By law, the party is then allowed to submit a list with six candidates of which two are women.

Chapter 8

Analysis of the lists of candidates submitted for the parliamentary elections of June 1999 shows that the outcome was very much as might have been expected.[39] Almost all parties respected the law, with an average of 40 per cent women candidates, but most women candidates were at the bottom of the lists. The Belgian Green Party, Agalev, nominated 43 per cent women in safe seats, the Christian People's Party (CVP) and Ecolo 35 per cent, the Flemish Liberal Party (VDP) and the Christian Socialist Party 22 per cent women, the Liberal Party (*Volksunie*) 17 per cent, the Flemish Socialist Party 14 per cent, the Wallonian Socialist Party 16 per cent and the ultra right-wing party Vlaams Blok only 6 per cent. Consequently, the number of women elected did not increase greatly. In the end, 18 per cent women were elected to the national parliament – far less than the 33.3 per cent stipulated by the quota law.

Table 8.6: Representation of Women in the Belgian Federal Parliament, 1999, 2003.

Wallonian parties	% Women 1999	% Women 2003	Flemish parties	% Women 1999	% Women 2003
MR	22	44	N-VA	38	38
Ecolo	55	33	Agalev	44	55
CdH	10	30	SP.A.Spirit	0	23
PS	11	36	Vlaams Blok	6	25
FN	0	0	CD&V	18	23
VLD	17	36			

Source: P. Meier, 2003, pp.7, 8.

---

[39] P. Meier, 'Necessaire mais Insuffisante: la Loi Smet-Tobback', in P. Saavedra (ed.) *Vers une Democratie Paritaire. Analyse et Revision des Lois Electorales en Vigueur*, Madrid, CELEM, 2000, pp. 197-210.

Since then, there have been several attempts, mainly in the Upper House, to amend the quota law in such a way that it will guarantee the desired result. One proposal has been to raise the quota to 50 per cent and other initiatives concerned the list order. The coalition that came into power in 1999 was headed by a Liberal prime minister and promised to review all possible mechanisms designed to increase the participation of women in political decision-making.[40] In July 2002, another law passed through parliament stating, first, that for each list the difference in the total number of male and female candidates cannot be greater than one and secondly, the top two candidates on the list should not be of the same sex. As a temporary provision, the first condition does not have to be met in the first election to which the law applies and, with regard to the top candidates, the law states that in the first election the top *three* positions cannot all be held by members of the same sex.[41] Further, in 2002 both Houses of the Belgian parliament passed a law enforcing the nomination of at least one woman in the executive bodies, such as national, regional and local bodies, as well as in certain advisory bodies.

The double quota laws certainly had an impact. Table 8.6 shows the results for the 1999 and 2003 parliamentary election for each party.

In the election of 1999, 16 (18 per cent) of 91 MPs were women. After the addition in the electoral law with regard to the *place on the list* the effect of the quota law is much larger: the 2003 federal parliament exists of 31 women, 34 per cent.[42] In the Senate the percentage raised from 27 in 1999 to 40 in 2003. As in the parliament, one third of the 2003 government members are women, with five women ministers and two women junior ministers.

GREECE

Quota legislation was introduced in Greece in 2000 and 2002. In 2000, parliament approved an amendment to Article 4 of the Constitution creating the possibility to take temporary positive measures. The passage of this amendment was preceded by lengthy discussions, in both parliamentary and juridical circles, on the

---

[40] See www.db-decisiob.de (Belgian expert).

[41] P. Meier, 'De Kracht van de Definitie. Quotawetten in Argentinië, België en Frankrijk Vergeleken', in *Res Publica*, vol. 46:1, 2004, pp. 80-100.

[42] P. Meier, 'De Hervorming van de Kieswet, de Nieuwe Quota en de M/V Verhoudingen na de Verkiezingen van Mei 2003', paper Politicologenetmaal, 22-23 May 2003, pp. 7, 8.

constitutionality of laws requiring parties to nominate a certain percentage women candidates. But the State Council eventually ruled in favour, and decided that 'the taking of positive measures in favour of women is not contrary to the constitution to the extent that these measures aim at precipitating the restitution of a true equality between men and women'.[43] The extremely low representation of women at local and regional level enhanced the pressure on the Greek Government to change the electoral laws. In 2002, only 1.5 per cent of mayors were women (14 in all), there were two women out of 55 prefects, while 7.1 per cent of the municipal and 11 per cent of the regional councils were women. Two government bills passed through the Greek parliament in 2002, requiring at least one third of each list of candidates for municipal and regional elections to be from either sex. No stipulation was given with regard to the order of the list. The quota law did exert an impact on the results of the local and regional elections held in 2002 and in 2003. The proportion of candidates on the lists for the regional elections who were women increased from 14 per cent in 1998, to 34 per cent in 2002. The percentage of those elected to the regional councils who were women went from 11 to 18 per cent. In the local elections in 2003 the proportion of councillors who were women increased by 5 per cent, from 7 in 1998 to 12 in 2003.

So far there is no quota law for candidates to the national parliament.

ITALY

The number of women in elective offices in Italy is still one of the lowest in Europe. For the parliament elected in 2001, only 10 per cent were women – a mere two per cent more than in 1948, the first parliament elected by female and male voters together. This low rate, as well as the limited progress being made, was an important reason to introduce quota laws during the 1990s.

Guadagnini (1998, 2000, forthcoming) describes how Italy eventually adopted quotas. She argues that a governmental organisation established in 1984, the National Committee for Equality and Equal Opportunities, was very active in getting a quota law adopted. Women who were active in the different parties formed an alliance on this issue through the Committee. During the 1987 parliamentary election, the Committee launched a campaign for more equal opportunities for women candidates. It put pressure on parties to nominate more women candidates and on

---

[43] See www.db-decision.de.

voters to vote for them. In the years following this election, the Committee organised debates, round-tables and meetings with party leaders in order to keep up the pressure. At the same time there was an ongoing debate about changing the political institutions. The collapse of the Italian party system as a result of a number of corruption scandals led to the adoption of a series of reforms, including changes to the electoral system. A majority favoured replacing the list-PR system with a plurality system, with the intention of reducing the number of parties and enhancing the stability of government. In the eyes of the citizens, the SMP electoral system would weaken the domination of the party elites. In August 1993, the system for electing the legislature was changed into a mixed-member system, under which 75 per cent of seats were to be elected by a first-past-the-post system in single-member constituencies and 25 per cent of the seats by list-PR in regional multi-seat constituencies.[44]

Against the background of a collapsing political system, the Italian parliament adopted the first quota law in March 1993. For the election of mayors, presidents of provincial governments and members of municipal and provincial councils, the law stated that neither sex could represent more than two thirds of the electoral lists.[45] According to Guadagnini, important reasons for the law to be adopted by the male-dominated parliament were, first, that one third of MPs were under investigation for corruption, so that allowing women to enter parliament may have been seen as a way to re-legitimise the political elite, and secondly, that many MPs were convinced that this law was going to be overruled by the Constitutional Court.[46]

In the same year another quota law was adopted by the parliament dealing with parliamentary elections. Given the change to an SMP system, which was going to penalise women's representation, several women MPs demanded the introduction of quotas in the new voting system. A clause was included to the new Electoral Law stating that for the 25 per cent (155) proportionally elected seats, lists should

---

[44] M. Guadagnini, forthcoming, pp. 11, 12.

[45] For the election of the municipal council in municipalities with up to fifteen thousand inhabitants, the maximum quota was set for either sex at three quarters. M. Guadagnini, 'The Debate on Women's Quotas in Italian Electoral Legislation', in *Swiss Political Science Review*, vol. 4:3, 1998, pp. 97-102.

[46] M. Guadagnini, 2000, p. 8.

consist of candidates of both sexes in alternate order. This new law provided for parity with regard to the seats elected by PR. In practice this meant that, even if not one woman was elected in a constituency, at least 12.5 per cent of all MPs were going to be women. The third quota law was adopted in 1995 and was similar to the first, but applied to regional councils.[47]

Resistance to these moves not only came from men. Women, both outside and inside parliament, were also very much divided on the matter and, interestingly enough, the division was not along party lines. In both left-wing and right-wing parties, women could be found who very much opposed the quota laws. Opponents called it the 'Panda' law, as if it were a means to safeguard an endangered species.[48]

The impact of the quota laws became apparent in the elections held in 1993 and 1995. Representation of women increased in local and regional councils from 6 to 9 per cent. In parliament, the increase was from 8 per cent women MPs in 1992 to 15 per cent in 1994.

However, as many had predicted, in July 1995 the Constitutional Court declared all quota laws unconstitutional. The Court declared that

> the fundamental right of equal access to elective offices, as established by Article 3 (All citizens are equal before the law, without distinction of sex, race, etc.) and Article 51 (All citizens of either sex can have access to public offices and elective posts under equal conditions) of the Constitution, cannot be subjected to special treatment on the basis of sex.[49]

The effect of this ruling became apparent in the elections that followed: in the Chamber of Deputies, the percentage of women MPs dropped from 15 per cent to 11 per cent in 1996, and to 10 per cent in 2001, while the number of women mayors dropped from 8 to 7 per cent.

But the debate on the need for electoral quota laws continued and between 1996 and 2000, several bills aiming at revising the Constitution and demanding balanced political representation were put forward. Eventually, a bill initiated by the government led by Prime Minister Berlusconi, passed both chambers of parliament in January 2003. This bill proposed to change the Constitution by adding to

---

[47] M. Guadagnini, 1998, pp. 97-102.

[48] *Ibid.*, p. 98.

[49] *Ibid.*, p. 99.

the existing paragraph 'All citizens of either sex can have access to public offices and elective posts under equal conditions' the following sentence: 'For this purpose the Republic promotes, by means of special measures, equal opportunities for women and men'.[50] This text opened up the possibility for other laws on gender quotas or for other regulations such as the reduction in financial aid to parties if their representation of women is too low.

Interestingly enough, the resistance to the constitutional reform of 2003 was much less than in 1993. Women from right-wing parties, such as Forza Italia and the National Alliance Party who were then very much opposed, now voted in favour. A reason for this change in attitude may be the extremely low level of women's representation in these two parliamentary parties, respectively 7 and 4 per cent. Another reason, according to Guadagnini, is that this time more and more women voters were aware of the issue, and these were voters that the parties did not want to lose, especially not at a time when, due to budget cuts, policies unfriendly to many citizens, had to be taken.

> Passing a bill that states a general principle in favour of equal opportunities is a good rhetorical strategy. It allows a government to show a women friendly image, while at the same time adopting policies, such as cuts to the welfare state funds, that have negative effects on women's lives.[51]

PORTUGAL

As in the other countries, the slow progress of women in parliament since the first democratic elections in 1975, triggered active women to lobby more aggressively for quota legislation. In Portugal too this started in the 1990s when several women's organisations concerned with parity were founded. This movement was very much influenced by the developments in France and Italy and stimulated, as in Greece, by the activities of the European Network 'Women in Decision-Making'. One initiative was the 'Parity Parliament', which took place in January 1994 in the Portuguese parliament. At that time only 21 out of 230 MPs were women (9 per cent) and 115 women, former or present members of parliament, invited the same number of men parliamentarians to sit with them in parliament

---

[50] M. Guadagnini, forthcoming, p. 18.

[51] M. Guadagnini, forthcoming, p. 20.

Chapter 8

and debate the situation of women in Portugal, citizenship and parity democracy. This and other activities created a lot of support for the issue and in the end government was convinced of the need for action with regard to the political participation of women.

In 1997, when the Portuguese Constitution was being revised, an article referring to the political participation of women was included. Article 109 states that:

> direct and active participation of men and women in political life is a condition and fundamental instrument of the consolidation of the democratic system. The law must promote equality in the exercise of civic and political rights and non-discrimination based on sex in the access to political office.

The aim of the constitutional reform was to allow the legislature to submit electoral laws designed to secure equal participation. Anticipating a revision of the Electoral Law, the Portuguese Government set up a small working group with the task of making legal suggestions how to promote access of women to decision-making positions. This group came up with several proposals, but in the end the Electoral Law they proposed was rejected by parliament. The government then decided to submit a quota law guaranteeing a more balanced division of seats between men and women. This law referred to the selection of candidates for the national parliament as well as for the European Parliament. The proposal was to impose, for the next two elections, a maximum of 75 per cent of all *eligible* places on the lists of candidates for one sex. In future elections, the quota would be 66.7 per cent. The proposal further stipulated that, in order to apply these quotas, female and male candidates should alternate: not more than two (or three in the first and second elections following the enforcement of the bill) candidates in a row should be of the same sex. If a list of candidates submitted by a party did not meet the conditions of the law, it would be denied participation in the election.

In the document accompanying the text of the bill, the government explicitly denounced the principle of parity. The text states that the Portuguese Constitution 'persists in prohibiting the creation of restrictions on the indivisible principle of unity and universality of active suffrage, as well as the representative mandate principle'. The government agrees that there may be a maximum limit on the participation of each sex or minimum quotas for candidates and/or representatives, but it does not want any division of voters or legislators: 'All voters vote for all candidates irrespective of gender; the representatives represent all citizens irrespective of gender'. In this text the Portuguese Government rejects all proposals of parity democracy 'with a tendency towards a type of "parallel democracy", a sexual "apartheid" in political representation'.[52] In March 1999, the Portuguese parliament discussed and then rejected this government proposal, parliamentarians being more in favour of alternative solutions, such as the adoption of internal rules by parties.[53]

DISCUSSION

With regard to the political empowerment of women, the 15 countries under investigation vary not only in actual representation figures, but also in the strategies used to reach a gender balance in parliament and other representative bodies. In contrast with the situation 20 years ago, governments and political parties do not differ in opinion about the *desirability* of a substantial participation of women in politics, but there is a deep schism over the *methods* used to achieve this, in particular the use of *legislation* to guarantee equal representation. The differences in opinion are driven not only by ideology. The introduction of gender quota laws can also be viewed as a kind of last remedy, since we only find quota laws for political offices in countries where the representation of women in the 1990s was still less than 10 per cent, and where there had been hardly any progress over the years. In such cases, political parties and other selectors of political personnel have been so determined in their resistance to including more women in politics that legal enforcement became necessary.

Party quotas and quota legislation have always been controversial, but the debate grew very intense with the introduction of the concept of 'parity'. This was introduced in 1989 by Elisabeth Sledziewski, a professor of political science in Strasbourg, at a conference of the Council of Europe. She rejected the 'sociological approach' which analyses women's position in terms of roles and cultural lag, but instead called for an examination of 'political laws', such as the working of universalism and the principles of democracy. Sledziewski and others pleaded for the recognition in political terms of the existence of two sexes.[54] Parity is about

---

[52] Proposal of law for introduction of quotas in parliamentary elections, June 1998, Article 5.

[53] See for example www.db-decision.de.

[54] E. Sledziewski, 'Report', in Council of Europe, *The Democratic Principle of Equal Representation. Forty Years of Council of Europe Activity*, Strasbourg, Council of Europe Press, 1992, pp. 17-28, cited in Outshoorn, 1993, pp. 6, 7, 8.

permanent representation on the basis of sex; it sees sexual difference as basic and prior to other differences. Parity is to be regarded as a goal, not as a redress of previous wrongdoing or as a catch-up manoeuvre for women.[55] Opponents of parity sometimes referred to the kind of representation operating in South Africa before 1990, *apartheid*: representation of whites by whites, of coloureds by coloureds, of blacks by blacks. It is understandable that some feminists who fought for equal opportunities and equal treatment and viewed sexual inequality as a temporary condition that could be overcome, rejected parity fiercely. In their opinion gender difference must not be written into law, because any measure endorsing a difference was a step backwards. Outshoorn (1993) phrases several other objections to the concept of parity democracy. A major problem is that parity implies that women are a homogeneous segment of the population and that, according to the parity advocates, being a woman overrides all other differences such as class, ethnicity, race, religion, age and life situation, like marital status, motherhood and sexual preference. Parity denies the diversity among women and it suggests common interests. Another criticism is the lack of reflection on the concept of representation in a parity democracy: who should the women representatives elected by parity laws represent in parliament once elected: all citizens or all female citizens?[56]

In the 1980s, feminists opposed to parity democracy on the grounds that it seeks its legitimacy in the fact that humankind consists of two sexes, got unexpected support from a series of constitutional rulings in different jurisdictions. Favouring one group over another by demanding that political parties select a certain number of women candidates was found by a number of different courts to be in conflict with the constitutional articles on equality before the law and on discrimination. These constitutional rulings posed a problem to the advocates of quota laws; they could either challenge the ruling by presenting bills in which it was argued that parity (or other quota laws) were not unconstitutional, or they could try to have the constitution changed. Following the first option, one can say that parity is not opposed to the principle of equality, but merely translates the principle of equality into reality. For example, Article 3 of the Italian Constitution says:

> All citizens have equal social dignity and are equal before the law, without distinction of gender, race, language, religion, political opinions or personal and social conditions. It is the responsibility of the Republic to remove eco-

---

[55] Outshoorn, 1993, p. 19.

[56] *Ibid.*, p. 21.

nomic and social obstacles which limit the liberty and equality of citizens and which are opposed to the full expansion of the human person and to the participation of all workers in the political, economic and social organisation of the country.

The law on electoral organisation in Italy can then also be interpreted as the measure required by Article 3 of the Italian Constitution to ensure the rebalancing of the starting conditions of men and women in the political world, in order to achieve substantial equality of access to elected positions as well as an 'appropriate measure' to guarantee women's presence in the representative bodies. Along the same line of reasoning, one can argue that this kind of electoral reform is a logical consequence of the constitutional right to gender equality and of the ratification by the European countries of the Convention on the Elimination of All Forms of Discrimination Against Women (CEDAW). Article 7 of CEDAW states that governments:

> shall take all appropriate measures to eliminate discrimination against women in the political and public life of the country and, in particular, shall ensure women, on equal terms with men the right to vote … to participate in the formulation of government policy … and to hold public office and perform all public functions at all levels of government.

The second option to counteract the constitutional bans on quota legislation is to amend the constitution (or where there is no written text, as in Britain, to amend existing legislation) to make it explicitly possible to differentiate in law between men and women candidates. We have seen that this happened in France, Greece, Italy and Great Britain. But also in Germany the constitution was amended to open the doors for affirmative action. Here Article 3 of the Constitution stipulating equality was amended in 1994 as follows: 'Men an women have equal rights. The State ensures the implementation of equality for women and men and takes action to abolish existing discrimination', thus making it possible for any government to introduce legislation guaranteeing equal participation in politics.[57]

While the concept of parity democracy is associated with a fierce debate on the meaning of universalism, democracy and citizenship, it is also possible to favour parity on purely pragmatic grounds. Gender quota legislation, when implemented, guarantees success: laws have a mandatory effect and impose an obligation to

---

[57] See www.db-decision.de.

Chapter 8

produce results. The higher numerical presence of women politicians in the representative bodies of the countries that passed quota legislation speaks for itself. A clear example is in Italy where between 1993, when the law on the municipal and provincial elections came into effect, and the summer of 1995, when the quota law was abolished, the percentage of women councillors more than doubled (from 6 to 13 per cent). Since abolition, the representation of Italian women in politics has decreased again.

So far we find no true parity democracy in Europe. In most of the laws that have been passed, there is no 50 per cent quota and there is no stipulation about the list-order, meaning that women candidates often find themselves in ineligible places. The Belgian law stipulates the specific placement of the under-represented sex on the candidate lists, but only for the top positions. The French law is more restrictive demanding, at least for local and regional elections, that in a block of six slots, three have to be fulfilled by women, but here too it is still possible for parties to place women candidates in the lower slots thus decreasing their chances of being elected. For the national elections, when SMP is used, the law is even more ineffective, because the parties can decide to 'give' unwinnable constituencies mainly to women. In the French parliamentary elections of 2002, despite the fact that 38 per cent of all party candidates were women, only 12 per cent of those elected were women.

But despite all these shortcomings in the actual texts of the quota laws now in use, the ultimate effect should not be under-estimated. The advantage of the parity argument is that, as a demand, it appeals to both traditional and feminist women and, as a slogan, it conveys a simple and easily understood message. Consequently the issue of the under-representation of women in political bodies has never been so much discussed as during governmental and parliamentary debates on parity and gender quotas. The general public seems to be in favour of measures taken by governments and parties in order to reach a kind of gender balance and so are most political parties. So, despite flaws in the laws in the countries with quota legislation, parties have presented many more women candidates than before and the actual representation figures have also increased. Given the relative success of quota legislation in terms of an increase in the representation of women, it is to be expected that other countries, where there has hardly been any increase in the representation of women, will follow the examples of France, Belgium, Italy and Greece. Groups of women, inside and outside parliament and the political parties, will put more pressure on party leadership to select many more women for political office. It is also to be expected that the demand will be for parity and not for lower quotas.

Compared with 20 years ago, there is now a more positive attitude towards the political integration of women. Governments, parliaments and parties all admit that unbalanced representation in political decision-making implies a democratic deficit. This combined with the fact that these are problematic times for political parties, given the low membership rates and decreasing turnout, create a window of opportunity for advocates of parity. As parties think about changing their institutional arrangements, policy-makers and political players can make use of the best practice policies on the inclusion of women. After all, a balanced participation by both men and women means that the scope of politics is enlarged at the same time as the networks of people involved in politics are made more inclusive. In the next chapter some examples are presented how parties and governments can define new rules and procedures that guarantee a more balanced participation of men and women.

CHAPTER 9

WINDOW OF OPPORTUNITY: THE CRISIS OF POLITICS

This chapter deals with the European debate on the so-called 'crisis of politics'. The fact that a large proportion of European citizens are now seen by many to be turning their backs on (party) politics is crucial to any analysis of the role of women in politics, since this increases pressure on the political system to change and find ways of involving more people, including women. In the context of this book, therefore, the 'crisis of politics' of the 1990s and 2000s can be viewed as a window of opportunity for women.

Regardless of the level of decision-making, political body or political post under consideration, many people these days challenge the legitimacy, fairness, democratic character, transparency and accountability of European politics. Politics and politicians have a bad image. For example, in each of the 15 countries under analysis, we find examples of dishonest politicians being exposed by the media. A striking case was the joint resignation of all European Commissioners in the spring of 1999, having been accused of mismanagement, favouritism and lack of transparency. There is also a general lack of involvement of European citizens in politics. Electoral turnout is decreasing in all European countries and membership of political parties is also declining. Explanations offered for these phenomena include, *inter alia*, increasing individualism and a growing lack of collective orientation. In addition, it is also argued that the Europeanisation of politics has not helped the image of politics, since decision-making has become more complex and opaque. For many European citizens, the processes and outcomes of political decision-making have come to seem remote and alienating. It is increasingly common for national politicians to defend the introduction of unpopular policies by referring to European agreements.

These trends and developments, in their turn, called for a reaction. Politicians, policy-makers and also academic researchers have been coming up with alternatives for political institutions, procedures and methods of decision-making. The debate on institutional reform is clearly having a revival, stimulated not only by the crisis of politics but also by new technologies for improving communication between decision-makers and citizens. Governments and parliaments as well as the European Parliament have initiated changes, for example, in the electoral system, or by introducing the referendum as a way of deciding tough political questions. Parties have in turn changed their selection criteria for candidates for political office, in order to increase the representativeness of their parliamentary party. Experiments with new forms of decision-making, such as citizens' juries and interactive policy-making have been introduced, especially at local level.

Reforming political institutions offers a unique opportunity for the greater political participation of women, since at the heart of the crisis there is the perceived exclusiveness of political decision-making. Only a few participate in the decision-making process and political selection mechanisms tend to be biased in favour of those who belong to the same networks as those who are already in power. The effect of this is that the institutions of a representative democracy make it much easier for some citizens to participate in decision-making than others. One way to make political decision-making more inclusive is to adapt the relevant political institutions to enable equal power-sharing by men and women. A win-win situation can thereby be created: the campaign to promote a better representation of half of the population, women, may in this way be viewed as a possibility to reaffirm democratic credentials.[1]

This chapter discusses four subjects. First we turn to a description of the crisis of politics in Europe: What are the developments that have contributed to the crisis? How is it manifested? The second part contains an overview of institutional arrangements that may help political institutions to regain the trust of citizens. We discuss new forms of policy-making such as referendums, interactive decision-making and citizens' juries. The third part deals with the effect of these new institutional arrangements on women's participation. The fourth part sets out a women-friendly electoral system for electing Members of the European Parliament, based on the best practice policies discussed in the previous chapters.

---

[1] E. Vogel-Poslky, 'Belgium', in *Panorama Strategies, Expert Network Women in Decision-Making*, Equal Opportunities Unit, European Committee, Brussels, 1993.

Chapter 9

THE CRISIS OF PARTY POLITICS

In most European countries, citizens seem to be less and less willing to play according to the rules of representative democracy. The traditional political parties, the classic intermediaries between government and citizens, find themselves in rough water at the beginning of a new century. First, in nearly all European countries, there is an increasing lack of involvement of citizens in both parties and elections. Gallagher, Laver and Mair (2001) provide some recent information on membership figures.[2]

Table 9.1: Party membership as a percentage of the electorate (2001).

Country	% of electorate that belongs to a party	Country	% of electorate that belongs to a party
Austria	19, down from 28% in '80s	Italy	4, down from 10% in '80s
Belgium	7, slight decline past 20 yrs	Luxemb'g	no information
Denmark	5, down from 20% in '60s	Neth'lands	2, half of the '80 figure
Finland	11, down from 16% in '80s	Portugal	5, modest increase since '80
France	2, little change	Spain	3, modest increase since '80
Germany	3, little change	Sweden	7, slight decline past 20 yrs
Greece	7, figure has doubled since late '70s	UK	2, a third of '50s figures
Ireland	4, slight decline past 20 yrs		

Source: M. Gallagher, *et al.*, 2001, p. 275.

---

[2] M. Gallagher, *et al.*, 2001, p. 275.

Only in Greece, Spain and Portugal, the countries with 'new' democracies starting in the 1970s, has party membership increased somewhat. In all other countries, the trend is downwards. In the Netherlands, membership went down from 12 per cent in the 1950s to 7 per cent in the 1960s to 2 per cent in 2003.[3] In Denmark, more than 20 per cent of citizens carried a membership card in the 1960s, while in 1995 this was only 5 per cent. In the UK, more than a million people were members of the Labour Party in the 1950s, but by the 1990s this figure had declined to 300,000.[4] The loss of members poses a problem to the political parties, not only because of a decline in membership fees, but more because fewer and fewer people are available to fill representative positions. The active members of the parties have always been the political decision-makers of the future, but more and more this particular function of parties, recruiting public representatives, is under pressure. The fact that fewer people are inclined to join a party is also a sign that the political party is less important than it used to be as a vehicle to advance certain policy goals. These days other groups, whether single-issue groups or large and diverse interest groups, are much more popular with citizens. In several European countries, political activities outside parties have increased and membership of organisations such as Greenpeace or National Heritage is much higher.[5]

Compared to voting at elections, the personal costs of becoming a member of a political party are much higher: often a membership fee is required and a certain degree of attendance at party meetings, as well as participation in activities for the well-being of the party, are expected of each member. But, although voting is the least strenuous form of political participation, electoral participation is also declining.

Each country uses different suffrage rules. In five of the subject countries of our study, voting is still compulsory, but then the degree of enforcement differs among these five countries as well as the sanctions for not obliging. Despite the dissimilarities, the conclusion that turnout is diminishing all over Europe is clearly valid. According to table 9.2, only in Denmark did voter turnout increase in the most recent election.

---

[3] G. Voerman, 1996, pp. 194, 195.

[4] P. Seyd and P. Whitely, *Labour's Grassroots: The Politics of Party Membership*, Oxford, Clarendon Press, 1992.

[5] For a Dutch example, see *Sociaal en Cultureel Rapport 1998, 25 Jaar Sociale Verandering*, Rijswijk, SCP, 1998, p. 758.

Chapter 9

Table 9.2: Levels of electoral participation.

Country	Mean level 1960s	Mean level 1980s	Year and turnout for parliamentary election	
Austria	93.8	91.6	2002	84.3
Belgium	92.9	93.9	2003	91.1
Denmark	87.5	85.6	2001	89.3
Finland	85.0	78.7	2003	66.6
France	76.6	71.9	2002	64.4
Germany	87.1	87.1	2002	79.1
Greece	–	83.5	2000	75.0
Ireland	74.2	72.9	2002	63.0
Italy	92.9	89.0	2001	81.3
Luxembourg	89.6	88.1	1999	86.5
Netherlands	95.0	83.5	2003	79.9
Portugal	–	78.0	2002	62.3
Spain	–	73.5	2000	70.6
Sweden	86.4	89.1	2002	80.1
UK	76.6	74.1	2001	59.4

Source: 1960s and 1980s M. Gallagher *et al.*, 2001, p. 260; www.elections.org.

A decline in turnout makes politicians nervous since it is a clear demonstration of the lack of political interest and involvement of citizens. Although some politicians denounce this by arguing that abstention may be a statement of satisfaction with the activities and behaviour of politicians, research into motives for voting (or for not voting) demonstrates that the main reason for non-voting is a loss of interest in politics, followed by cynicism and distrust.[6]

---

[6] C.W.A.M. Aarts, 'Opkomst', in J.J.A. Thomassen, C.W.A.M. Aarts and H. van der Kolk (eds.), *Politieke Veranderingen in Nederland 1971-1998, Kiezers en de Smalle Marges van de Politiek*, Den Haag, SDU, 2000, pp. 57-76.

Not only are citizens less willing to vote, but those who do vote have a more erratic voting behaviour than 10-20 years ago. Electoral volatility increased in the 1990s as did support for new political parties.[7]

All these developments are related to the second indicator of a crisis of (party) politics, the negative image most people have of politics and politicians. Although the 15 countries in general score well on the Transparency International Corruption Perception Index (CPI) measuring perceptions in each country of the degree of corruption that exist among public officials and politicians,[8] on a smaller scale citizens are often confronted with news stories of pay-offs, nepotism and personal greed. It is possible to come up with examples in almost every European country. Apart from actual fraud and corruption by politicians, citizens are fed up with the arrogance of many politicians who have been in the job for ages and who no longer seem to speak the same language as their electors. The electoral success of newcomers in politics such as Silvio Berlusconi and Pim Fortuyn tells us that many citizens would like to see different types of politicians.

A REACTION: POLITICAL REFORM

The protest movements of the 1960s and 1970s also attacked the elitist character of politics. Then too the lack of transparency and the exclusiveness of decision-making were heavily criticised. All over Europe, there was a lot of pressure for more direct say in decision-making, for example through referendums or through direct election of the prime minister. Many citizens joined interest groups, such as environmental and peace organisations and demanded government attention for these issues through large protest meetings and demonstrations. But their protests did not result in structural reforms of the political system. What happened in the Netherlands, for example, was that parliamentary and government committees were established to *study* possible institutional reform, but that in the end not one proposal survived parliamentary debate.

---

[7] M. Gallagher *et al.*, 2001, p. 263.

[8] 133 countries are ranked on the CPI index. The 15 countries under observation received the following ranking scores: Finland, 1; Denmark 3; Sweden 6; Netherlands 7; Luxembourg / UK 11=; Austria 14; Germany 16; Belgium 17; Ireland 18; France / Spain 23=; Portugal 25; Italy 35; Greece 50.

In the 1990s, due to the developments discussed above, we saw a revival of the debate on institutional reform, but this time these debates often resulted in institutional changes and in the introduction of new policies to improve dialogue and cooperation between citizens and representatives, often at local level.

Examples of institutional reforms can be found in Italy, where discontent of citizens with politics turned into a crisis of the party system in the early 1990s. The dominance of the traditional parties suddenly collapsed. Lega Nord, a party that did not fit into the traditional party system, gained a lot of support in the elections of 1992 at the expense of the Christian Democratic Party. At the same time a thorough judicial investigation exposed a widespread pattern of corruption among the political elite. As a result the traditional party system fell apart and many of its parties were replaced. In the parliamentary elections of 1994, all the parties that had governed between 1945 and 1992 entered the election with a new name.[9] Another reform was the changing of the electoral system, which has already been discussed in chapter 8. A third reform was the granting of more power to local government.

A second example of institutional reform was the devolution of political power in the United Kingdom. The wish for a certain degree of political autonomy was granted to the people of Wales and Scotland and, in 1999, legislatures were established in the two countries. In Belgium, again in order to increase involvement of citizens with politics, the electoral rules on preferential voting were changed. In the Netherlands in 2000, a proposal for the introduction of a corrective referendum did pass the Second Chamber, but was defeated (by a single vote) by the Senate.[10] In 2004, the Dutch parliament again discussed changing the electoral system, with a cabinet proposal to have 75 seats elected through national lists and 75 seats distributed through multi-member constituencies. What we can find in all 15 countries is a trend towards more decentralisation of political decision-making. The demands for greater effectiveness, efficiency, responsiveness and support for policy decisions have resulted in a shift of responsibilities towards local government.[11]

---

[9] M. Guadagnini, forthcoming, p. 1. See also L. Morlino, 'Crisis of Parties and Change of Party System in Italy', in *Party Politics*, vol. 2:1, 1996, pp. 5-30.

[10] A corrective referendum can be called on the initiative of a certain number of citizens in order to prevent the enactment of specified types of legislation.

[11] M. Gallagher, M. Laver and P. Mair, 2001, p. 166.

Apart from institutional reforms at national level, and the trend towards more decentralisation, many examples can be provided of reforms at local level: old forms of 'command and control' have been replaced by so-called 'new politics' of inclusion and participation. An ever-developing infrastructure for telecommunications contributed to these 'new politics'. Let us discuss briefly two 'new' trends for strengthening democracy: the use of information and communications technology (ICT) and face-to-face deliberation in small groups. In the next section we then focus on the effects of the new politics on the political participation of women.

The widespread use of mobile phones and of internet access in the majority of the 15 counties has triggered several experiments in democratic decision-making. Public access to political decision-making is greatly enhanced by providing all relevant information such as political documents and data underpinning political decisions. Local governments daily post all relevant information on the internet so that everyone is capable of familiarising themselves with the issues. Apart from providing the necessary information, ICT also makes it possible for citizens to offer their views on political issues. For example, in the Netherlands, regular polling through computers has been in practice since the beginning of the 1990s. The city of Delft surveys a representative sample of 1000 citizens each month with all kinds of questions that are useful for decision-making and implementation. More recently, there are possibilities for citizens to communicate directly with (local) politicians through electronic interfaces set up for the public and for companies. Websites offer now electronic conferences where people can conduct a dialogue with other citizens or with political representatives. There are examples in Sweden where local authorities have enabled citizens to follow the council debates live via computers and submit comments and proposals to the councillors by e-mail while the debate is ongoing.[12] The internet seems to be a new forum for an informed dialogue with local people on decisions that have to taken, such as the plans for a major new airport in a region or a restructuring of the marketplace.[13] The next step

---

[12] L. Iilshammar, 'Sweden as an IT Nation', published on the internet (www.sweden.se), 2000.

[13] The Civil Aviation Administration in Sweden set up this forum in order to democratise planning and decision-making on a major new airport in the Stockholm region. The local government of the city of Delft in the Netherlands asked citizens by using scale models for the restructuring of the city centre (the Marketplace) to cooperate in the development of the plans.

Chapter 9

in using ICT as a decision-making tool will be electronic voting from home via the internet at general elections. Teams of experts are now trying to solve problems of voter identification.

A second trend can be seen in the new types of policy-making that involve consultation, negotiation and/or deliberation between representatives of government, civil society and citizens. The objection to the use of polling and surveys via computers and the internet is that they only register opinions without giving people the opportunity to think through the issues and form an opinion while 'deliberating' with other people. In contrast to traditional methods of public inquiry, such as voting or opinion polling, interactive policy-making involves the formation of public opinion.[14] Interactive policy-making is an informal and *ad hoc* form of policy-making, including as many citizens as possible. However it is still mainly a top-down initiative. Common local practice is that the initiative for interactive projects comes from the town hall or district boards. In the Netherlands these practices became trendy in the 1990s and since then there have been many projects in small and large municipalities all over the country.[15] An example is decision-making on the restructuring of a square in a small town of Leerdam in the Netherlands. The issue involved was the rearrangement of a large square located in the middle of a rather deprived neighbourhood. The upkeep of the square had been neglected, but several large food chains had shown interest for setting up new businesses. The council decided to set up a planning group which main task was to present an integrated plan for the square that was agreeable to all players involved. This planning group consisted of citizens, representatives of companies and shops involved, and local civil servants and politicians. Before the whole process started, the mayor and aldermen had promised the group that in principal their plan would pass the local council, given a few natural preconditions. The whole process took five months and the outcome was very satisfying for all participants. The plan passed through the council unchanged.[16]

---

[14] T. Akkerman, 'Urban Debates and Deliberative Democracy', in *Acta Politica*, vol. 36, Spring 2001, p. 73.

[15] J. Edelenbos and R. Monnikhof (eds.), *Spanning in Interaktie. Een analyse van interactief beleid in lokale Democratie*, Amsterdam, IPP, 1998; F. Henriks and P.W. Tops, 'Tussen Democratie en Verzakelijking. Trends in de Hervorming van het Lokaal Bestuur in Nederland en Duitsland', in *Bestuurswetenschappen*, 1997, vol. 51:4, pp. 198-217.

[16] T. Akkerman, M. Leyenaar and B. Niemöller, 'Reforming Government in the Netherlands', paper presented at the ESF Explanatory Workshop, Nijmegen, 8-10 November 2001, p. 11.

Examples like this can be found in many European countries, with a majority of cases in the Scandinavian countries. This part of Europe is also a frontrunner when it concerns experiments in decision-making through so-called citizens' juries. Citizens who have been randomly selected are invited for a period of time (weekend or one whole day) to deliberate on a particular problem. They are given carefully balanced briefing material, have the chance to interact with competing sets of experts and are given extensive opportunities for discussion and debate, moderated by trained moderators. In Denmark, for example, deliberations have taken place on the future of county hospitals and on the introduction of the euro. In Dublin a citizens' jury of 50 residents were first thoroughly informed by pro and contra 'witnesses' and then deliberated in small groups before making a judgement on the building of a waste incinerator in the area. Apart from the greater legitimacy of a decision taken by a random sample of involved citizens, several other benefits are claimed to result from involving in this debate the very people who are subject to its outcomes. These include:

- an improvement in the levels of interest, awareness, information and analytical capacity among citizens;

- an increased sense of efficacy and involvement;

- a general increase in the willingness of citizens to take account of the arguments of others, leading to a broadening of the social consensus around the eventual decision; and

- an increase in the legitimacy of decisions eventually taken, even among those who disagree with them.[17]

GENDER AND POLITICAL REFORM

We now turn to the significance of gender representation in these new institutional arrangements and forms of citizens' participation at local level. Has the building of new institutions created opportunities for women and other newcomers on the political scene? And if so, is this because of strategic behaviour of women activists

---

[17] J. Fishkin, *The Voice of the People*, New Haven, Yale University Press, 1997; J. Elster, *Deliberative Democracy*, Cambridge, Cambridge University Press, 1998.

in and outside political parties or because of a change in attitude of the selectors? We have seen in chapters 2 and 3 that one of the strategies of Scandinavian women working inside parties for getting more women appointed to party boards was to have the number of seats expanded. Since no men had to give up their seats, selectors were more willing to allow women to take up these new seats. Now that women inside parties and at universities are much more aware and knowledgeable about the biases in institutions and selection procedures, influencing institution-building in a positive way for women can be done more effectively.

Another question is whether party leaders and other selectors are now more willing to share power with women because they view this as a way to improve the image of politics. Women are still newcomers to politics, often communicating differently with citizens and the media and thus sending out a less traditional image. Shaping new political institutions with a large share of women representatives may be way to introduce a new sort of politics.

In Italy, for example, political parties were forced to reform given people's total lack of trust in party politics. Women involved in the 'old' Communist Party (PCI) took advantage of this and demanded numerical and substantive representation in the new party to be formed. By giving their support to the formation of a new party, the Democratic Party of the Left (PDS), women were in turn backed by the new party leadership in their demands for quotas and for the integration of women's issues in the party programme.[18] Guadagnini is also of the opinion that support for the women's demands was because these party leaders and officials were convinced that this would help

> consolidate a new image of the party in contrast with the old PCI, both in terms of its political elite and in its ideological content and programmes. Many thought that reform would help increase the appeal of the party to women voters who, in Italy, had always tended to vote for centre parties, especially for the Christian Democratic Party.[19]

Something similar happened with the debate on electoral reforms in Italy. Before the 1990s, gender was not an issue in the debates on political representa-

---

[18] M. Guadagnini, forthcoming, p. 8. In this article Guadagnini also points to the lack of results. Despite the formal rules of quotas and attention to gender, in 2003 women do not constitute 40 per cent of the internal party bodies and the women's committee of the party complains about their lack of influence in party policy-making.

[19] Ibid., p. 8.

tion within parliament and parties. Until the second half of the 1980s, the feminist movement did not bother to discuss the under-representation of women in politics.[20] The discussion on the electoral laws created the opportunity to gender mainstream the debate on representation, and led to the acceptance by parliament of the quota laws of 1993, albeit that the effect was only short-term, since the laws were declared unconstitutional by the Constitutional Court in 1995 (see chapter 8).[21]

Another intriguing example is the constitutional reform in Britain, introducing devolution and creating new legislatures in Scotland, Wales and Northern Ireland. Mackay and Brown have written extensively on how the devolution process in Scotland has resulted in a distribution of power between the sexes.[22] In 1989, the Scottish Constitutional Convention was established to discuss the future government of Scotland. When only 10 per cent women found themselves appointed in this Convention, a broad coalition of women's organisations, both partisan and non-partisan, was created, the Scottish Women's Coordination Group (SWGG), who lobbied the Convention and other political players constantly in order to guarantee a fair women's representation in the future institutions. They pleaded for an electoral system of proportional representation instead of the SMP-system used in the British elections and they convinced the Scottish Labour Party and the Scottish Liberal Democrats to accept the principle of gender balance in winnable seats. The first Scottish legislature consisted of 37 per cent women MPs and 5 out of 22 cabinet ministers were women. Apart from the discussion on numerical representation the SWGG was able to demand attention for women's interests and had the parliament adopt a gender mainstreaming approach.[23] Although it has taken place within a total different context, the case of Northern Ireland is also part of the British devolution process. Here too all kinds of women's groups realised in time that joint action was necessary in order to be guaranteed inclusion in the institutions. The Northern Ireland Women's Coalition (NIWC) was founded and they

---

[20] *Ibid.*, p. 1.

[21] *Ibid.*, p. 13.

[22] See among others, F. Mackay, F. Myers and A. Brown, 'Towards a New Politics? Women and Constitutional Change in Scotland', in A. Dobrowolsky and V. Hart (eds.), 2003, pp. 84-98.

[23] A. Brown *et al.*, 'Women and Constitutional Change in Scotland and Northern Ireland', in *Parliamentary Affairs*, 2002, vol. 55, pp. 75, 76.

succeeded through elections to gain two seats in the forum of political parties where the debate on the constitutional changes was going to take place. In the end, however, only 13 per cent women were elected in the Northern Ireland Assembly, because the parties had placed the majority of women candidates in unwinnable seats.[24] However, the NIWC played a substantial role, according to the memoirs of Mo Mowlam, the Secretary of State for Northern Ireland at that time, in the Good Friday agreement. Given their cross-party character, they were often able to pull the talks out of stalemate situations.[25]

These examples teach us that the goal of fairer representation for women forms a basis for women to cross party lines and form coalitions. In Italy, Scotland and Northern Ireland – and we have seen similar developments in the debates on quotas and parity in Belgium and France – women from different political backgrounds and organisations joined each other in pursuit of a common goal. Another similarity is the strategic and self-confidence approach. Not only are the women involved very knowledgeable of the pitfalls of particular electoral systems, selection and nomination procedures, and do they share this knowledge with the architects of the new political institutions, but they are also more than ever convinced of their own capacities to stand for political office.

Turning to direct democracy, there is a growing interest in referendums as a means for citizens to participate regularly in the political decisions of their parliaments and regional or local councils.[26] For example, in the Netherlands, more than 50 communities passed a regulation that allows for a referendum. Referendums are open to all voters and therefore are not as gender biased, as are selection procedures of candidates for election lists.

In many of the 15 countries, especially at local level, we find experiments involving citizens more directly in policy-making. These experiments differ in many aspects such as the kind of issue, the number of people involved and whether the outcome of the process is binding. However, many of them involve a kind of deliberation among decision-makers and citizens. Deliberative decision-making goes beyond the mere aggregation of individual preferences that characterises

---

[24] *Idem*, pp. 78, 79.

[25] M. Mowlam, *Momentum. The Struggle for Peace, Politics and the People,* Coronet Books, Hodder & Stoughton, 2002, p. 233.

[26] M. Gallagher and P. Vincenzo Uleri (eds.), *The Referendum Experience in Europe*, London MacMillan Press, 1996.

institutions such as elections and referendums. Reasoned discussion, dialogue and debate allow a range of options to be developed, examined, challenged and evaluated. Because of the many different types of 'interactive policy-making' it is difficult to estimate the effect on the participation of women. It is known, however, from earlier research on gender and political participation, that women tend to participate more often in less institutional and more informal processes of decision-making than in institutionalised processes.[27] More informal ways of decision-making are often more accessible for people with little organisational experience and with few contacts as well. It is also true that many women view these more informal and less institutional ways of decision-making as more effective. A third reason is that, since these initiatives happen at local level, they more often concern concrete subject matters to which women feel more attracted.[28]

Although an important reason to initiate new forms of local decision-making is to involve as many citizens in the process as possible in order to increase the legitimacy of political decision-making, there is not much exact information available on numbers and types of citizens that participate. In a study of ten cases of these local initiatives carried out in 2003 in the Netherlands it appeared that hardly any systematic monitoring of the involvement of citizens is done. Participation figures were very difficult to obtain and often had to be calculated from attendance records or from estimates made by people who were present. This research confirms some of the above-mentioned expectations. Openly announced meetings and public hearings tend to be attended by equal numbers of women and men. When participation is decided upon through selection, the number of women reduces. Fewer women tend to be present when it concerns meetings with experts and delegates from interest organisations. In this case, the presence of women is dependent on the professional group it concerns: in one of the cases where the decision-making process was about the chronically unemployed, half of the participants were women, since many women work in welfare. But in two other cases relatively few women participated in the decision-making process on the future structuring of the community, because here it concerned mainly representatives of local interest organisations and they were often men. In the more institutionalised

---

[27] J. Lovenduski, *Overview State of the Art Study of Research on Women in Political, Economic and Social Decision-Making in Europe, Final Report*, 1998, p. 18.

[28] See for example, J. Lovenduski, 1986; M. Leyenaar, 1989; B. Nelson and N. Chowdhury, 1994.

forms of citizens' participation, such as village councils, in two of the cases, less than 30 per cent were women. A final finding of this study was that women participate less then men in decision-making initiatives using ICT. In three of the four cases using ICT one-third women and two-thirds men participated in the internet debates.[29]

In the above-mentioned study, the number of women reduced when experts and delegates of interest groups were the target of local government. This was so because the issues to be decided upon often included shopkeepers, farmers' organisations and chambers of commerce which mainly represent men. However including the less formal part of civil society in the decision-making process is favourable to the participation of women, because community and voluntary sections are often primarily female. An interesting example is the establishment of the Civic Forum in Northern Ireland. The previously mentioned Northern Ireland Women's Coalition proposed the formation of the Civic Forum 'as a way of bringing civil society into the political arena to ensure that the new arrangements were participatory and inclusive'.[30] The Civic Forum was to be a consultative body for the new government institutions. It consists of 60 members of which six are nominated by the cabinet and the remainder by extra-Assembly bodies, for example from business, agriculture, trade unions, churches, the arts, sports and education. It was finally established in 2001 and it included 37 per cent women (in contrast to the 13 per cent women appointed in the Northern Ireland Assembly).[31]

A final example is the emergence of so-called citizens' juries as a means to involve people in decision-making. The selection of a citizens' jury should always be done through random sampling. To be able to carry the decision to a much larger public, the representativeness of the sample is extremely important. Random sampling means that women and men have an equal chance of being selected for the jury. A systematic observation in the deliberation groups in the Citizens Jury on Waste Incineration in Ireland in November 2003 did not show any significant gender differences in attendance as well in behaviour: in each group a few men

---

[29] M. Leyenaar and B. Niemöller, 'Lokale Beleidsbeinvloeding in 2003: een Gender Analyse van de Participatie van Burgers', in Ministerie van Sociale Zaken en Werkgelegenheid, *Werkdocumenten no. 297*, Voorburg, 2003, pp. 66-71.

[30] E. Meehan, 'The Civic Forum', paper presented at the ESF Exploratory Workshop, Nijmegen, Netherlands, 8-10 November 2001, p. 3.

[31] *Ibid.*, pp.7, 8.

and women dominated the discussion and the moderator ensured that the others joined in as well.

In the previous chapters, the gender impact of many existing political institutions has been discussed, while in this chapter we looked at the opportunities for the participation of women in newly created institutions. In the last section of this chapter we bring the acquired knowledge into practice when we define a system to elect future Members of the European Parliament.

A NEW INSTITUTIONAL REGIME FOR SELECTING MEPS

The enlargement of the European Union from 15 to 25 countries demanded an adaptation of the statutes involving the Unions' competencies and institutions. This was a clear window of opportunity to increase opportunities for women to participate in these newly created institutions. In 2001, the European Council meeting in Laeken, announced the Declaration on the Future of the European Union 'thereby committing the Union to becoming more democratic, more transparent and more efficient and preparing the way for a Constitution for the citizens of Europe'.[32] A Convention was set up consisting of representatives of the Heads of State or government, of national parliaments, of the European Parliament, of the European Commission, of the Heads of State or government from the accession countries and of the national parliaments from the accession countries. From February to July 2003 in total 102 participants in the Convention drafted a Constitutional Treaty. This document has served as the basis for negotiations of the Intergovernmental Conference comprised of the Heads of State and governments of the Member States and the accession countries.

Before discussing the content of the Draft Constitution with regard to women's representation, we discuss the composition of the Convention, the politicians who drafted the Constitution. Table 9.3 provides the background of the members.

While the separate, national institutions carry relatively much more women, this important, institution-building committee consisted only of 16 per cent women. Again we see that when there is no central coordination guaranteeing a fair balance of men's and women's representation, male politicians win the individual, national competitions and are delegated to these powerful bodies. The European

---

[32] Citation at the website www.european-convention.eu.int. See also Laeken Declaration, *The Future of the European Union*, 15 December 2001.

Chapter 9

Table 9.3: Composition of the European Convention, 2002-2003.

Heads of State or Government		
15 total	2 women	Finland, Sweden
Representatives of national parliaments		
30 total	3 women	Greece, Portugal, UK
Representatives of European Parliament		
16 total	5 women	Netherlands, UK, Belgium, Denmark, Italy
Representatives of European Commission		
2 total	0 women	
Heads of State or Governments accession countries		
13 total	4 women	Poland, Romania, Latvia, Bulgaria
MPs accession countries		
26 total	3 women	Latvia, Slovakia, Cyprus
Observers		
13 total	2 women	Committee of the regions; Economic & Social Committee
115 total	19 women	16.5%

Women's Lobby did protest in 2002 against the unbalanced composition with the slogan: 'Women 16% of the Convention, 50% of the European Population: Is Decision-Making in Europe a Men Only Space?', but their lobby was not successful. So, contrary to the Scottish and Northern Ireland experience, women have not been present from the start in the shaping of the new European Constitution. It is hardly surprising, therefore, that the Draft Constitution is not a very gender-friendly document. To give an example, the English version of the Preamble to the draft

Constitutional Treaty uses the word 'mankind' in the very first sentence, and uses the male possessive pronoun. The European Women's Lobby is also trying hard to have 'Equality of men and women' explicitly mentioned as a basic value.[33] There is just one article in the Draft Constitution that mentions gender in regard to political representation. In Part I, Title IV, Article 26 the following text prescribes the selection of the members of the European Commission:

> Each Member State determined by the system of rotation shall establish a list of three persons, in which both genders shall be represented, whom it considers qualified to be a European Commissioner. By choosing one person from each of the proposed lists, the President-elect shall select the thirteen European Commissioners for their competence, European commitment, and guaranteed independence.[34]

Although this article is an acknowledgement of the current existing gender biases in selection procedures, the selection of one out of three is no guarantee at all for a future gender balanced European Commission.

But the Draft Constitutional Treaty offers a window of opportunity for a gender-balanced future European Parliament. The Draft Constitution embraces the principle of democratic equality (all citizens shall receive equal attention from the Union's institutions) as well as the principle of representative democracy.[35] 'Citizens are directly represented at Union level'; 'every citizen shall have the right to participate in the democratic life of the Union' and 'political parties at European level contribute to forming European political awareness and to expressing the will of Union citizens'.[36] Given these principles much further on in the Draft Constitutional Treaty a provision is made for the future election of the European Parliament. In Part III of the Constitution, Title VI, Article III-232 the following text is mentioned:

> A European law or framework law of the Council of Ministers shall establish the necessary measures for the election of the Members of the European Parliament by direct universal suffrage in accordance with a uniform procedure

---

[33] See www.womenlobby.org.

[34] English version of the text of the draft constitution, www.european-convention.eu.int.

[35] Draft European Constitution, Part I, Title VI, Article 44, English version, 2004, p. 38.

[36] *Ibid.*, Article 45.

Chapter 9

in all Member States or in accordance with principles common to all Member States.

The Council of Ministers shall act unanimously on a proposal from and after obtaining the consent of the European Parliament, which shall act by a majority of its component members. This law or framework of law shall not enter into force until it has been approved by the Member States in accordance with their respective constitutional requirements.[37]

According to this article, the Council of Ministers and the European Parliament have to address in the near future the question of introducing a single common electoral system and what this is going to be. The introduction of a common electoral system provides an excellent opportunity to introduce best practice policies on gender representation and to define a European electoral system that is friendly to women and to other newcomers to politics.

At present each country organises its own election for the Members of the European Parliament and each party runs its own process of candidate selection.

Table 9.4 summarises the methods of election to the European Parliament used in the 15 countries that are object of this study. It is clear that almost all countries use proportional representation, nearly always in a single national constituency. There is some diversity within the group of countries using list-PR systems on the matter of thresholds and on the use of preferential voting. More uniformity is found on the matter of constituency size and structure. In defining a women-friendly system the strategy is to stay as close as possible with the present systems in use for electing the members of the European Parliament, because that will make acceptance of national legislatures and therefore implementation more feasible.

Taking the best practice policies set out in the previous chapters together with the characteristics of the current electoral systems in use, key elements of the new electoral system should be:

- A list-PR voting system;
- A single national constituency;
- A 4 per cent threshold;
- Preferential voting;

---

[37] Draft European Constitution, Part 3, Title VI, Article III-232. English version, 2004, p. 177.

- Gender indication of candidates;
- A term limit for MEPs;
- No '*cumul des mandats*'.

Our overview of gender representation in the 15 countries in chapter 2 showed that, whatever electoral system is used, women are under-represented in all European legislatures. Considering only the manner in which votes cast are translated into seats won, all voting systems used in modern democracies are formally gender blind. They contain no internal mechanism that might induce them to favour one gender over another. Despite the fact that no electoral system formally favours men over women, some electoral systems, notably list-PR systems, do in practice tend to result in the election of greater proportions of women. Under a common electoral system therefore seats should be allocated using a list-PR method. Since nearly all 15 countries use this system at present, introduction of a list-PR system will not be adversary. A European list-PR system should be used in single national constituencies. We have seen that large constituency sizes make it easier for even smaller political parties to achieve a more gender-balanced legislative representation. Of the 15 Member States analysed in this study, 11 already use a single national constituency, so again it should not be hard to accept this element.

There should be a four per cent electoral threshold. While on balance fewer countries use thresholds than do not, we should bear in mind the argument that thresholds help in the creation of a gender balance by favouring the larger parties that in practice find it easier to elect a more balanced parliamentary group. For this reason I suggest to introduce a four per cent threshold for the elections of the European Parliament, which is roughly the average of the percentages currently used in the 15 countries. To set against this, one might consider the argument that thresholds lessen party competition. The threat of losing voters to new, for example green, parties has been a strong driving force for the main parties to allow organisational changes, including party quotas.

The main outstanding issue in relation to list-PR systems concerns the distinction between preferential and non-preferential lists. While the received wisdom is that non-preferential (or 'closed') lists are most friendly to the election of more women legislators, there is no compelling evidence either way in this regard. This is almost certainly because the main argument in favour of closed lists is that these take the choice of candidate away from voters, who may be prejudiced against women. So far, however, there is no evidence suggesting systematic voter prejudice against women candidates. This implies that the distinction between preferential and closed lists should not make a difference to the legislative recruitment of women.

Chapter 9

Table 9.4: Systems for electing MEPs in the 15 countries under observation.

Country	No. of seats	Electoral system	Constituency structure	Who can nominate candidates/lists?	Preferential voting?
Austria	21 (18)	List-PR 4% threshold	Single national constituency	Parties or candidates endorsed by 3 MPs or 1 MEPs or by 2600 voters (signatures)	Yes
Belgium	25 (24)	List-PR	4 regional constituencies	5 MPs from the same linguistic group or 5000 signatures of voters in a certain region	Yes
Denmark	16 (14)	List-PR	Single national constituency	Parties winning seats, or at least 2% vote, in last national election	Yes
Finland	16 (14)	List-PR	Single national constituency	Political parties or association of 2000 voters (signatures)	Yes
France	87 (78)	List-PR 5% threshold	Single national constituency	Parties, € 15,000 deposit	No
Germany	99 (99)	List-PR 5% threshold	Single national constituency	Land or national party lists proposed by 5 members of Bundestag (or Landtag) or 4000 federal (2000 land) voters (signatures)	No
Greece	25 (24)	List-PR 3% threshold	Single national constituency	Political parties	No

Ireland	15 (13)	STV	4 regional constituencies	Candidates may nominate themselves, signatures needed	Yes
Italy	87 (78)	List-PR	5 regional constituencies	Parties with one seat or more in previous EP; or new parties with 50,000 signatures of voters in each constituency	Yes
Luxembourg	6 (6)	List-PR	Single national constituency	One national MP, one MEP or 250 voters may propose a party list	Yes
Netherlands	31 (27)	List-PR	Single national constituency	Political parties. Deposit of € 11,000 for parties not in EP	Yes
Portugal	25 (24)	List-PR	Single national constituency	Political parties	No
Spain	64 (54)	List-PR	Single national constituency	Parties or associations endorsed by 50 legislators or 15,000 voters	No
Sweden	22 (19)	List-PR 4% threshold	Single national constituency	Parties or candidates may nominate themselves	Yes
United Kingdom	87 (78)	List-PR in regions	11 regions	Parties or independent candidate, deposit of £5000 in each region	No

Source: www.europarl.eu.int/election/law In the column indicating the number of seats the distribution of seats in the European Parliament as of the elections of 2004 can be find in brackets.

Empirically, furthermore, while Sweden, the country with the highest proportion of women legislators, used an effectively closed list until very recently, the other countries with high levels of women's representation – Finland, Denmark and the Netherlands – all use preferential lists. Of far greater importance for women's political recruitment is ensuring that party lists are gender-balanced and that women are placed in positions on them that are as good as those of men. It is obviously better if parties adopt such policies voluntarily, since this avoids having to tackle the difficult matter of breaching the principle of free political association in order to legislate for the internal affairs of political parties. It is equally clear, however, that not all political parties can be relied upon to do this, so that methods of enforcing such policies must be explored. It is also clear that any policies that are adopted must be able to withstand challenges under equal opportunities legislation. These considerations interact in complex ways, and it may be that working with preferential lists, and relying upon what does appear to be a lack of prejudice against women among voters, offers the best way forward. This is because a preferential list leaves the final decision on candidate selection with voters. In effectively removing this decision from parties, we may not only have a system that has greater legitimacy among voters, but may also remove the threat of legal challenges based upon the argument that parties are threatening the livelihood of particular groups of individuals by adopting particular candidate-selection policies. This issue certainly deserves detailed legal and constitutional exploration, but for now we can conclude that preferential lists, in which voters have the final say about who is going to represent them in parliament, may in the long term be more effective and resistant to challenge than closed lists as mechanisms for achieving a more gender-balanced legislative representation. For this reason European voters should have the possibility to express their preference for a specific candidate. The majority of the 15 countries already offer preferential voting.

Each ballot paper used in the election of the members of the European Parliament should indicate the sex of the candidate. This provides not only a way for voters to express their preference for a male or female candidate if they wish to do so, but it also forces political parties to show the electorate whether or not they are serious about having a gender balance in their parliamentary parties.

The new electoral provisions should include a term limit for MEPs. Being an incumbent gives by far the best chance of being selected. This has a negative impact on all newcomers to politics, including women. A term limit of, say, 10 years, would guarantee a higher turnover of MEPs and allow for the arrival of more newcomers into the European representative system.

In the description of legislative representation in France, the practice of accumulating political offices is an important explanation for the extremely low participation of women in parliament and regional councils. High-level French women politicians suggested ending the practice of the *'cumul des mandats'* as an alternative for the inclusion of parity in the French Constitution. From a gender perspective, governments should not only impose a term limit on representative positions, but also allow representatives to hold only one political position.

So far we described a woman-friendly *electoral system*. However, as was argued over and over again in chapter 2 and 3, the nomination of candidates and the ranking of lists is the single most important feature if we are seriously concerned with the issue of gender balance. As table 9.4 shows, by far the greatest diversity between the 15 countries under observation has to do with the procedures used to nominate candidates or lists. It is no exaggeration to say that every Member State arranges this matter in a completely different way. However, given the highly valued principle of free political association, there is no way that the European Parliament, Commission, Council of Ministers, national governments or parliaments can force parties to conduct their candidate selection in a specific way. Or they have to interpret Article III-233 of Part 3 of the Draft Constitutional Treaty very broadly. This article reads:

> A European law shall lay down the regulations governing political parties at European level referred to in article I-45/4 and in particular the rules regarding their financing.[38]

The most likely way forward is that the parties represented in the European Parliament will put pressure on their national party leaderships to adopt best practice policies while defining their candidate selection procedures for European elections. The following set of principles for a woman-friendly procedure to select the candidates for the European Parliament can therefore be recommended:

- Control over party lists by party leaderships;
- A profile of the ideal list;
- A transparent and open recruitment practice;
- Scrutinising the performance of incumbents;
- A 'zipper' system.

---

[38] Draft European Constitution, Part 3, Title VI, Article III-233. English version, 2004, p. 178.

Chapter 9

A list-PR electoral system operating in a single, national constituency makes it possible for the leadership of a party to control the recruitment and selection process. National party leaders will then be able to balance the list according to different criteria, including gender.

The chances of women candidates will be enhanced when party leaderships explicitly put forward, for example in a profile of the ideal composition of the Euro delegation, their wish to have a gender-balanced list of candidates. This will make selectors aware of the need to search actively for women candidates.

One reaction to the crisis political parties found themselves in has been to change traditional selection procedures. Lately, many parties have altered their image of what it takes to be an attractive candidate, pressured by low turnout at elections and a decrease in their own membership. The behaviour of voters is much less predictable than it used to be, and short-term factors such as the personality of candidates are becoming more important in deciding which party people vote for.

Given the lower rates of female party membership, it is not sufficient for parties to recruit candidates exclusively from among their own members. A more active recruitment policy, which will involve approaching non-party organisations and other groups, improves the prospect of mobilising women to put themselves forward as candidates. In the same vein, parties should also be more flexible in the criteria they apply when selecting candidates. The importance many parties still attach to a long party career and previous political experience should be reduced and replaced by a greater emphasis upon professional and organisational experience in a range of diverse fields. Women will be much more encouraged to bring themselves forward as candidates with a transparent and professionally conducted candidate-selection process, based upon an agreed profile of the ideal composition of parliamentary party, implemented by a selection committee and including assessment interviews. Searching for candidates outside the party, for example by placing advertisements in newspapers, enhances the number of women aspirants. In order to be able to select 50 per cent women candidates, a party needs at least 50 per cent women aspirants. In most countries the rate of party membership of women tends to be lower than that of men, while women party members tend to be less active in the party. Special care, therefore, has to be given to the recruitment stage in the selection process. Parties should recruit as openly and widely as possible so as to convince women to bring themselves forward as aspirant candidates.

One similarity among the various candidate selection procedures is that incumbents have by far the best chance of being reselected. This happens in every electoral system and has an obvious negative impact on all newcomers to the political arena, including women. One might say in defence of this practice that experience in the job is a very important asset. On the other hand, being a politician is not an ordinary job. Communication with individual voters and legitimacy among the electorate as a whole are vital parts of the job. Involving as many people as possible, ensuring a turnover of politicians and above all making possible the injection of 'new blood' into the representative system are very important in this context. Incumbency should not lead automatically to reselection. The performance of incumbents should be taken into account in the selection procedure.

The final matter at issue concerns how to ensure that parties nominate equal numbers of men and women candidates. Given the unbalanced representation of men and women in political decision-making, specific policies are still needed to ensure the nomination of sufficient numbers of women to good places on party lists. By far the most obvious alternative is the zipper system of alternating men and women candidates on the party list. In a large list, electing to large constituencies, with a preferential element in the voting system, it is difficult to see how this could legally be challenged on equal opportunities grounds. It is important, however, that a zipper system, or indeed any other quota system, is combined with other policies to increase the participation of women in the internal life of political parties, including training programmes for female cadres.

Imposing the zipper system on recalcitrant parties would involve interfering with the principle of free political association. In several European countries this is felt to be unacceptable. Then the alternative is to leave the policy as voluntary but use public policy grounds to argue that public funding should only be available to parties implementing gender-balanced party lists. Such a condition would definitely fit in the above-mentioned Article III-233 on a European law on political parties.

CONCLUSION

Politics is in need of a thorough cleansing. Citizens are making this clear by not playing according to the rules of representative party democracy. Long-standing political parties are in particular trouble, also because some of their own leaders have been seen as corrupt and have lost the trust of many adherents. The public image of party politics is bad and citizens' interest in political decision-making is low. In the past decade governments and political parties have introduced many different reforms in order to stem this tide of disillusionment. In some countries, radical change of institutional arrangements has taken place, and efforts have been made to introduce new ways of involving as many citizens as possible in political decision-making. Changing the institutions is one way to address the crisis.

Chapter 9

Another is to replace the kind of people who have been in charge in politics over the past decades.

Not only are governments and parties convinced of the need to improve the image of politics, amongst other ways by widening their recruitment pool, but women activists in and outside parties also perceive the opportunities created by this need for reform. Thirty years of studying the question of 'why so few' now bears fruit. Their knowledge of gender biases in recruitment, selection and nomination procedures for political jobs is used to lobby for institutions that guarantee a fair representation of women. However, as was the case in the previous century, women still need to combine their efforts to fight for this. Only when there is a broadly based women's coalition present in the debate on constitutional reforms, will success be feasible. When there is no strong women's coalition, as was the case in the European Convention, there is not much chance for guarantees on numerical and substantive representation of women, notwithstanding the many formal commitments to achieving gender equality in political decision-making at national and European level.

The need to make political decision-making more inclusive is clearly present in Europe. The possibilities to do so are there, as the sketch of a 'women or newcomer friendly' electoral system and candidate selection procedure shows us. The final question is whether there is the political will to implement these changes.

CHAPTER 10

THE FUTURE OF EUROPEAN GENDER DEMOCRACY

This final chapter brings together the main reasons for writing this book. The first reason is to satisfy our curiosity about the results of 30 years of struggle for a greater representation of women in politics. At the end of the 1960s, women inside and outside political parties started a crusade for a piece of the political action. Since then, many strategies have been developed and implemented and women activists have intensely lobbied parties and governments to put mechanisms in place guaranteeing the inclusion of women. Feminist civil servants within Departments of Internal Affairs and Equal Opportunities Units have written policy programs directed at increasing women's political participation. Female, as well as a few male, academics have researched the question of 'why so few'. What has been the outcome of all this diligent labour? Now that we see an improved social and economic status of women in the majority of the 15 EU countries, what has happened to women's political role? In the first section we shall summarise the state of the art on women's political representation in the 15 countries under investigation, in the Netherlands and in the ten countries that joined the EU in May 2004.

The overall conclusion for Europe is that at the start of the 21st century, the numerical presence of women in representative bodies and in governments is higher than before. The second question addressed in this chapter is how this success can be explained. Sharing political positions is about sharing power. How have women succeeded in convincing the long-term tenants of power – men – to start sharing this precious commodity with women? Which strategies have been successful under which conditions? Are quota laws the only real guarantee for a balanced representation of political bodies in the future?

The third question concerns whether this success in numbers will be permanent. Can we expect more diverse and colourful pictures of newly installed cabinets or of European summits in the near future? There are many factors that may reverse the positive trend in women's political representation. Young, well-educated,

Chapter 10

women, who themselves experienced no sex discrimination may yet turn against positive action measures for women, including women in politics. The embracing of a gender mainstreaming approach at both international and national levels provides excuses for governments to discard Equal Opportunities Units with a coordinating competence, as well as specific women's policies. The same is true for political parties where women's sections may be abolished. A third danger is the rise of populist parties in Europe, the majority of which advocate conservative views on the role of women in society. Last but not least is the danger that women as a group choose against politics as a career in favour of other spheres of life. We have seen examples in the previous chapters of women political leaders who voluntarily make room for male contenders or women council members who give up after one term under the pressure of time constraints and a perceived lack of results.

In the fourth section we shall consider whether a 'New Politics' is appearing on the scene; if so, what does this look like? The fabric of representative democracy is unravelling, with regard both to the relationship between citizens and their representatives and to the role that parties play in society. We have seen in chapter 9 that there are numerous ways to renew politics in order to make it more inclusive. The institutions of representative party democracy can easily be revamped, while new institutions of direct or deliberative democracy can be created.

In the final section we conclude that the debate on gender relations in general and in politics in particular will not disappear from the political agenda of Europe and may even gain in importance.

RESULTS OF 30 YEARS' STRUGGLE FOR REPRESENTATION

The 15 European Countries

In each of the 15 countries we have been discussing here women have fought for a fair representation of women and men in politics. Suffrage for women was not easy to gain and when it became clear that voting *rights* did not automatically lead to balanced representation, a permanent lobby of women activists, both in and outside political parties, developed. The role women play in politics is strongly related to their social and economic status. We have seen in chapter 2 that, in those countries where women take an active part in the labour force, their participation rate is relatively higher than in countries where the employment figures of women lag behind. The social and economic status of women has improved steadily. In the majority of countries women have caught up with men in education, fulfil their roles at the labour market and, in some of the northern countries, (mainly younger) men have taken over some of the care of children as well. In some countries childcare facilities have been greatly improved. In all of the 15 countries some kind of gender equality government policy, together with a so-called women's machinery, have been instrumental in the general advancement of women. But the degree of advancement differs among the 15 countries, depending on factors such as the dominance of conservative values on gender roles, often proclaimed by the Church, on other cultural values such as machismo, but also on access to education and on the availability of welfare state provisions. However, examples of *formal* inequality between men and women are hard to find at the start of the 21st century. This does not mean, of course, that there are no longer any wrongs or abuses. The difficult circumstances of many women should not be under-estimated, nor should the persistent gender differences in pay, employment, taxes and so on, as well as continuing sexual violence against women, be overlooked. The world is still far from perfect in the 21st century but, at least in the 15 European countries we have been discussing here, the world is socially and economically less imperfect for women than it was a century ago.

So the fight for political equal representation was in most cases part of the general struggle for gender equality, often led by the same women activists. But the strategies and the players to be lobbied were different. The objective was to influence those who dominated the recruitment and selection procedures for political office: the political parties. It was either to cultivate the existing political parties or to launch a women's party. This latter strategy has not been used very often although, unknown to many political scientists, we do find examples of women's parties in Sweden (1990s), in Denmark and Great Britain (around 1918), in Ireland (1982), in Belgium (1972), in (West) Germany (1986), in France (1978), in Spain (1980) in Italy (1982) and in the Netherlands (around 1918 and in the 1970s and 1980s).[1] Most of these parties however were neither very successful in elections nor long-lasting. The other strategy, of working within existing parties and changing institutions and procedures, has appeared to be more fruitful. The women's sections of political parties have been very creative and persuasive in their attempts to change the party leaderships' views on women's representation. These sections were also important as recruitment pools: many women cabinet ministers started their careers in women's groups.

---

[1] M. Leyenaar, 'Women's Parties: A Strategy for Power', paper presented at the Global summit of Women, 16-19 February 1994, Taipei, Taiwan, p. 1.

Chapter 10

Figure 10.1: Percentage of women MPs in 1980/1981 and in 2002/2003.

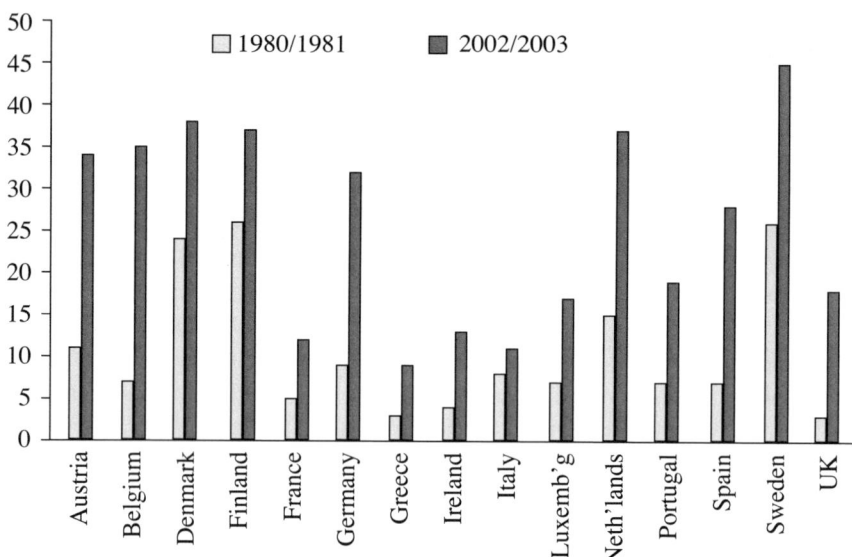

Figure 10.1 shows the development of women's representation in 23 years in the national parliaments.

In *all* 15 countries women's representation in parliament increased between 1980 and 2003. In seven of the countries more than 30 per cent of parliamentarians are women. The stragglers are France, Greece, Ireland and Italy. In these four countries the partition between public and private in relation to men's and women's roles has persisted for the longest time. The elitist and masculine culture of the *Ecole Nationale d'Administration* (ENA), the gateway to high-level political and administrative jobs in France, has worked as an almost impenetrable bastion for women. The culture of machismo in Greece and Italy is responsible for a resilient old boys' network to which women can never belong. The practice of clientelism, combined with a tendency for voters to rely more on male than on female representatives, is another firm barrier in these two countries. In Ireland women suffer from longstanding, though fading, cultural values that have for many years deemed women's proper place to be at home. The practice of electing MPs by SMP, both in France and Italy does not help women either. Given the very low representation figures, it is hardly a surprise that three of these four countries, France, Greece and Italy have already introduced, or are thinking of introducing, quota laws guaranteeing a greater gender balance in the legislatures.

The Dutch Case

What is the outcome of the demand for a greater representation of women in politics in the Netherlands? Chapters 4-7 presented a case study of the empowerment of women in this country. The narrative started in 1883 when Aletta Jacobs confronted the government of Amsterdam with her demand to be put on the list of voters, since she satisfied all conditions for eligibility. At that time it was still possible to laugh the matter off, but 34 years later suffrage for women was inserted in the Constitution. The Netherlands is an example of a country where the representation of women has increased steadily since the 1970s to reach about 37 per cent in the 2004 parliament. It has outlived the confessional background of Dutch society and practices such as pillarisation and consocationalism with their negative influence on women's participation in politics. It has been a long and difficult road for women. At first the only women allowed to enter the political game were those who equalled men – in the sense that they had no caring tasks. They were unmarried and childless. They were professionals and as such were let in the game. Only in the 1970s and later with the rise of feminism, were gender differences recognised. In politics this meant acknowledgement of both women's and men's interests, and of the importance of having women in politics, who would have a better eye and ear for women's needs and demands. Women MPs contributed by expanding the political agenda with issues such as the legalisation of abortion, the need for child-care facilities and legislation against the trafficking and abuse of women.

Without under-estimating the role that women's organisations have played, for example in demanding women's policies and an Equal Opportunities Department, an important player has been the government, and more specifically feminist civil servants working on the issue of the empowerment of women in the Ministry of Internal Affairs and the Ministry of Social Affairs. Their continuous pressure from the inside, helped by women in the political parties, created an atmosphere that allowed for numerous policy plans on the issue which were implemented over the years. Governments' approach has always been one of convincing the main players and not compelling them. Party leaders were asked over and over again to address the issue and recruit, nominate and select more women in political offices.

The steady monitoring practice that started in 1992 by the Ministry of Internal Affairs has contributed heavily to the success of this 'soft approach'.

The importance of taking measures, of directing and steering from above and of constant monitoring becomes even clearer when we analyse women's political participation at the decentralised levels of government. Since 1990, the overall figure of women local councillors has stayed the same, while the percentage at the national level steadily increased. A close analysis of the candidate nomination process showed that this is not the result of fewer women candidates, but rather because women local councillors leave the office after one term. With each local election, more women candidates can be found at eligible places on the lists but, by the time they enter the council, their predecessors have left. Women councillors, more than their male colleagues, give up after one term, often because of time constraints and because of a lack of concrete results. The steady rise of independent, local, lists is another explanation for the lack of results at the local level. These parties have fewer incentives to actively search for women candidates.

The overall conclusion on the political representation of women in the Netherlands is positive. Party leaderships have shown to be willing to share power with women. The parties on the left use a 50-50 policy in their recruitment and selection procedures, while the centre parties nominate between 30-40 per cent women candidates. There is a clear overtone of political correctness to appoint women in the cabinet and in other high-level political offices.

An Enlarged Europe

The EU administration also helped to keep the issue of gender representation on the agenda. Several resolutions and recommendations have been issued calling upon the Member States to take policy measures improving women's political role. The European Parliament took its own advice seriously and managed to have a mere 30 per cent women in its midst. But the selection of MEPs of course happens nationally, so the explanations for the success of women have to be found at that level. In chapter 2 we mentioned as an important reason that, since it was a new institution in 1979, no men had to step down in order to share power with women. Since women joined in right from the beginning, there was no culture of values and traditions shaped by male politicians. Women MEPs declared in interviews that the European Parliament always had a much more women-friendly image and this had its impact on the nominating parties as well.

Women's presence in the European Commission is another matter. In both the 1994-1999 and the 1999-2004 terms, women composed only 25 per cent of the Commission. Here too the problem is that the final composition of the Commission is the result of many negotiations and decisions at many different levels, European and nationally, since there is not one coordinating body with an oversight into the overall nomination process.

So far the EU never issued a binding directive on gender equality in political representation. In the opinion of most political leaders, politics is a too sensitive field in which sovereignty must be respected. Nor has it been an issue in the negotiations with the accession countries. The latter would have been difficult, of course, given the fact that some of the 'old countries' have not complied either.

EXPLAINING THE SUCCESS

The steadily growing presence of women in the 15 legislatures is the result of the application of a range of strategies by several groups of women. In order to discuss this range of strategies, we turn back to the five stages of representation distinguished in the analytical framework in chapter 3.

Voting

We learned from the Dutch case that the struggle for women's suffrage was one of the first true clashes between groups of women and the male political elite on the issue of power sharing. All over Europe women had literally to struggle for voting rights. Although a range of methods have been used to convince the respective parliaments to vote women in, the successful ending has been very much a result of the *joint* effort of so many women. We have seen at both ends of the 20th century, the power of women's rights activists working together with women from different political parties, with feminists working in governments and with feminist academics. Collectively they have been capable of gaining voting rights, of demanding quotas within parties or quota legislation and of securing women-friendly electoral systems in new constitutions.

Recruitment

The previous chapters have illustrated that political recruitment is closely related to gender equality in the wider society. In countries where the gendered division of roles has been persistent, such as Ireland, Greece and Italy, women's participation in politics has hardly increased. Greater gender equality in education, in professional status and in the caring for children and the elderly also had a positive impact on political interest and political efficacy, both important attitudes when deciding to take up a political career.

Another successful strategy for women has been the expansion of the recruitment pool by turning to individuals who are not party members. More transparent recruitment practices, such as broad advertising campaigns, resulted in relatively more women potential candidates for political office, than the use of the traditional party networks. The general appeal of politics should also be boosted. More knowledge about the functioning of the political system and one's own role in it, as well as a better understanding of the democratic principles for decision-making, may lead to greater interest and participation. Given the lack of political interest in national and, especially, European politics, a greater concern for civic education does seem an important way forward.

Selection

It is by now crystal clear that selection procedures and criteria have formed important barriers for newcomers wanting to gain access to representative office. A crucial asset has been the gaining of knowledge of the existing gender biases in selection procedures. After all, these procedures often pass themselves off as gender-neutral. To ask (former) aldermen to apply when there is a vacancy for a mayor position seems a logical step. However, when there are fewer women aldermen available than male, this is a gender biased selection criterion. Insight into these types of gender bias, in the dominant use of the 'old boys' networks' as recruitment pools, in the dealing among male party elites from different parties on political jobs, such as cabinet posts, the position of state commissioner and a mayoral position in the large cities and in the formal ways selection of candidates should take place, has been one of the important tools of women striving for a gender balance in politics. Again the joining of forces by feminist academics, feminist bureaucrats, women party members and women activists has led to successful attempts of changing constitutions and party statutes. Having knowledge of the effects of certain aspects of electoral systems on the selection, such as the fact that incumbents are very difficult to defeat, it becomes possible to define the right strategy (in this case, a term limit). An essential tool has been quota-setting in parties and the introduction of quota legislation. In the 1970s and 1980s in particular, when local party leaderships were not yet convinced of the justification for demands for a higher representation of women, quota-setting by the national party leaders was often the only way to get attention. Quotas functioned as an eye-opener: local selectors realised for the first time that there were hardly any women party members present in the meetings and, as a result, they started to approach women more explicitly during candidate selections. Quota legislation was more in fashion in the 1990s and 2000s than previously, because it is a policy that governments can implement when political parties fail to select more women as representatives. Quotas are still a very effective strategy to get more women selected. The zipper system that alternates men and women candidates seems to be the most promising procedure for achieving a balanced participation.

Election

In the early days, women candidates for political office were confronted with a biased image of how a politician should look and behave. Women simply did not fit the traditional image of a political leader. These days, voters have as much trust in women politicians than they have in men. The increasing distrust in, even disgust for politicians who have been in office for years may even have a positive effect on the electoral attractiveness of women. Women political leaders project, almost by definition, an image of the new, fresh and (therefore) more honest and more responsive politician.

In electoral systems were a lot of money is needed for campaigning, the fact that in general women have less money available than men do, can be a serious drawback. Funds, such as Emily's List, set up to support women running for office financially have been a great success.

As we have seen in the previous chapters, it happens now and then that the systems for electing representatives are being reformed or that other forms of democratic decision-making are being introduced. Many examples of such reform have shown the utmost importance of *being there right from the start*. A timely presence makes it possible to force the architects of new constitutional arrangements or other political institutions to integrate a gender perspective in the plans, as we have seen in examples from Scotland and Wales. For the future, binding agreements are necessary enforcing a gender assessment of each new plan to change political institutions.

Representation

The phrase 'from token to player' accurately describes the development of women's political representation. The first women in parliament were eccentric and watched closely by their colleagues, press and public. They suffered from the heightened effects of tokenism. They also paved the path for those who followed: male colleagues now knew that women MPs did not burst into tears during a harsh dispute and were equally capable of performing the job. A successful strategy therefore has been the demand for a *larger* share of the pie. The argument in favour of quotas has always been that quotas guarantee the access of a *group* of women at the same time. Many scholars point to the link between numerical and substantive representation. Dahlerup (1988) showed that when women moved from a 'small minority to a large minority' they were able to influence the institutional culture, the political agenda and the outcome of decision-making in a more women-friendly way.[2] Participating in decision-making is one of the surest strategies to remove gender bias from policies and programmes. When enough women entered positions of power, they were able to shape and alter the systems and institutions of power. Female MPs themselves had to improve working conditions. Examples are the new rules on pregnancy leave for women MPs and the child-care facilities one finds in most legislative bodies.

A final successful strategy has been the constant monitoring of the presence of women in the representative bodies and the dissemination of these statistics. By doing this political parties and other selectors have been kept aware of the (lack of) progress in the empowerment of women.

In the previous chapters we have read how different players and selectors used a wide range of strategies in order to increase women's political representation. These strategies ranged from knowledge building and awareness rising to facilitating training for women aspirants, to quota legislation. Here we have highlighted a few of the main strategies and policies, such as:

- the necessary precondition of joining forces;
- having at one's disposal the exact knowledge of the formal selection procedures and the existing gender biases;
- the extension of the recruitment pool by widening it to people outside the political parties;
- a thorough scrutiny of selection criteria;
- the setting of quotas;
- applying a gender assessment of political reforms; and
- constant monitoring.

---

[2] D. Dahlerup, 1988, pp. 275-298.

All this have resulted in a political scenery where there is no gender balance yet, but where there are enough women on the stage able to pave the path for more women.

DANGERS THAT LIE IN WAIT

Having registered that in 7 of the 15 countries under investigation there are more than 30 per cent women MPs and that the overall percentage of women MEPs is 30 per cent, does not mean that a 50-per cent representation is close and just a matter of time. We have learned from the Dutch experience that sudden turmoil in politics, in this case the sudden extreme popularity of a new political leader and his party, may lead to a decrease of women's representation both in parliament and in government. With just one woman minister in the 2002 cabinet, the Netherlands had turned the clock back to 1956 when the first woman minister was appointed. A public outcry by high-level women in the parties and women's organisations resulted in the appointment of five women in the next cabinet. We should not forget that sharing political positions is about sharing power and power is a commodity which is in demand and not easy to part with. This becomes clear again when you look at top positions in politics. The higher the rank and status of the position, the fewer women you find, because the competition for these rare jobs is fierce. A very illustrative example is the European Convention, with only 16 per cent women. Since only one or two persons from each category were eligible, mostly men won these mini-competitions and were delegated off. At these moments the drive for power takes over all rational arguments about the need for a Convention in which many different perspectives are reflected in order to come up with a document recognisable and legitimate for as many different kinds of citizen as possible. Apart from the eternal threat of men taking back the positions of power, there are a few other dangers to a gender balanced political representation in the future.

First, a feminist backlash is noticeable in many parts of Europe. Especially young, highly educated, women in their 20s, who themselves experienced no gender discrimination in their education and in finding a job, do not see any problems for women as a group. They perceive feminism and the separate treatment of women, using devices such as positive action and quota-setting as degrading. In chapter 8 we mentioned the group Italian women who referred to the quota laws as 'panda' laws. It fits the *zeitgeist* from the 21st century to say that women should no longer be viewed as 'victims', as people in need of special treatment. In chapter 2 it was mentioned that this was the main reason for several parties in the Scandinavian countries to abolish quotas. Individual women are now more difficult to mobilise

Chapter 10

on the issue of women's political representation. Another consequence is that the nature of women's organisations has changed. With regard to the Dutch case we noticed that women's organisations tend to be more professional these days and they focus more on the lack of *economic* power of women. Only in those countries where women's representation is still below 15 per cent, do we still find large women's coalitions lobbying consistently for more women in politics, like the Women's Political Association in Ireland, the Women for Parity in France and the Political Association of Women in Greece. So in the majority of the countries where we find around one-third women legislators, it is more difficult than it used to be to form large coalitions of individual women and of separate women's groups in order to lobby during elections, formation of cabinets or during constitutional changes for more women.

This feminist backlash is also present inside the legislatures. Now that women MPs are a substantial group in some of the EU Member States, with most women MPs having a high educational background and considerable working experience, these women do not want to focus too much on gender differences. In the 1970 and 1980s women MPs were very successful in changing the content of the political agenda. As previously mentioned, issues as child care, sexual violence, the difficult combination of caring and work became fully fledged political issues. These gender differences in parliamentary behaviour have mostly disappeared and, in some cases, so have the parliamentary committees on equal opportunities.

A second, related, danger refers to the practice of gender mainstreaming. To attain equality and to reach a balance of power, we have seen that equal opportunities departments have presented many 'women-specific' policies. The danger is that mainstreaming might be used to displace or eliminate these specific women's programmes before there is any *guarantee* of an integration of women's needs and interests in general policies. By referring to the now accepted approach of gender mainstreaming, some political parties in the Netherlands have already abolished their women's sections. Representation of women in politics as well as gender equality policies is from now on the sole responsibility of the party leadership. The same may happen with the governmental departments on equal opportunities, as in the Netherlands where the regional women's bureaus already disappeared. The danger exists that in those countries where women's social, economical and political advancement is clearly visible, governments and parties will decide unilaterally that *the emancipation of women is complete* and specific structures and policies are no longer necessary. This will then mean a standstill in these countries. Other, less-developed EU Member States, may follow suit as well as politicians at the European level. Future binding agreements on gender equality and on gender representation will then be out of the question. This could be a risky development as the example of the composition of the European Convention shows us. When there is no coordinating body in charge of selection procedures, women tend not to be chosen. Other examples are the European Commission and the local, independent, parties.

To avoid this threat, both approaches – mainstreaming and separate programming – should be simultaneously promoted. The integration of a gender perspective in general policies should obviously be carefully *monitored* enabling national and European equal opportunities departments to keep an eye on progress.

Another factor that can stop the progress in women's political representation is the rise of populist parties in Europe. In the 1990s, new populist parties came to the fore, such as the Freedom Party Austria (*Freiheitliche Partei Österreichs*, FPÖ), Lega Nord in Italy and the LPF in the Netherlands. These parties placed a strong emphasis on the defence of their own countries' cultural values. They mobilised support against two things that they saw as threats to the survival of Western European values – globalisation and Islam. Playing into citizens' dissatisfaction with the long-standing political parties and politicians, they mobilised people against these political elites. Another characteristic was a hostility towards the expansion of the public sector and the welfare state. Right-wing populist parties embrace liberal individualism and want to maximise the autonomy of the individual.[3] In the 1990s populist parties became successful in Europe, especially in attracting first-time voters.[4] Interestingly enough all available research points to a gender gap in voting preferences for these populist new-right parties. Men are much more likely than women to support the new right.[5] Explanations are the greater dependency of women on the welfare state and hence a reluctance to support a party wanting to dismantle it and women's greater loyalty to Christian Democracy given their greater church attendance.[6] Other factors of importance are men's greater emphasis on law and order and the fact that political cynicism is less important for women than

---

[3] E. Gidengil *et al.*, 'The Gender Gap in Support for the New Right: The Case of Canada', paper prepared for the conference on 'Populism in North America, South America and Europe: Comparative and Historical', Italy, January 2003, pp. 3, 4; see also P. Taggert, 'New Populist Parties in Western Europe', in *West European Politics,* 1995.

[4] Center for Applied Research, *The Changing Austrian Voter*, 2000.

[5] H. Betz, *Radical Right-Wing Populism in Western Europe*, New York, St. Martin's Press, 1992, pp. 142-146.

[6] H. Kitschelt, *The Radical Right in Western Europe: A Comparative Analysis*, Ann Arbor, University of Michigan Press, 1995, p. 297.

men. In a Canadian study of the support for the Alliance, a populist party in the 2000 federal election, it appeared that women were as cynical as men, but that they attached less significance to this.[7] The danger is that many of these populist parties who put an emphasis on traditional family values will not be much in favour of nominating women as their candidates. The huge electoral success in 2002 of the LPF, the populist party in the Netherlands, was the main reason for the decrease in women's parliamentary representation there.

A final possible threat to a future balanced participation of men and women in politics comes from women themselves. We mentioned in chapter 3 the fact that fewer women than before are willing to adhere to the demands of leadership positions, both in politics and in business. An important reason for women politicians to quit after one term in a representative office is the view they take of the time that is needed and the results that can be achieved. Politics is time consuming, while the concrete results can be few and far between. Woodward and Lyon (2000), using interviews with 1647 male and female leaders in politics and business from 27 different countries, concluded that women politicians work on average about 66 hours a week, compared to 36 hours by other women in the same age group. Further, they conclude, 'politicians of both genders have the highest occurrence of a 90+ hour week'.[8] They explain these 'super-human weeks' by the need to be available, not only during those working hours when civil servants are present, but also in their private time on weekends, evenings and early mornings. Spending so much time on the job means of course less time for other aspects of life. In these interviews, politicians were also asked about their perceptions of the sacrifices and trade-offs they made in the pursuit of their careers (table 10.2).

More women than men sacrifice their own personal time and time spent with friends, while they claim to make fewer sacrifices in time spend with children and partner. A relatively small percentage of both genders emphasise a sacrifice in relation to children.[9]

Another aspect is the culture of politics. Looking at the debates in the British Lower House, it is perfectly understandable why many women (and men) decide

---

[7] E. Gidengil *et al.*, 2003, pp. 11, 12.

[8] A. Woodward and D. Lyon, 'Gendered Time and Women's Access to Power', in M. Vianello and G. Moore (eds.), 2000, pp. 92, 93.

[9] *Ibid.*, pp. 100, 101.

Table 10.2: Sacrifices in time (percentages).

	% male	% female
Personal free time	75	83
Friends and social time	54	62
Time with children	54	29
Time with partner	51	40
Delay having children	12	16

Source: A. Woodward and D. Lyon, 2000, p. 101.

not to become involved in party politics. Part of the feminine culture is to solve problems through negotiation and compromise and not through fighting and conflict.[10] It seems that women as a group do care about the policies and outcome of decision-making, but they care less about office in and for itself. Office-seeking is less important than policy-seeking as a motive for women to become involved in politics.

TIME FOR NEW POLITICS

Behind the demand for a greater representation of women in politics has always been the suggestion that the presence of women will improve the quality of politics. In the early days of the suffragettes, gender differences in character, opinions and behaviour were very much emphasised. Women parliamentarians were going to improve the world in the sense that more attention would be given to the conditions of children and mothers and less to the military and war. Chapter 4 discussed

---

[10] M. Brouns and M. Sibbes, *Research and Support. Beeldvorming in Taal en Bedrijf*, Universiteit Groningen, 1999, p. 20.

the women's parties of the 1920s, which homed in on the typical qualities of women, like being pacifist, caring and sensitive. We saw that the early women MPs were expected to deal with issues related to motherhood and care for the elderly. In the 1970s and 1980s, the ideology shifted from a focus on 'women's qualities' to the defence of 'women's interests'. Women as such were not 'better human beings' but, given their different upbringing and socialisation, only they themselves could defend the interests of women in politics. At that time the emphasis was more on broadening the political agenda to include issues such as child care and, later, the legalisation of abortion and abolition of sexual violence. At that time, too, debate started on the possible effect of having more women politicians on the procedures of political decision-making. Because women were supposed to be less hierarchical and less power oriented, political decision-making would change when women entered politics in greater numbers. The argument for more women in politics altered once more in the 1990s and 21st century. Now, a more inclusive politics is demanded, because traditional representative governance is seen as no longer working properly. New faces and new procedures seem to be necessary in order to keep citizens interested and participating.

More often, the term 'New Politics' is used, especially in the context of devolution campaigns of the type that happened recently in Great Britain. As a counterpoint to the (British) Westminster parliament, the newly created parliaments in Scotland and Wales would involve smaller parties as well because they would use proportional representation instead of SMP; the influence of MPs would be guaranteed by a strong parliamentary committee system and power sharing would take place through multi-party bargaining and coalition government.[11]

These features of New Politics are not so 'new' for those EU Member States where list-PR systems are already in use. Other defining characteristics of New Politics, however, are also valid for other European countries. We refer here to better relations between parliament and civil society, as well as greater access for, and participation by, citizens. A more inclusive parliament in terms of gender, as well as the application of gender mainstreaming, also fits under the heading of New Politics. The new Scottish Parliament, for example, has included in its Standing Orders the requirement that 'all Executive Bills are accompanied by a statement

---

[11] F. Mackay, F. Myers and A. Brown, 'Towards a New Politics? Women and the Constitutional Change in Scotland', in: A. Dobrowolsky and V. Hart (eds.), Palgrave, 2003, p. 4.

of their potential impact on equal opportunities'. It also established an Equal Opportunities Parliamentary Committee.[12]

New Politics and Gender

In order to change the image of politics, women candidates are now in demand. Women political leaders are still the exception rather than the rule and once appointed, therefore, transmit to citizens a sense of change. There are also examples of women becoming presidents, prime ministers or cabinet ministers, because they were either the only candidates acceptable to competing political parties or because circumstances were difficult and violent and a woman political leader was more likely to calm down the situation. Examples of the first case are Mary Robinson and Mary McAleese who both became presidents of Ireland in, respectively, 1990 and 1997. Examples of women political leaders as 'saviours' are Mo Mowlam, Secretary of State for Northern Ireland in the 1997 cabinet of British Prime Minister Tony Blair and Tansu Çiller, who served Turkey as prime minister from 1993-1995.

With regard to the introduction of so-called women's interests, we can conclude that most such issues are now part of the normal political routine. The more women MPs there are, the easier it is to articulate these issues in legislative debates. In chapter 7, we discussed gender mainstreaming as a relatively new approach to ensuring that policy effects on women are taken into account. When more parliaments make gender mainstreaming part of their Standing Orders, as the Scottish and Dutch Parliaments have done, articulation and defence of women's interests will be more strongly guaranteed. However as was mentioned in the previous section, strict monitoring is also needed. When women are in a clear minority in legislative or advisory bodies, such as happened in the European Convention, then chances are high that a gender perspective is lacking in the resulting policy documents.

The third element of New Politics is the promotion of a more participatory democracy, in the sense that more citizens and civil society groups can take part in political decision-making. In chapter 9 it was shown how local governments experiment extensively with forms of decision-making that include as many citizens as possible. Governments are really trying to increase the legitimacy of decision-making and to involve citizens from the very beginning of the planning of new

---

[12] *Ibid.*, pp. 4-6.

policies. The spread of internet and other ICT applications support these developments. Another approach has been the creation of new institutions of participatory democracy, such as the introduction of a referendum or citizens' juries. Both institutions are not discriminatory on gender. Citizens' juries and civic forums have the advantage that there is ample room for discussion and deliberation, which guarantees the input of both women and men. A final example of making political institutions more inclusive is the introduction of quota laws. Chapter 8 made it very clear that the advantage of quota laws is that, when implemented, they guarantee success since laws have a mandatory effect. In those countries where there is hardly any progress in women's political representation, quota legislation will be the only way forward.

The hope for the future is that policy-makers acknowledge the need for applying a kind of gender assessment to each proposal to reform political institutions and procedures. Thus a decision by the Dutch parliament on reforming the electoral system from a list-PR system with one national district into a mixed system with 20 multi-member districts should not be taken without looking at the consequences this has for the (s)election of women.[13] In chapter 9, it was shown that there are many ways to make political institutions more women-friendly. A good example is the practice of 'twinning', mentioned in chapter 2 in relation to the selection of candidates in Scotland. This is a perfect solution to the obstacles the SMP electoral system form for electing women candidates.

GENDER DEMOCRACY AS A CONDITION OF GOOD EUROPEAN GOVERNANCE

National states as well as European institutions need to reform political decision-making. This is true for national states because too many citizens are disinterested in politics and do not participate. It is true for European institutions because of a similar lack of interest on the part of citizens, and because of the recent enlargement, which has added 10 more Member States. The intention to create a large numerical and substantive representation of women in politics should be embedded in any debate on institutional or policy reform. The chapters in this book have provided many examples of how this can be done.

---

[13] The Dutch government tabled a reform law on the electoral system in 2004 stating that a mixed system should replace the list PR system.

The Future of European Gender Democracy

Despite the progress in enhancing women's political involvement, the issue of gender representation is likely to stay on the political agenda. In those countries with relatively low percentages of women legislators, demands for quota laws will become louder. In countries where there has been progress that was followed, due to certain developments, by a relapse, women will stand up, demonstrate and demand their fair share. An example is the reduction of the number of women in the Swiss government in December 2003. Instead of the expected three out of seven positions, only one female minister was selected by the parliament. The reaction was the largest demonstration of women ever. The old slogan, 'no taxation without representation', used by women at the time of the Declaration of Sentiments at Seneca Falls, New York in 1848, may come back in use, for example during the referendums on the Draft European Constitution.[14]

A balanced gender representation in politics is strongly correlated with gender equality in the wider society. The issue of gender equality will also grow in importance, now that more countries where traditional Catholicism still has a strong impact on gender roles have become part of European's decision-making structures. Another factor is the debate in some of the EU states on the growing influence of Islam in relation to gender roles.

In order not to lose the ground that has been won in recent years, there is a need for great clarity on the importance of gender equality and gender political representation. The simplest way to achieve this is to embed these as conditions for good European governance in a European Constitution, combined with sanctions against those Member States that do not comply. European funding should only be available to Member States implementing gender equality, as well as gender balanced governments and representative bodies. It is clearly time to introduce the best practice policies outlined in this book. The result will be a genuinely gender-balanced Europe, and national political bodies that will stand as outstanding examples of inclusiveness and legitimacy to the rest of the world.

---

[14] The Declaration of the Seneca Falls Convention, using the model of the US Declaration of Independence, forthrightly demanded that the rights of women as right-bearing individuals be acknowledged and respected by society. It was signed by 68 women and 32 men.

ABBREVIATIONS OF POLITICAL PARTIES

DUTCH PARTIES

AOV	General Association for the Elderly
ARP	Anti-Revolutionary Party
CD	Centre Democrats
CDA	Christian Democratic Party
CHU	Christian Historical Union
CPN	Communist Party Netherlands
CU	Christian Union
D66	Democrats 66
DS'70	Democratic Socialists 70
EVP	Evangelical People's Party
GL	Green Left
GPV	Reformed Political League
KVP	Catholic People's Party
LN	Livable Netherlands
LPF	List Pim Fortuyn
LSP	Liberal State Party
PPR	Progressive Radical Party
PSP	Pacifistic Socialist Party
PvdA	Labour Party
RPF	Reformed Political Federation
SDAP	Social Democratic Labour Party
SGP	Political Reformed Party
SP	Socialist Party
VDB	Liberal Democratic League
VVD	People's Party for Freedom and Democracy

Abbreviations of Political Parties

PARTIES MENTIONED IN TABLE 8.1

CDU	Christliche Demokratische Union Deutschland
DL	Democratic Left
DS	Democratici di Sinistra
MPG	Miljopartiet de Grona
ÖVP	Österreichische Volkspartei
PDS	Partei des Demokratischen Sozialismus
PPI	Partito Populare Italiano
PRC	Partito della Rifondazione Comunista
PS	Parti Socialiste
PS	Partido Socialista
PSOE	Partido Socialista Obrero Espanol
PvdA	Partij van de Arbeid
SAP	Socialdemokratiska Arbetare Partiet
SDI	Socialisti Democratici Italiani
SP	Socialistische Partij
SPD	Sozialdemokratische Partei Deutschland
SPÖ	Sozial Demokratische Partei Österreichs
VP	Vänsterpartiet

BIBLIOGRAPHY

Aarts, C.W.A.M., 'Opkomst', in J.J.A. Thomassen, C.W.A.M. Aarts and H. van der Kolk (eds.), 2000, pp. 57-76.

Akkerman, T., 'Urban Debates and Deliberative Democracy', in *Acta Politica*, vol. 36, spring 2001, pp. 71-88.

Akkerman, T, M. Leyenaar and B. Niemöller, 'Reforming Government in the Netherlands', Paper presented at the ESF Explanatory Workshop, Nijmegen, 8-10 November, 2001.

Andeweg, A. and G. Irwin, *Governance and Politics of the Netherlands*, New York, Palgrave, 2002.

Andreasen, T, A. Borchorst, D. Dahlerup, E. Lous, H.R. Nielsen (eds.), *Moving On. New Perspectives on the Women's Movement*, Aarhus, Aarhus University Press. 1991.

Angerman, A. and R. Meines, *Meer Vrouwen in de Politiek*, Leiden, Stichting Burgerschapskunde, Nederlands Centrum voor Politieke Vorming, 1993.

Arioli, K. (ed.), *Quoten und Gleichstellung von Frau und Mann*, Basel, Heibing & Lichtenhahn, 1996.

Astellarra, J., 'Spanien. Politische Partizipation und Repräsentation von Frauen in Spanien', in B. Hoecker (ed.), 1998, pp. 333-352.

Bergman, S, 'Finland. Frauen in die Finnischen Politik Auf dem Weg zur Halfte der Macht?', in B. Hoecker (ed.), 1998, pp. 91-114.

Bergqvist, C. *et al.* (eds.), *Equal Democracies? Gender and Politics in the Nordic Countries*, Oslo, Scandinavian University Press, 1999.

Betz, H., *Radical Right Wing Populism in Western Europe*, New York, St. Martin's Press, 1992.

Borchert, J. and J. Zeiss (eds.), *The Political Class in Advanced Democracies*, Oxford, Oxford University Press, 2003.

Borchorst, A., 'What is Institutionalised Gender Equality?' in C. Berqvist *et al.* (eds.), 1999, pp. 161-166.

Braun, M., 'Beginselvast staatkundig gereformeerde vrouwenstemmen', in *De Groene Amsterdammer*, vol. 117, no. 46, 1993, pp. 14-14.

Braun, M., 'Staatkundig gereformeerde gewetensnood: beginselvastheid door de eeuwen heen', in *Nemesis*, vol. 10, no. 1, 1994, pp. 12-16.

Braun, M., 'De hoogmoed van het mannelijk lid: de SGP, de nationale constitutie en de rechten van de mens', in *Nemesis*, vol. 12, no. 1, 1996, pp. 1-3.

Bremmer, C. (ed.), *ARP. Personen en momenten, uit de geschiedenis van de Anti-Revolutionaire Partij*, Franeker, Wever, 1980.

Brouns, M. and M. Sibbes, *Research and Support. Beeldvorming in Taal en Bedrijf*, Groningen, Rijks Universiteit Groningen, 1999.

Brown, A. et al., 'Women and Constitutional Change in Scotland and Northern Ireland', in *Parliamentary Affairs*, 2002, vol. 55, pp. 71-84.

Bussemaker, J. and R. Voet (eds.), *Gender, Participation and Citizenship in the Netherlands*, Aldershot, Ashgate, 1998.

Bussemaker, J. and R. Voet, 'Introduction', in J. Bussemaker and R. Voet (eds.), 1998, pp. 1-10.

Bussemaker, J., 'Gender and the Separation of Spheres in Twentieth Century Dutch Society: Pillarisation, Welfare State Formation and Individualisation', in, J. Bussemaker and R. Voet (eds.), 1998, pp. 25-37.

Bustelo, J., 'Spain, Analytical Statement', in *Panorama*, Brussels, European Network Women in Decision-making, 1993.

Cacoullos, A., 'Greece. Women Confronting Party Politics in Greece', in B. Nelson and N. Chowdury (eds.), 1994, pp. 311-325.

Campbell, B., *The Iron Ladies*, London, Virago, 1987.

Carroll, S.J. and W.S. Strimling, *Women's Routes to Elective Office. A Comparison with Men's*, Rutgers, Centre for the American Woman and Politics, 1985.

Castenmiller, P., M. Leyenaar, B. Niemöller and H. Tjalma, *Afscheid van de raad*, Den Haag, VNG-Uitgeverij, 2002.

Castenmiller, P., *De levende werkzaamheid. Politieke betrokkenheid van burgers bij het lokaal bestuur*, Den Haag, VNG-uitgeverij, 2002.

Castle, B., *Fighting All the Way*, London, Macmillan, 1993.

Charlot, M., 'Women and Elections in Britain', in H.R. Penniman (ed.), 1981, pp. 241-261.

CBS, *Statistisch Zakboek*, Den Haag, Staatsuitgeverij, 1979, 1982.

CDA, *Vrouwen en mannen van de partij. Een onderzoek in het kader van een positief actiebeleid voor vrouwen in het CDA*, Den Haag, CDA-uitgeverij, 1989.

Centre for Applied Research, *The Changing Austrian Voter*, 2000.

Chaney, P., 'Increased Rights and Representation: Women and the Post-Devolution Equality Agenda in Wales', in A. Dobrowolsky and V. Hart (eds.), 2003, pp. 173-184.

Childs, S., 'In Their Own Words: New Labour Women and the Substantive Representation of Women', in *British Journal of Politics and International Relations*, vol. 3, no. 2, 2001, pp. 173-190.

Childs, S., 'Hitting the Target: are Labour Women MPs "Acting For" Women?', in K. Ross (ed.), 2002, pp. 143-153.

Chodorow, N., *The Reproduction of Mothering*, Berkeley, University of California Press, 1978.

Craske, N. and M. Molyneux (eds.), *Gender and the Politics of Rights and Democracy in Latin America*, England, Palgrave, 2002.

Costera Meijer, I., *Het persoonlijke wordt politiek: feministische bewustwording in Nederland*, Amsterdam, Het Spinhuis, 1996.

Council of Europe, *Gender Mainstreaming: Conceptual Framework, Methodology and Presentation of Good Practices*, Strasbourg, Council of Europe, May 1998.

Council of Europe, *Women in Politics in the Council of Europe Member States*, Strasbourg, Council of Europe, December 2002.

Daalder, H. and H. Gosman (eds.), *Compendium voor Politiek en Samenleving*, Deventer, Kluwer, 2000.

Dahlerup D. and L. Freidenvall, 'Quotas as a Fast Track to Equal Political Representation for Women. Why Scandinavia Is No Longer the Model', Paper presented at the 19th International Political Science Association World Congress, Durban, June 2003.

Dahlerup, D., 'Using Quotas to Increase Women's Political Representation', in A. Karam (ed.), 1998, pp. 91-108.

Dahlerup, D., 'From a Small to a Large Minority Women in Scandinavian Politics', in *Scandinavian Political Studies*, 1988, vol. 11, no. 4, pp. 275-298.

Darcy, R., S. Welch and J. Clark, *Women, Elections and Representation*, New York, Longman, 1987.

Derksen, W. (ed.), *De burgermeester, van magistraat tot modern bestuurder*, Deventer, Kluwer, 1984.

Derksen, W., *Lokaal Bestuur*, Amsterdam, Elsevier, 2001.

Diemer-Lindeboom, F.T., *Man én vrouw in het volle leven*, Utrecht, Libertas, 1949.

Diemer-Lindeboom, F.T., 'Honderd jaar ARP en de vrouw', in C. Bremmer (ed.), 1980.

Dobrowolsky A. and V. Hart (eds.) *Women Making Constitutions New Politics and Comparative Perspectives*, Basingstoke and New York, Palgrave, 2003.

Dubois, J.P., 'Le Cumul des Mandats', *Après Demain*, 399, pp. 7-11, 1997.

Duverger, M., *The Political Role of Women*, Paris, UNESCO, 1955.

Ebbenhorst-Tengbergen, K. van, 'Presentation of International Programme of Action to Promote the Participation of Women in Decision-Making', Dublin, CDEG, 1996.

Edelenbos, J. and R. Monnikhof (eds.), *Spanning in Interaktie. Een analyse van interactief beleid in Lokale Democratie*, Amsterdam, IPP, 1998.

Eijk, C. van der, and B. Niemöller (eds.), *In het spoor van de kiezer. Aspecten van 10 jaar kiesgedrag*, Meppel, Boom, 1984.

Elster, J., *Deliberative Democracy*, Cambridge, Cambridge University Press, 1998.

Emancipatie Kommissie, *Organisatie Emancipatiebeleid*, Nota aan de kabinetsformateur, Den Haag, Emancipatie Kommissie, 26 May 1977.

Emancipatie Kommissie, *Aanzet voor een vijfjarenplan, revisie positie van de vrouw, rolverdeling vrouw-man*, Den Haag, Emancipatie Kommissie, 17 March 1977.

Emancipatieraad, *Vrouwen in politiek en openbaar bestuur*, Den Haag, Emancipatieraad, 1992.

European Commission, *European Constitution* (Draft), Part I, Title VI, article 44, English version, 2003.

Fishkin, J., *The Voice of the People*, New Haven, Yale University Press, 1997.

Freedman, J., 'Women in the European Parliament', in K. Ross (ed.) 2002, pp. 179-189.

Grabijn-van Putten, R., *Ik wil het gewoon vertellen: over vrouwenlidmaatschap van de SGP*, Zoetermeer, Boekencentrum, 1996.

Gallagher, M. and P. Vincenzo Uleri (eds.), *The Referendum Experience in Europe*, London, MacMillan Press, 1996.

Gallagher, M. and M. Marsh (eds.), *Candidate Selection in Comparative Perspective*, London, Sage, 1988.

Gallagher, M., M. Laver and P. Mair, *Representative Government in Modern Europe, Institutions, Parties and Governments*, New York, McGraw Hill Higher Education, 2001.

Galligan, Y., 'Party Politics and Gender in the Republic of Ireland', in J. Lovenduski and P. Norris (eds.), 1993, pp. 147-167.

Galligan, Y., 'Irland. Die politischen Repräsentation von Frauen in der Republik Irland', in B. Hoecker (ed.), 1998, pp. 189-210.

Gardiner, F., and M. Leyenaar, 'The Timid and the Bold. Analysis of the "Women Friendly State" in Ireland and in the Netherlands', in F. Gardiner (ed.), 1997, pp. 60-90.

Gardiner, F. (ed.) *Sex Equality Policy in Western Europe*, London, Routledge, 1997.

Gardiner, F., 'Ireland, Analytical Statement', in *Panorama*, Brussels, European Network Women in Decision-making, 1993.

Gaspard, F., 'Assessment. Women Elected Representatives in French Municipalities' in CEMR, *Men and Women in European Municipalities*, Paris, CEMR, 1998, pp. 35-42.

Gaspard, F., 'La Parité Pourquoi Pas?', in *Pouvoirs*, 82, 1997, pp. 115-125.

Gaspard, F. and C. Servan-Schreiber, 'De la Fraternité à la Parité', *Le Monde*, 1993.

Gidengil, E., *et al.*, 'The Gender Gap in Support for the New Right: the Case of Canada', Paper prepared for the conference on 'Populism in North America, South America and Europe: Comparative and Historical', Italy, January 2003.

Gilder, D. de, N. Ellemers, H. van de Heuvel and G. Blijleven, 'Arbeidssatisfactie, committment en uitstroom. Overeenkomsten en verschillen tussen mannen en vrouwen', in *Gedrag en Organisaties*, vol. 11, 1998, pp. 25-35.

Gilligan, C., *In a Different Voice*, Cambridge, Harvard University Press, 1982.

Greenstein, F., *Children and Politics*, Yale, Yale University Press, 1965.

Groen, A., *Vrouwen en het Binnenhof*, Den Haag, Staatsuitgeverij, 1985.

Guadagnini, M.,'A Partitocrazia without Women: the Case of the Italian Party System', in J. Lovenduski and P. Norris (eds.), 1993, pp. 168-204.

Guadagnini, M., 'Gendering the Debate on Political Representation in Italy, an Open Challenge', Paper prepared for the 96th Annual Meeting of the APSA, Washington, 2000.

Guadagnini, M., 'Gendering the Debate on Political Representation in Italy, a Difficult Challenge', forthcoming.

Guadagnini, M., 'The Debate on Women's Quotas in Italian Electoral Legislation', in *Swiss Political Science Review*, vol. 4, no. 3, 1998, p. 97-102.

Gustafsson, S., 'Childcare and Type of Welfare States', in D. Sainsbury (ed.), 1994, pp. 45-62.

Haavio-Manilla E., *et al.* (eds.), *Unfinished Democracy. Women in Nordic Politics*, Oxford, Pergamon Press, 1985.

Halimi, G. (ed.), *Femmes: Moitié de la Terre, Moitié du Pouvoir*, Paris, Gallimard, 1994.

Handelingen der Staten Generaal 1916/1917, 1918/1919, 1976/1977, Den Haag Tweede Kamer.

Henriks, F. and P.W. Tops, 'Tussen democratie en verzakelijking. Trends in de hervorming van het lokaal bestuur in Nederland en Duitsland', in *Bestuurswetenschappen*, 1997, vol. 51, no. 4, pp. 198-217.

Hernes, H. and K. Voje, 'Women in the Corporate Channel: a Process of Natural Exclusion?', *Scandinavian Political Studies*, vol. 3, no. 2, 1980, p. 163-186.

Hernes, H. and E. Hänninen-Salmelin, 'Women in the Corporate System', in E. Haavio-Mannila *et al.* (eds.), 1985, pp. 106-133.

Hillebrand, R., *The Antichambre van het Parlement*, Leiden, DSWO Press, 1992.

Hoecker, B. (ed.), *Handbuch Politischen Partizipation von Frauen in Europa*, Opladen, Leske Verlag, 1998.

Hooghiemstra, B.T.J. and M. Niphuis-Nell, *Sociale Atlas van de vrouw, Deel 2, Arbeid, inkomen en faciliteiten om werken en de zorg voor kinderen te combineren*, Rijswijk, SCP, 1993.

Hoskyns C. and Rai, S., 'Gender, Class and Representation: India and the EU', *European Journal of Women's Studies*, 1998, no. 5, pp. 345-365.

Htun, M. and M. Jones, 'Engendering the Right to Participate in Decision-Making: Electoral Quotas and Women's Leadership in Latin America', in N. Craske and M. Molyneux (eds.), 2002, pp. 32-56.

Iilshammar, L., 'Sweden as an IT-nation', published on the internet (www.sweden.se), 2000.

International Centre for Parliamentary Documentation. Series Reports and Documents, no. 14, Geneve, IPU, March 1988.

Jacobs, A., *Herinneringen*, Nijmegen, Sun reprint, 1978/1924.

Janova, M. and M Sineau, 'Women's Participation in Political Power in Europe: an Essay in East-West Comparison', in *Women's Studies International Forum*, vol. 11, 1992, pp. 115-128.

Janssen, L. and M. Leyenaar, 'Growing Minority. Background and Behaviour of Women in Local Politics', Paper presented at the Joint Sessions of Workshops, ECPR, Florence, 1980.

Jansz, U., *Vrouwen ontwaakt*, Amsterdam, Bert Bakker, 1983.

Kampen, J. (ed.), *Schrift en Historie, Gedenkboek bij het 50-jarig bestaan der georganiseerde ARP 1878-1928*, Den Haag, ARP, 1928.

Karam, A. (ed.), *Women in Parliament: Beyond Numbers*, Stockholm, IDEA, 1998.

Kelly, R.M. and M. Boutilier, *The Making of Political Women. A Study of Socialization and Conflict*, Chicago, Nelson-Hall, 1978.

Keuzenkamp, S. and K. Oudhof, *Emancipatiemonitor 2000*, Den Haag, SCP/CBS, 2000.

Kitschelt, H., *The Radical Right in Western Europe: A Comparative Analysis*, Ann Arbor, University of Michigan Press, 1995.

Kleszcz-Wagner, A., 'Frankreich. Frauen in Frankreich heiss geliebt und politisch kaltgestellt', in B. Hoecker (ed.), 1998, p. 115-146.

Koeneman, L. *et al.*, 'Het Partijgebeuren: kroniek van de partijpolitieke gebeurtenissen van het jaar 1984', in Documentatiecentrum Nederlandse Politieke Partijen, *Jaarboek 1984*, Groningen, DNPP, 1985, pp. 10-60.

Kolinsky, E., 'Party Change and Women's Representation in Unified Germany', in J. Lovenduski and P. Norris (eds.), 1993, pp. 113-146.

Kool-Smit, J., *Hé zus ze houen ons eronder. Een boek voor vrouwen en oudere meisjes*, Utrecht, Bruna, 1972.

Koole, R., and M. Leyenaar, 'The Netherlands: The Predominance of Regionalism', in M. Gallagher and M. Marsh (eds.), 1988, pp. 190-209.

Koopman, M.J. and M. Leyenaar, 'Het vergeten electoraat vrouwen en verkiezingen', in C. van der Eijk and B. Niemöller (eds.), 1984, pp. 241-261.

Knijn, T., 'Participation through Care? The Case of the Dutch Housewife', in J. Bussemaker and R. Voet (eds.), 1998, pp. 65-78.

Kuyper, H.S.S., 'De anti-revolutionaire vrouw en het staatkundig leven', in J. Kampen (ed.), 1928.

Leyenaar, M., *De Geschade Heerlijkheid. Politiek gedrag van vrouwen en mannen in Nederland, 1918-1988*, Den Haag, Staatsuitgeverij, 1989.

Leyenaar, M.H., *et al.*, *De helft als meerderheid. Verslag van een onderzoek naar vrouwen in politieke functies*, Den Haag, VNG-uitgeverij, 1983.

Leyenaar, M. and H. van de Velde, 'Belangenbehartiging door vrouwen. Vrouwenpartijen', in *Acta Politica*, vol. 24, no. 1, 1989, pp. 3-29.

Leyenaar, M., 'Women's Parties: A Strategy for Power', Paper presented at the Global Summit of Women, 16-19 February 1994, Taipei, Taiwan.

Leyenaar, M.H., *How to Create a Gender Balance in Political Decision-Making*, Brussels, European Commission, 1997.

Leyenaar, M., B. Niemöller, M. Laver and Y. Galligan, *Electoral Systems in Europe: a Gender Impact Assessment*, Brussels, European Commission, 1999.

Leyenaar, M., B. Niemöller and A. van der Kooy, *Kandidaten gezocht. Politieke partijen en het streven naar grotere diversiteit onder gemeenteraadsleden*, Amsterdam, IPP, 1999.

Leyenaar, M. and B.Niemöller, 'The Netherlands', in P. Norris (ed.), 1997, pp. 114-136.

Leyenaar, M., 'Vrouwen en Politiek in Nederland', in H. Daalder and H. Gosman (eds.), *Compendium voor Politiek en Samenleving*, Deventer, Kluwer, 2000, pp. 1600/1-87.

Leyenaar, M. and B. Niemöller, 'Lokale beleidsbeïnvloeding in 2003: een gender analyse van de participatie van burgers' in Ministerie van Sociale Zaken en Werkgelegenheid, *Werkdocumenten no. 297*, Voorburg, Ministerie van SZW, 2003.

Leyenaar, M. and S. Saharso, *Vrouwen en politieke macht*, Den Haag, Ministerie van WVC, 1983.

Lemke, C., 'Women and Politics: the New Federal Republic of Germany', in B. Nelson and N. Chowdhury (eds.), 1994, pp. 261-284.

Lovenduski, J., *Overview State of the Art Study of Research on Women in Political, Economic and Social Decision-making in Europe, Final Report*, 1998.

Lovenduski, J., *Women and European Politics. Contemporary Feminism and Public Policy*, Brighton, Wheatsheaf Books Ltd., 1986.

Lovenduski, J. and P. Norris, 'Westminster Women: The Politics of Presence', in *Political Studies*, vol. 51, 2003, pp. 84-102.

Lovenduski, J., 'Grossbritannien. Grossbritanniens sexistische Demokratie Frauen, Männer und die Politik im Parteienstaat', in B. Hoecker (ed.), 1998, pp. 167-188.

Lovenduski, J., 'Great Britain. The Rules of the Political Game: Feminism and Politics in Great Britain', in B. Nelson and N. Chowdhury (eds.), 1994, pp. 298-310.

Lijphart, A., *Verzuiling, pacificatie en kentering in de Nederlandse Politiek*, Amsterdam, De Bussy, 1968.

Mackay, F., F. Meyers and A. Brown, 'Towards a New Politics? Women and the Constitutional Change in Scotland', in A. Dobrowolsky and V. Hart (eds.), 2003, pp. 84-98.

Mandel, R.B., *In the Running. The New Woman Candidate*, New Haven, Ticknor and Fields, 1981.

Marques-Pereira, B., *La Representation Politique des Femmes en Amerique Latine*, Brussels, L'Harmattan, 2001.

Matland, R. and D. Studlar, 'The Contagion of Women Candidates in Single-Member District and Proportional Representation Electoral Systems: Canada and Norway', in *The Journal of Politics*, vol. 58, no. 3, pp. 707-733.

Meehan, E., 'The Civic Forum', Paper presented at the ESF Exploratory Workshop, Nijmegen, Netherlands, 8-10 November 2001.

Meier, P., 'Gender as Part of Political Identity. Gender Quota in Parliament, Government and Advisory Committees in Belgium', Paper presented at the APSA, Washington DC, 2000.

Meier, P., 'Necessaire mais insuffisante: la loi Smet-Tobback', in P. Saavedra (ed.), 2000, pp. 197-210.

Meier, P. 'On the Theoretical Acknowledgement of Diversity in Representation', in *Res Publica*, vol. 43, no. 4, 2001, pp. 551-570.

Meier, P., 'De kracht van de definitie. Quotawetten in Argentinië, België en Frankrijk vergeleken', in *Res Publica*, vol. 46, no. 1, 2004, pp. 80-100.

Meier, P., 'De hervorming van de kieswet, de nieuwe quota en de m/v verhoudingen na de verkiezingen van mei 2003', Paper presented at the Politicologenetmaal 22-23 May 2003.

Ministerie van Binnenlandse Zaken, *Vrouwen in politiek en openbaar bestuur*, Voortgangsrapportage, Den Haag, Ministerie van Binnenlandse Zaken, 1992-2004.

Ministerie van Binnenlandse Zaken, *Kabinetsstandpunt Vrouwen in Politiek en Openbaar Bestuur*, Kamerstuk 22 777, no. 1, Den Haag, Ministerie van Binnenlandse Zaken, 1992.

Ministerie van Binnenlandse Zaken, *Vrouwen in Politiek en Openbaar Bestuur. Kabinetsstandpunt 1996*, Den Haag, Ministerie van Binnenlandse Zaken, 1996.

Ministerie van Onderwijs, Cultuur en Wetenschappen, *Emancipatie. Proces van Verandering en Groei*, Den Haag, Ministerie van OC&W, 1977.

Ministerie van Sociale Zaken en Werkgelegenheid, *Plan of Action on Gender Mainstreaming*, Voorburg, Ministerie van SZW, 2002.

Ministerie van Sociale Zaken en Werkgelegenheid, Directie Coördinatie Emancipatie beleid, *Multi-Year Plan on Emancipation Policy. Short and Medium Term*, Voorburg, Ministerie van SZW, 2000.

Ministerie van Sociale Zaken en Werkgelegenheid, *Beleidsbrieven 2002* and *2003*, Voorburg, Ministerie van SZW, 2002, 2003.

Ministerie van Sociale Zaken en Werkgelegenheid, Directie Coördinatie Emancipatie beleid, *Netherlands Interdepartmental Plan of Action and Final Report on Gender Mainstreaming*, Voorburg, Ministerie van SZW, 2002.

Ministerie van Sociale Zaken en Werkgelegenheid, Department for the Coordination of Emancipation Policy, *The Netherlands Five Years after Beijing*, Voorburg, Ministerie van SZW, 2001.

Molle, L. van, and E. Gubin, *Vrouw en Politiek in België*, Lannoo, Tielt, 1998.

Morlino, L., 'Crisis of Parties and Change of Party System in Italy', in *Party Politics*, vol. 2, no. 1, 1996, pp. 5-30.

Moss Kanter, R., *Men and Women of the Corporation*, New York, Basic Books, 1977.

Mossuz-Laveau, J., 'Les conceptions politiques des homes et des femmes ou de la four casse de la RMIste', in M. Riot-Scarcey, *Democratie et Representation*, Paris, Kimé, 1995, pp. 259-279.

Mossuz-Laveau, J. and M. Sineau, *Women in the Political World in Europe*, Strasbourg, Council of Europe, 1984.

Mowlam, M., *Momentum. The Struggle for Peace, Politics and the People*, London, Hodder & Stoughton, 2002.

Neale, J., 'Family Characteristics', in M. Vianello and G. Moore (eds.), 2000, p. 157-168.

Nelson, B. and N. Chowdhury (eds.), *Women and Politics Worldwide*, New Haven, Yale University Press, 1994.

Norris, P. and J. Lovenduski, 'Gender and Party Politics in Britain', in J. Lovenduski and P. Norris (eds.), 1993, pp. 35-59.

Norris, P. and J. Lovenduski (eds.), *Political Recruitment. Gender, Race and Class in the British Parliament*, Cambridge, Cambridge University Press, 1995.

Norris, P. (ed.), *Passages to Power. Legislative Recruitment in Advanced Democracies*, Cambridge, Cambridge University Press, 1997.

Oldersma, J., *De vrouw die vanzelf spreekt*, Leiden, DSWO Press, 1996.

Oldersma, J., 'More Women or more Feminist in Politics? Advocacy Coalitions and the Representation of Women in the Netherlands, 1967-1992', in *Acta Politica*, vol. 37, 2002, pp. 283-317.

Ophuysen, T. and I. Sjerps, 'Van vrouwen en de dingen die haar binden', *Katijf*, no. 21, 1984, pp. 19-23.

Oud, P.J. and J. Bosmans, *Honderd jaren. Een eeuw van staatkundige vormgeving in Nederland, 1840-1940*, Assen, Van Gorcum, 1982.

Oudijk, C., *De Sociale Atlas van de Vrouw*, Den Haag, Staatsuitgeverij, 1984.

Outshoorn, J., *Vrouwenemancipatie en socialisme, een onderzoek naar de houding van de SDAP ten aanzien van het vrouwenvraagstuk tussen 1894 en 1919*, Nijmegen, SUN, 1973.

Outshoorn, J., *De politieke strijd rondom de abortuswetgeving in Nederland 1964-1984*, Den Haag, Vuga, 1986.

Outshoorn, J., 'Parity Democracy: a Critical Look at a "New" Strategy', Paper presented at the ECPR Joint Sessions of Workshops, Leiden, Netherlands, 1993.

Outshoorn, J. 'A Distaste of Dirty Hands: Gender and Politics in Second Wave Feminism', in T. Andreasen *et al.* (eds.), 1991.

Outshoorn, J., 'Furthering the Cause: Femocrat Strategies in National Government', in J. Bussemaker and R. Voet (eds.), 1998, pp. 108-121.

Pantelidou Maloutas, M., 'Griechenland. Frauen als Akteurinnen in der politischen Kultur Griechenlands', in B. Hoecker (ed.), 1998, pp. 147-166.

Penniman, H.R., (ed.) *Britain at the Polls 1997*, Washington, American Enterprise Institute, 1981.

Plantenga, J., 'Double Lives: Labour Market Participation, Citizenship and Gender', in J. Bussemaker and R. Voet, (eds.), 1998, pp. 51-64.

Plantenga, J., *Een afwijkend patroon. Honderd jaar vrouwenarbeid in Nederland en (West) Duitsland*, Amsterdam, SUA, 1993.

Plesch, B., 'Strategies for a Gender Balance in Political Decision-Making', Paper presented at the conference Women and Public Power, organised by the European Network Women in Decision-Making, Dublin, 23, 24 March 1995.

Portegijs, W., A. Boelens and S. Keuzenkamp, *Emancipatiemonitor 2002*, Den Haag, SCP/CBS, 2002.

Posthumus van der Goot, W.H. *et al.*, *Van moeder op dochter, de maatschappelijke positie van de vrouw in Nederland vanaf de Franse tijd*, Nijmegen, SUN-reprint, 1977.

Pothuis-Smit, C., *Wat deden de vrouwen met haar kiesrecht? Het al.gemeen vrouwenkiesrecht in de praktijk 1919-1940*, Arnhem, Van Loghum Slaterus, 1946.

Rendel, M. (ed.), *Women, Power and Political Systems*, London, Croom Helm, 1981.

Riot-Scarcey, M. (ed.), *Democratie et Representation*, Paris, Kimé, 1995.

Ross, K. (ed.), *Women, Politics and Change*, Hansard Society Series in Politics and Government, Oxford, Oxford University Press, 2002.

Rubart, F., 'Der Fall der Norwegen', in B. Hoecker (ed.), 1998, pp. 353-378.

Sainsbury, D., 'The Politics of the Increased Women's Representation, the Swedish Case', in J. Lovenduski and P. Norris (eds.), 1993, pp. 363-290.

Sainsbury, D., *Gendering Welfare States*, London, Sage, 1994.

Sainsbury, D., *Gender, Equality and Welfare States*, Cambridge, Cambridge University Press, 1996.

Sande, M. van de, 'Mevrouw de burgemeester ...', in W. Derksen (ed.), *De burgermeester, van magistraat tot modern bestuurder*, Deventer, Kluwer, 1984, pp. 165-187.

Saavedra, P. (ed.), *Vers une Democratie Paritaire. Analyse et Revision des Lois Electorales en Vigueur*, Madrid, CELEM, 2000.

Schokking, J.C., *De Vrouw in de Nederlandse* Politiek, Assen, Van Gorkum, 1958.

SCP, *Sociaal en Cultureel Rapport 1998, 25 Jaar Sociale Verandering*, Rijswijk, SCP, 1998.

Seeland, A., 'Germany', in *Panorama,* Brussels, European Network Women in Decision-making, 1993.

Seyd, P. and P. Whitely, *Labour's Grassroots. The Politics of Party Membership*. Oxford, Clarendon Press, 1992.

Sineau, M., 'Parité et Principe d'Egalité: le Debat Francais', in Ephesia (ed.), *La Place des Femmes*, Paris, Editions de la Decouverte, 1995, pp. 518-523.

Sinkkonen, S. and E. Haavio-Mannila, 'The Impact of the Women's Movement and Legislative Activity of Women MPs on Social Development', in M. Rendel (ed.), 1981, pp. 195-215.

Skeije, H., 'Norway: a Case History of Political Integration', Paper presented at the UNESCO meeting of experts, Oslo, February 1990.

Sledziewski, E., 'Report', in Council of Europe, *The Democratic Principle of Equal Representation. Forty Years of Council of Europe Activity*, Strasbourg, Council of Europe Press, 1992, pp. 17-28.

Sledziewski, E., 'Rapport sur les ideaux et les droits des femmes', in Reseau Femmes Ruptures, *Bulletin d' Information, de liaisons et d'echanges*, 90, March 1993, pp. 23-33.

Smit, J., 'Afscheid van de gemeenteraad', in J. Smit, 1988.

Smit, J., *Er is een land waar vrouwen willen wonen. Teksten 1967-1981*, Amsterdam, SUA, 1988.

Spanning, H. van, *De Christelijk Historische Unie. Enige hoofdlijnen van haar geschiedenis*, dissertation RUL, Leiden, 1988.

Steiniger, B., 'Österreich. Zwischen Konflikt und Konsens Frauen im politischen System Österreichs', in B. Hoecker (ed.), 1998, pp. 275-296.

Swiebel, J. and J. Outshoorn, 'Feminism and the State, the Case of the Netherlands', Paper presented at the Annual Meeting of the Dutch Political Science Association, Twente, Netherlands, 1991.

Swiebel, J., 'De vrouwenbeweging en de beleidsorganisatie bij de overheid', in *Katijf*, 45, 1988, p. 15.

Taggert, P., 'New Populist Parties in Western Europe', in *West European Politics*, vol. 18, 1995, pp. 34-51.

Thomassen, J.J.A., C.W.A.M. Aarts and H. van der Kolk (eds.), *Politieke veranderingen in Nederland 1971-1998, kiezers en de smalle marges van de politiek*, Den Haag, SDU, 2000, pp. 57-76.

Tingsten, H., *Political Behaviour: Studies in Election Statistics*, London, P.S. King & Son, 1937.

Tweede Kamer der Staten-Generaal, *Actieprogramma Emancipatiebeleid 1987-1990*, Vergaderjaar 1987-1988, 20255, no. 1-2,

United Nations Study, *Women in Politics and Decision-Making in the Late Twentieth Century*, Leiden/Boston, Martinus Nijhoff Publishers, 1992.

Valence, E. and E. Davies, *Women of Europe: Women MEPs and Equality Policy*, Cambridge, Cambridge University Press, 1986.

Valian, V., *Why So Slow. The Advancement of Women*, Cambridge, MIT Press, 1998.

Vallance, E., *Women in the House. A Study of Women Members of Parliament*, London, Athlone Press, 1979.

Velde, H. van de, and M.H. Leyenaar, 'Women's Access to Political Parties, the Netherlands', Paper presented at the Joint Sessions of the ECPR, Essex, Great Britain, 23-27 March 1991.

Velde, H. van de, *Vrouwen van de partij. De integratie van vrouwen in politieke partijen in Nederland, 1919-1990*, Leiden, DSWO-press, 1994.

Veldhuijzen, G., *Wat bezielde die vrouwen? Vijfenveertig jaar Centrale van CH-vrouwen*, De Meern, Centrale van CH-vrouwen, 1979.

Vianello, M. and G. Moore (eds.), *Gendering Elites. Economic and Political Leadership in 27 Industrialised Societies*, Basingstoke, Macmillan Press, 2000.

Vianen, A. van, and A. Fischer, 'Sexeverschillen in voorkeuren voor een "mannelijke" organisatiecultuur', in *Gedrag en Organisatie*, vol. 11, no. 5, 1998, pp. 249-264.

Visser, A., 'Aanpassen of dwarsliggen', in *Opzij*, vol. 13, no. 10, 1985, p. 10.

Vleuten, A. van der, *Dure Vrouwen, Dwarse Staten. Een institutioneel-realistische visie op de totstandkoming en implementatie van Europees beleid*, Nijmegen, Nijmegen University Press, 2001.

Voerman, G., 'De ledentallen van politieke partijen, 1945-1995', in *DNPP Jaarboek van Politieke Partijen 1995*, Groningen, DNPP, 1996.

Vogel-Poslky, E., 'Belgium' in *Panorama*, Brussels, European Network Women in Decision-making, 1993.

Vogel-Polsky, E., 'Les Actions Positives, les Quotas au Crible du Droit de l'Egalite', in K. Arioli (ed.), 1996, pp. 109-137.

Wagener, R., 'Luxemburg. Luxemburg Verspäteter politischer Einsteig der Frauen', in B. Hoecker (ed.), 1998, pp. 233-254.

Welch, S., 'Women as Political Animals? A Test of Some Explanations for Male-Female Political Participation Differences', in *American Journal of Political Science*, 1977, vol. 21, no. 4, pp. 712-716.

Woodward, A., 'Belgien. Politische Partizipation in Belgien Die gespaltene Frau', in B. Hoecker (ed.), 1998, pp. 17-40.

Woodward, A. and D. Lyon, 'Gendered Time and Women's Access to Power', in M. Vianello and G. Moore (eds.), 2000, pp. 91-103.

INDEX

A

Abortion 9, 111, 116, 118, 132, 147, 157, 158, 159, 160, 212, 283, 294
Accession countries 53, 218, 267, 268, 285
Additional Member System 45
Affirmative action 5, 41, 57, 75, 137, 143, 145, 168, 169, 173-178, 184, 186, 201, 206, 233, 249
All-woman shortlist 41
Aspirants 71-72, 75, 223, 225, 276, 288
Austria 8, 17-20, 43, 44, 47, 48, 51, 60, 61, 64, 80, 222, 254-257, 272, 282, 291

B

Ballot 19, 45, 68, 91, 102, 172, 187, 223, 274
Belgium 8, 13, 17-20, 30-36, 50, 51, 59, 60-64, 77, 148, 149, 217, 218, 222, 226, 227, 236, 237, 250, 253-258, 264, 268, 272, 281, 282
Britain 17, 20, 36, 39, 40, 41, 68, 73, 76, 80, 81, 149, 221, 249, 263, 281, 294

C

CEDAW 179, 249
Child care 3, 7, 81, 101, 118, 121, 133, 138, 147, 151, 159, 206, 212, 290, 294
Child-care facilities 3, 54, 62, 66, 67, 137, 152, 183, 184, 205, 210, 212, 281, 283, 288
Citizens' jury 261, 266
Civic education 57, 60, 286
Civic expertise 78
Civic forum 266, 296
Civil society 57, 64, 230, 260, 266, 294, 295
Cliental voting 26
Closed-list systems 30, 69
Commissioner 52, 92, 184, 206, 252, 269, 286
Consociational democracy 9
Constituency vote 30
Constitutional Court 28, 232, 235, 243, 244, 263
Corporate system 64
Corporatism 57, 64
Corruption 243, 257, 258
Council of Europe 209, 228, 247
Council of Ministers 2, 49, 238, 239, 269, 270, 275
Council of State 206, 208, 237, 239
Crisis of politics 252
Critical mass 6, 11, 133
Cultural climate 38, 57, 62, 63, 153
Culture of politics 57, 58, 82, 158, 292
Cumul des mandats 31, 271, 275
Cyprus 53, 268
Czech Republic 53

Index

D

Decentralisation 258, 259
Denmark 8, 17-24, 51-52, 59-62, 80, 219, 220, 222, 254-257, 261, 268, 272, 274, 281, 282
Department for the Coordination of Emancipation Policy 154, 197
Directive 49, 207, 285
Dual mandate 38, 224

E

Eastern Germany 43
Ecole Nationale d'Administration 32, 282
Election campaign 33, 34, 68, 69, 158
Electoral attractiveness 80, 191, 287
Electoral law 173, 224, 241, 243, 246
Electoral threshold 21, 68, 70, 71, 89, 271
Emancipation
  Bureaus 197
  Committee 154, 176, 177
  Council 154, 178, 179
  Policy Plan 177
Empowerment of women 1, 9-13, 17, 30, 50, 64, 75, 83, 84, 87, 117, 119, 133, 148, 164, 177, 182-186, 195, 201, 206, 212, 213, 217, 247, 283, 288
Enfranchisement 1, 99
Equal opportunities 36, 48, 49, 110, 157, 159, 162, 169, 177, 199, 210, 211, 242, 245, 248, 274, 277, 279, 280, 283, 290, 291, 295
Equality legislation 6, 21, 24, 156
Equality policies 7, 133, 153, 176, 184, 213, 290
Estonia 53
Ethnic minorities 13, 198, 199, 207
Eurobarometer 59, 61
European Constitution 268, 297
European Convention 52, 278, 289, 291, 295
European Parliament 13, 28, 49, 50, 54, 120, 138, 145, 148, 180, 246, 253, 267-271, 274, 275, 284
European Union 17, 28, 48, 52, 145, 149, 267
Explanatory framework 8, 55, 56

F

Family circumstances 66
Family connections 38
Feminism 110, 151, 160, 162, 169, 170, 178, 210, 283, 289
Feminists 27, 32, 44, 82, 132, 159, 162, 184, 212, 248, 285
Finland 8, 17-24, 36, 51, 54, 60-65, 80, 220, 222, 254-257, 268, 272, 274, 282
First-past-the-post 41, 45, 68, 243
Fortuyn, Pim 93, 187, 257
France 8, 9, 17-20, 30-38, 43, 50-52, 60-62, 68, 77, 149, 198, 217-218, 222, 226-229, 236, 237, 245, 249, 250, 254-257, 264, 272, 274, 281-283, 290

G

Gatekeepers 30, 47, 67, 164
Gender democracy 279, 296
Gender division of labour 63, 64, 137, 152, 161, 181
Gender gap 18, 48, 59, 61, 136, 223, 291
Gender ideology 26, 58, 62, 67, 77, 78
Gender mainstreaming 137, 202, 208-210, 213, 263, 280, 290, 294, 295
Germany 8, 17-20, 36, 43-45, 51-54, 60-62, 68, 69, 101, 181, 220, 222, 249, 254-257, 272, 281, 282

Greece 8, 17-20, 25-30, 43, 50-54, 59-61, 63, 67, 70, 82, 198, 217, 218, 222, 227, 241, 245, 249, 250, 254-257, 268, 272, 282-285, 290
Groeneweg, Suze 106, 120
Group representatives 11, 119, 123

H
Halonen, Tarja 24
Hungary 53

I
Incumbency/incumbents 32, 38, 50, 54, 69, 70-74, 80, 81, 181, 219, 275, 276, 277, 286
Individual factors 57, 67
Institutional factors 18, 57, 58, 62
Integration of women 9, 11, 87, 89, 92, 98, 99, 108, 135, 168, 175, 188, 195, 201, 211, 251, 262, 290
Interactive policy-making 253, 260, 265
Ireland 1, 8, 17-20, 36-39, 50-53, 60-65, 76, 80, 82, 198, 222, 254-257, 263-266, 268, 273, 281, 282, 285, 290, 295
Italy 8, 9, 17-20, 25-30, 43, 51-53, 59-63, 67, 68, 76, 82, 217, 218, 220, 222, 225, 226, 242, 245, 249, 250, 254-258, 262, 264, 268, 273, 281-285, 291

J
Jacobs, Aletta 11, 87-90, 112, 283

K
Katz, Frida 103, 104, 109
Klompé, Marga 107, 124

L
Latvia 53, 268
Liberal feminism 110

List Pim Fortuyn 93, 187-193, 291, 292
Lithuania 53
Local alderman 74, 146
Local councillors 31, 138, 145, 164, 187, 200, 232, 236, 284
Local elections 28, 30, 117, 139, 145, 148, 180, 183, 193, 211, 232, 236, 238, 242
Local level 12, 31, 93, 108, 109, 112, 118, 138, 140, 143, 144, 156, 163, 164, 174, 185, 200, 213, 253, 258, 259, 261, 264, 265, 284
Luxembourg 8, 17-20, 30, 31, 35, 36, 51, 52, 59-62, 222, 254-257, 273, 282

M
Machismo 57, 281, 282
Malta 53
Mayor 31, 74, 88, 92, 141, 142, 143, 146, 260, 286
McAleese, Mary 37, 295
Merkl, Angela 79
Ministry of Culture, Recreation and Social Work 155
Ministry of Education 182
Ministry of Internal Affairs 141, 143, 148, 178-182, 201, 213, 283, 284
Ministry of Social Affairs and Employment 154, 155
Municipality 115, 117, 141, 143, 144

N
National machinery 27, 154, 213
Neo-corporatism 97, 98
Netherlands 4, 7, 8-12, 17-20, 37, 51, 54, 60, 61, 70, 72, 74, 76, 79, 80, 84, 85, 87-214, 219, 222, 254, 255, 256, 257, 258, 259, 260, 264, 265, 266, 268, 273, 274, 279, 281-283, 284, 289-292

Index

New politics 28, 259, 280, 293, 294, 295
Nijpels, Jet 94

O

Old boys' networks 282, 286

P

Pacifistic 118
'Panda' laws 217, 244, 289
Parity 12, 33, 155, 217-251, 264, 275
Parity democracy 12, 217, 246, 248, 249, 250
Parliamentary committee on women's affairs 133
Parliamentary committee on women's rights 50
Parliamentary elections 12, 25, 27, 41, 44, 46, 72, 79, 80, 88, 93, 115, 116, 187-193, 258
Party competition 57, 77, 271
Party lists 23, 25, 28, 46, 68, 98, 218, 221, 235, 239, 272, 274, 275, 277
Party membership 29, 48, 78, 103, 106, 109, 165-167, 219, 255, 276
Party quotas 23, 247-251, 271
Pillarisation 9, 90, 96, 97, 103, 283
Pioneers 11, 119-120, 123, 126, 211
Players 11, 119, 133-138
Poland 53, 268
Poldermodel 87
Political agenda 93, 118, 129, 147, 148, 164, 187, 202, 212, 230, 280, 283, 288, 290, 294, 297
Political elite 65, 97, 129, 229, 243, 258, 262, 285, 291
Political experience 74, 219, 276
Political expertise 78
Political interest 48, 57, 58, 60, 64, 76, 78, 82, 256, 285, 286

Political parties
  Catholic 30, 87, 92, 96, 100, 101, 103, 121, 124, 125, 128, 144
  Communist 33, 76, 93, 96, 161, 169, 221, 233, 262
  Confessional 91, 94, 100, 102-112, 117, 118, 124, 126, 128, 141, 187, 193
  Conservative 40, 42, 223
  Green 23, 33, 36, 44-48, 78, 93, 96, 135, 143, 146, 165, 166, 170, 173, 174, 199, 201, 220, 225, 233, 239, 240
  Labour 38, 40-42, 72, 73, 76, 92, 110, 120-124, 129, 132, 137, 155, 161, 165, 167, 172, 173, 178, 186, 218, 220, 221, 224, 255
  Liberal 23, 102, 104-107, 121, 169, 220, 240, 263
  Protestant 87, 117, 121, 128
  Social Democratic 9, 21, 23, 36, 76, 102, 123, 219, 220, 225
  Socialist 23, 29, 33, 36, 44, 48, 76, 77, 93, 104-107, 200, 220, 225, 233, 236, 240
Political reform 93, 257, 261, 288
Political segregation 9
Portugal 8, 17-20, 25, 26, 29, 30, 51, 59-62, 217, 218, 222, 245, 246, 254-257, 268, 273, 282
Potential candidates 34, 42, 64, 72, 73, 173, 183, 212, 225, 286
Preferential voting 21, 25, 68, 80, 270, 191, 258, 270, 274
Proportional representation 21, 28, 46, 68, 87, 89, 91, 92, 98, 145, 180, 181, 234, 235, 263, 270, 294
Provincial councillors 119, 193
Provincial deputy 146
Provincial elections 193, 250
Psychological factors 64-67

Q

Quality of life 57, 78
Quota legislation 12, 28, 217, 218, 223, 226, 227, 236-238, 241, 245, 247, 249, 250, 285, 286, 288, 296
Quotas 217-218, 218-225

R

Regional level 33, 138, 146, 175, 178, 193, 242
Resistance 107, 124, 166
Robinson, Mary 37, 38, 295
Roudy, Yvette 77
Rutgers, Jaqueline 108

S

Schouwenaar-Franssen, Johanna 124
Scotland 5, 42, 43, 54, 224, 258, 263, 264, 287, 294, 296
Selection criteria 57, 58, 73, 171, 175, 181, 184, 212, 253, 288
Selection process 24, 57, 58, 67, 71-75, 78-81, 99, 109, 145, 167, 172, 176, 181, 276
Senate 33, 124, 125, 131, 180, 232, 234, 235, 241, 258
Single transferable vote 37
Situational factors 64, 65
Slovakia 53, 268
Slovenia 53
Smet, Miet 33, 77, 238
Smit, Joke 158
Social climate 57, 62
Spain 8, 17-20, 25-30, 51, 52, 60-63, 76, 217, 222, 254-257, 273, 281, 282
State governor 90, 138, 139, 146, 180, 181, 213
Structural factors 64, 65
Suffrage 11, 20, 30, 57, 58, 87, 89, 90, 91, 99-106, 112, 114, 117, 139, 150, 157, 246, 255, 269, 280, 283, 285, 293
Support structure 156, 197
Sweden 8, 17-24, 51, 52, 60-62, 74, 220, 222, 254-259, 268, 273, 274, 281, 282

T

Target figures 163, 167, 168, 180
Thatcher, Margaret 36, 39
Tokens 11, 119, 123, 211
Turnout 59, 229, 251, 252, 255, 256, 276
Turnover of candidates 71
Twinning 42, 224, 296

U

United Kingdom 8, 18-20, 41, 50, 51, 60, 61, 62, 222, 254-258, 268, 282

V

Veenendaal van Meggelen, Sophia van 96, 125
Vorrink, Irene 124
Voting 57, 58, 80, 285
Voting behaviour 4, 44, 48, 59, 101, 257
Voting procedures 57

W

Waal, Anna de 125
Wales 42, 43, 54, 224, 258, 263, 287, 294
Westerman, Johanna 121
Window of opportunity 10, 251, 252, 267, 269
Wittewaal van Stoetwegen, Lady Christine 109
Women's Contact groups 111
Women's factions 75-77, 167-171

Index

Women's organisations
  Association for Redistribution of Paid and Unpaid 161
  Association for Women in Politics 164
  Association for Women's Suffrage 102, 112, 162
  Catholic Women's Club 98, 160
  Clara Wichmann Institute 196, 197
  Dutch Organisation of Housewives 98, 160
  E-Quality 196, 197
  Foundation against Trafficking in Women 196, 197
  International Information Centre and Archives for 196
  Man/Woman: 50/50 162, 163, 178, 198
  Opportunity in Business 196
  Organisation for Women's Suffrage 89
  Platform for Economic Independence 161, 196
  PvdA Women's Network 199
  Roman Catholic Women's Organisation 103
  Toplink 182, 197
  Transact 196, 197
  We Women Demand 160
  Wild Mina 157, 158, 159
  Women's Alliance 196
  Women's Organisation for University Women 124
Women's parties
  Catholic Women's List 113, 117
  Dutch Women's Party 113, 115
  Feminist Party 34, 113, 114
  General Dutch Women's Organisation 113, 114
  Pragmatic Policy 113, 115
  Women's Action Party 113

Women's List of Leerbroek 113
Women's Party 116, 117
Women's Party Landgraaf 113
Women's sections
  AR Women's Group 109
  CDA Women's Council 168
  Centre for Christian-Historical Women's Groups 104
  Femnet 199, 200
  League of Social-Democratic Women's Clubs 106
  Liberal Democratic Women's Club 105
  Liberal Women's Network 199
  Organisation of Women in the VVD 110, 199
  Red Women 111, 112, 167
  Women/Men Rights Committee 200
Working conditions 57, 81, 83, 115, 288
World War I 114, 149
World War II 44, 48, 58, 66, 76, 94, 97, 99, 104, 107, 109, 112, 115, 123, 150, 154, 166

NIJHOFF LAW SPECIALS

1. D. Campbell: *Abortion Law and Public Policy.* 1984   ISBN 90-247-3107-0
2. J. Pictet: *Development and Principles of International Humanitarian Law.* 1985
   ISBN 90-247-3199-2
3. J. van Houtte: *Sociology of Law and Legal Anthropology in Dutch-speaking Countries.*
   1985   ISBN 90-247-3175-5
4. C.D. De Fouloy: *Glossary of NAFTA Terms.* 1994   ISBN 0-7923-2719-5
5. H.L. Zielinski: *Health and Humanitarian Concerns. Principles and Ethics.* 1994
   ISBN 0-7923-2963-5
6. K.S. Foster and D.C. Alexander: *Prospects of a US-Chile Free Trade Agreement.* 1994
   ISBN 0-7923-2885-X
7. F.J.M. Feldbrugge (ed.): *Russian Federation Legislative Survey. June 1990-December 1992.* 1995   ISBN 0-7923-3243-1
8. R. Platzöder (ed.): *The 1994 United Nations Convention on the Law of the Sea. Basic Documents with an Introduction.* 1995   ISBN 0-7923-3271-7
9. D. Warner (ed.): *New Dimensions of Peacekeeping.* 1995   ISBN 0-7923-3301-2
10. M. van Leeuwen (ed.): *The Future of the International Nuclear Non-Proliferation Regime.* 1995   ISBN 0-7923-3433-7
11. E.-U. Petersmann: *International and European Trade and Environmental Law After the Uruguay Round.* 1995   ISBN 90-411-0857-2
12. V. Gowlland-Debbas: *The Problem of Refugees in the Light of Contemporary International Law Issues.* 1996   ISBN 90-411-0085-7
13. A. Kaczorowska: *International Trade Conventions and Their Effectiveness. Present and Future.* 1995   ISBN 0-7923-3362-4
14. T.F. Acuña: *The United Nations Mission in El Salvador. A Humanitarian Law Perspective.* 1995   ISBN 90-411-0123-3
15. H. Wiggering and A. Sandhövel (eds.): *European Environmental Advisory Councils.* 1996   ISBN 90-411-0873-4
16. E.A. Ankumah: *The African Commission on Human and Peoples' Rights. Practice and Procedures.* 1996   ISBN 90-411-0130-6
17. B. de Rossanet: *Peacemaking and Peacekeeping in Yugoslavia.* 1996
    ISBN 90-411-0192-6
18. A. Webster and K. Packer (eds.): *Innovation and the Intellectual Property System.* 1996
    ISBN 90-411-0907-2
19. H. Bocken and D. Ryckbost (eds.): *Codification of Environmental Law. Draft Decree on Environmental Policy.* 1996   ISBN 90-411-0911-0
20. K. Lescure and F. Trintignac: *International Justice for Former Yugoslavia. The Working of the International Criminal Tribunal of the Hague.* 1996   ISBN 90-411-0201-9
21. G. de Nooy (ed.): *The Role of European Naval Forces after the Cold War.* 1996
    ISBN 90-411-0227-2

22. M. Bertrand and D. Warner (eds.): *A New Charter for a Worldwide Organisation?* 1997
    ISBN 90-411-0286-8
23. E.-U. Petersmann: *The GATT/WTO Dispute Settlement System. International Law, International Organizations and Dispute Settlement.* 1996   ISBN 90-411-0933-1
24. G. de Nooy (ed.): *Cooperative Security, the OSCE, and its Code of Conduct.* 1996
    ISBN 90-411-0316-3
25. M. Bertrand: *The United Nations. Past, Present and Future.* 1997   ISBN 90-411-0337-6
26. D. Dijkzeul: *The Management of Multilateral Organizations.* 1997   ISBN 90-411-0356-2
27. G. de Nooy (ed.): *The Role of European Ground and Air Forces after the Cold War.* 1997
    ISBN 90-411-0397-X
28. M. Hilaire: *International Law and the United States. Military Intervention in the Western Hemisphere.* 1997   ISBN 90-411-0399-6
29. D. Warner (ed.): *Human Rights and Humanitarian Law. The Quest for Universality.* 1997
    ISBN 90-411-0407-0
30. J.C. Hathaway (ed.): *Reconceiving International Refugee Law.* 1997
    ISBN 90-411-0418-6
31. G. de Nooy (ed.): *The Clausewitzian Dictum and the Future of Western Military Strategy.* 1997   ISBN 90-411-0455-0
32. Canadian Council on International Law and The Markland Group (ed.): *Treaty Compliance: Some Concerns and Remedies.* 1997   ISBN 90-411-0732-0
33. B. de Rossanet: *War and Peace in the Former Yugoslavia.* 1998   ISBN 90-411-0499-2
34. C.M. Mazzoni (ed.): *A Legal Framework for Bioethics.* 1998   ISBN 90-411-0523-9
35. M. Marín-Bosch: *Votes in the UN General Assembly.* 1998   ISBN 90-411-0564-6
36. L. Caflisch: *The Peaceful Settlement of Disputes between States: Universal and European Perspectives. Règlement pacifique des différends entre Etats: Perspectives universelle et européenne.* 1998   ISBN 90-411-0461-5
37. R. Wazir and N. van Oudenhoven (eds.): *Child Sexual Abuse: What can Governments do? A Comparative Investigation into Policy Instruments Used in Belgium, Britain, Germany, the Netherlands and Norway.* 1998   ISBN 90-411-1034-8
38. E.M. Barron and I. Nielsen (eds.): *Agriculture and Sustainable Land Use in Europe.* 1998
    ISBN 90-411-9691-9
39. K. van Walraven (ed.): *Early Warning and Conflict Prevention.* 1998
    ISBN 90-411-1064-X
40. S. Shubber: *The International Code of Marketing of Breast-milk Substitutes. An International Measure to Protect and Promote Breast-feeding.* 1999
    ISBN 90-411-1100-X
41. G. Prins and H. Tromp (eds.): *The Future of War.* 2000   ISBN 90-411-1196-4
42. Choung Il Chee: *Korean Perspectives on Ocean Law Issues for the 21st Century.* 2000
    ISBN 90-411-1301-0
43. K. Idris and M. Bartolo: *A Better United Nations for the New Millennium. The United Nations System – How it is now and how it should be in the future.* 2000
    ISBN 90-411-1344-4

44. E. McWhinney: *The United Nations and a New World Order for a New Millennium. Self-determination, State Succession, and Humanitarian Intervention.* 2000
    ISBN 90-411-1371-1
45. C.Y. Pak: *Korea and the United Nations.* 2000 ISBN 90-411-1382-7
46. G. Prins and H. Tromp (eds.): *The Future of War.* 2000 ISBN 90-411-1399-1
47. V. Gowlland-Debbas, H. Hadj-Sahraoui and N. Hayashi (eds.): *Multilateral Treaty-making. The Current Status of Challenges to and Reforms Needed in the International Legislative Process.* 2000 ISBN 90-411-1448-3
48. G. Simpson (ed.): *Detainees Denied Justice.* 2001 ISBN 90-411-1552-8
49. C.A. Magariños, G. Assaf, S. Lall, J.D.-Martinussen, R. Ricupero and F. Sercovich: *Reforming the UN System. UNIDO's Need Driven Model.* 2001 ISBN 90-411-1669-9
50. K. Wellens (ed.): *Resolutions and Statements of the United Nations Security Council (1946-2000). A Thematic Guide.* 2001 ISBN 90-411-1722-9
51. P. Soar (ed.): *The New International Directory of Legal Aid.* 2001 ISBN 90-411-1718-0
52. C.M. Mazzoni (ed.): *Ethics and Law in Biological Research.* 2002 ISBN 90-411-1742-3
53. I. Omar: *Emergency Powers and the Courts in India and Pakistan.* 2002
    ISBN 90-411-1775-X
54. M. O'Flaherty: *Human Rights and the UN: Practice Before the Treaty Bodies.* 2002
    ISBN 90-411-1788-1
55. Y. Beigbeder: *Judging Criminal Leaders. The Slow Erosion of Impunity.* 2002
    ISBN 90-411-1815-2
56. Marianne van Leeuwen (ed.): *Confronting Terrorism: European Experiences, Threat Perceptions, and Policies.* 2003 ISBN 90-411-1960-4
57. Ralf Bredel: *Long-term Conflict Prevention and Industrial Development: The United Nations and its Specialized Agency, UNIDO.* 2003 ISBN 90-04-13619-3
58. Raphael Walden: *Racism and Human Rights.* 2004 ISBN 90-04-13651-7
59. Monique Leyenaar: *Political Empowerment of Women: The Netherlands and Other Countries.* 2004 ISBN 90-04-14099-9

MARTINUS NIJHOFF PUBLISHERS – LEIDEN / BOSTON